WITTGENSTEIN
Sources and Perspectives

WITTGENSTEIN

Sources and Perspectives

Edited by C. G. LUCKHARDT

Cornell University Press

ITHACA, NEW YORK

First published 1979 by Cornell University Press.

Printed in the United States of America

Library of Congress Cataloging in Publication Data
Main entry under title:

Wittgenstein, sources and perspectives.

Includes bibliographical references and index.
1. Wittgenstein, Ludwig, 1889–1951—Addresses, essays, lectures. I. Luckhardt, C. G., 1943–
II. Title.
B3376.W564W56 192 78-58632
ISBN 0-8014-1122-X

Contents

Contributors

ROBERT L. ARRINGTON is Associate Professor of Philosophy at Georgia State University. He received his B.A. degree from Vanderbilt University and his M.A. and Ph.D. degrees from Tulane University. He was an Honorary Woodrow Wilson Fellow and an N.D.E.A. Fellow. Recently he was awarded a Fellowship by the American Council of Learned Societies. He has published several essays on topics arising out of the philosophy of Wittgenstein.

GORDON BAKER holds an A.B. degree from Harvard University and B.A., M.A., and D. Phil. degrees from Oxford University. He has been Assistant Lecturer at the University of Kent at Canterbury and is presently Fellow and Lecturer at St. John's College, Oxford. He is the author of various articles in philosophy, a coeditor of Friedrich Waismann's *Logik, Sprache, Philosophie,* and the coauthor, together with P. M. S. Hacker, of a forthcoming analytical commentary on the *Philosophical Investigations.*

JOHN BEVERSLUIS received his A.B. degree from Calvin College and his Ph.D. from Indiana University. He is currently Associate Professor and Head of the Department of Philosophy at Butler University.

BRUCE GILLETTE studied philosophy at the University of Tübingen and Munich, Czech at the Defense Language Institute, and Germanics at the University of Washington. He received an M.A. degree from the last institution, where he also completed all course-work requirements for a doctorate in Germanic and Slavic linguistics. He is presently a senior interpreter/translator with the U.S. Department of the Army.

P. M. S. HACKER took a B.A. at the Queen's College, Oxford, and a D. Phil. at St. Anthony's, Oxford. He was a Junior Research Fellow at Balliol and is presently a Fellow and Tutor in Philosophy at St. John's College, Oxford. He has been a Visiting Professor at Swarthmore College and at the University of Michigan. He has published numerous articles in philosophy and is the author of *Insight and*

Illusion: Wittgenstein on Philosophy and the Metaphysics of Experience. He is coeditor and contributor to *Law, Morality and Society: Essays in Honour of H. L. A. Hart* and is the coauthor, together with Gordon Baker, of a forthcoming analytical commentary on the *Philosophical Investigations.*

ALLAN JANIK studied philosophy and classics at St. Anselm's College. He took an M.A. in philosophy at Villanova University, where he wrote a thesis on Schopenhauer and the early Wittgenstein. His Ph.D. is in the History of Ideas and was taken at Brandeis University. He is the coauthor (with Stephen Toulmin) of *Wittgenstein's Vienna* and is currently at work on a companion volume treating of *Der Brenner* and twentieth-century philosophy.

KENT LINVILLE holds a B.A. degree from California State University, Northridge, and a Ph.D. from the University of California, Santa Barbara. He is presently an Associate Professor of Philosophy at Oxford College of Emory University and is the author of various articles in philosophy.

FANIA PASCAL, née Feiga Polanowska, was born in Shitomir, Ukraine. She studied philosophy at the University of Berlin and was awarded the Dr. Phil. in 1931. Her dissertation was entitled "Losskij's erkenntnistheoretischer Intuitionismus." She married Roy Pascal, now Emeritus Professor of German at the University of Birmingham, in 1931. For some years she was part-time lecturer in Russian at the University of Birmingham.

DAVID PEARS took an M.A. at Oxford. He is now a Student of Christ Church and Reader in Philosophy at Oxford. He was made a Fellow of the British Academy in 1971. He is the cotranslator of Wittgenstein's *Tractatus Logico-Philosophicus* and has written *Bertrand Russell and the British Tradition in Philosophy, Ludwig Wittgenstein,* and *Some Questions in the Philosophy of Mind.*

G. H. VON WRIGHT has been Professor of Philosophy at Helsinki University and at Cambridge University, where he succeeded Wittgenstein. He has served as Research Professor at the Academy of Finland and Andrew D. White Professor-at-Large at Cornell University. He is an executor of Wittgenstein's literary estate and has served as editor for many of his works. His own published work includes numerous essays and books in the areas of induction and probability, philosophical logic, ethics, and philosophy of science. Some of his more famous books are *Norm and Action, The Varieties of Goodness, Explanation and Understanding,* and *The Logical Problem of Induction.*

Abbreviations

BBB — L. Wittgenstein, *The Blue and Brown Books* (Oxford: Basil Blackwell; New York: Harper & Row, 1958).

"BT" — L. Wittgenstein, "Big Typescript" (von Wright Catalogue #213).

E — P. Engelmann, *Letters from Ludwig Wittgenstein with a Memoir,* trans. L. Furtmüller, ed. B. F. McGuinness (Oxford: Basil Blackwell, 1967).

F — L. Wittgenstein, *Briefe an Ludwig von Ficker,* ed. G. H. von Wright assisted by Walter Methlagl (Brenner Studien, I: Salzburg: Otto Müller, 1969). Translated by Bruce Gillette as "Letters to Ludwig von Ficker," Chapter 3, this volume.

LSP — F. Waismann, *Logik, Sprache, Philosophie,* ed. G. P. Baker, B. F. McGuinness, and J. Schulte (Stuttgart: Reclam, 1976).

NB — L. Wittgenstein, *Notebooks 1914–1916,* ed. G. H. von Wright and G. E. M. Anscombe, trans. G. E. M. Anscombe (Oxford: Basil Blackwell, 1961; New York: Harper and Row, 1969).

OC — L. Wittgenstein, *On Certainty,* ed. G. E. M. Anscombe and G. H. von Wright, trans. Denis Paul and G. E. M. Anscombe (Oxford: Basil Blackwell; New York: Harper & Row, 1969).

PB — L. Wittgenstein, *Philosophische Bemerkungen,* ed. Rush Rhees (Oxford: Basil Blackwell, 1964).

PG — L. Wittgenstein, *Philosophical Grammar,* ed. Rush Rhees, trans. Anthony Kenny (Oxford: Basil Blackwell; Berkeley: University of California Press, 1974).

PI — L. Wittgenstein, *Philosophical Investigations,* trans. G. E. M. Anscombe (Oxford: Basil Blackwell; New York: Macmillan, 1958).

PLP — F. Waismann, *The Principles of Linguistic Philosophy,* ed. R. Harré (London: Macmillan; New York: St. Martin's Press, 1965).

PR — L. Wittgenstein, *Philosophical Remarks,* ed. Rush Rhees, trans. Raymond Hargreaves and Roger White (Oxford: Basil Blackwell; New York: Barnes & Noble, 1975). (A translation of *Philosophische Bemerkungen.*)

PTLP L. Wittgenstein, *Prototractatus: An Early Version of Tractatus Logico-Philosophicus,* ed. B. F. McGuinness, T. Nyberg, and G. H. von Wright (London: Routledge & Kegan Paul; Ithaca, N.Y.: Cornell University Press, 1971).

R L. Wittgenstein, *Letters to Russell, Keynes, and Moore,* ed. G. H. von Wright, assisted by B. F. McGuinness (Oxford: Basil Blackwell; Ithaca, N.Y.: Cornell University Press, 1974).

RFM L. Wittgenstein, *Remarks on the Foundations of Mathematics,* ed. G. H. von Wright, R. Rhees, G. E. M. Anscombe, trans. G. E. M. Anscombe (Oxford: Basil Blackwell, 1956; Cambridge, Mass.: M.I.T. Press, 1964).

TLP L. Wittgenstein, *Tractatus Logico-Philosophicus,* trans. D. F. Pears and B. F. McGuinness (London: Routledge & Kegan Paul; New York: Humanities Press, 1961).

WWK F. Waismann, *Wittgenstein und der Wiener Kreis,* ed. B. F. McGuinness (Oxford: Basil Blackwell, 1967).

Z L. Wittgenstein, *Zettel,* ed. G. E. M. Anscombe and G. H. von Wright, trans. G. E. M. Anscombe (Oxford: Basil Blackwell, 1967; Berkeley: University of California Press, 1970).

WITTGENSTEIN

Sources and Perspectives

Editor's Introduction

C. G. LUCKHARDT

Most of the essays in this volume were written on request, and with three exceptions all appear here for the first time. They are related to each other by two sets of family resemblances, which themselves reflect two recent and important changes in the course of studies on Wittgenstein. It may be helpful therefore to introduce the essays in this volume by first describing these two changes and then relating the essays to them *seriatim* and in some detail.

First, in the past decade a large amount of Wittgenstein's *Nachlass*, and several of his lectures and letters, have been made available to the public for the first time. Some of this material has appeared only in German, but much has also been made available recently in English. The result has been that Wittgensteinian scholarship has become more complex than ever before. It is no longer possible to speak only of Wittgenstein's "earlier" and "later" periods of philosophy, and to mean by those terms simply the *Tractatus* and the *Investigations*. For the "period" of the *Tractatus* is now seen as encompassing the *Prototractatus* and the *Notebooks 1914–1916*, as well as several of his letters, whereas the "period" of the *Investigations* now includes the *Remarks on the Foundations of Mathematics, Zettel, On Certainty*, and *On Colour*, as well as various lectures, letters, remarks, and conversations. Further, it is only in the last few years that much attention has been paid to Wittgenstein's works of the 1930s, so that now *The Blue and Brown Books* are no longer seen simply as early versions of the *Investigations*, but as forming part of a whole "middle period" of development which includes the *Philosophical Remarks* and *Philosophical Grammar*.

With the advent of these new materials, however, there have naturally resulted a series of new ways of viewing Wittgenstein's philosophy. New points of view about various details of his works have been developed, and perhaps more important, whole new perspectives on his philosophy have emerged, and with them, of course, new arguments defending the more traditional interpretations of his works. Many of the essays in this book relate directly to this change in Wittgensteinian scholarship, for, as I shall show in describing the essays, one of them makes material by Wittgenstein available for the first time in English, while seven others refer to previously neglected or unavailable material, such as the "Big Typescript," *Notebooks 1914–1916, Philosophical Remarks, Philosophical Grammar,* and the Letters to von Ficker, either to develop new perspectives on Wittgenstein's philosophy or to challenge previously accepted ones. One essay has the added interest of presenting and analyzing some material from an unpublished MS of Bertrand Russell entitled "Theory of Knowledge."

A second recent and important change in Wittgenstein studies has been a move to relate Wittgenstein to other figures in the history of philosophy. Wittgenstein's own comment that no assistant lecturer in philosophy in England had read fewer books on philosophy than he seems to have been taken quite seriously by many scholars writing in the 1960s, as if Wittgenstein's own professed unfamiliarity with the history of philosophy meant that his philosophy bore little relation to that of past philosophers. Indeed, many authors seemed to regard him as having written in a philosophical void, isolated from others in thought, influence, and outlook. But, of course, references to other philosophers do occur throughout his writings, and Wittgenstein's own remark was probably an overstatement, and certainly said in jest. The initial bashfulness in relating his work to others, and in locating his place in the history of philosophy, has inevitably given way to allow for essays which draw the lines either connecting him with or separating him from other philosophers. Six of the essays included here reflect this abandonment of the ahistorical approach by relating him to figures as diverse as Russell, Descartes, von Ficker, Augustine, Moore, Frege, Aristotle, and Waismann.

The first essay in the book relates directly to the first change I have mentioned, for in it Mrs. Fania Pascal conveys a personal impression of Wittgenstein quite different from most of those that have gone before. Based on her experiences as his Russian teacher, her memoir is an illuminating and often moving account written from the unusual perspective of a teacher, rather than a student, of Wittgenstein. She contributes much valuable historical detail about his interest in Russia and his trip there, and she provides many interesting clues to his character, including his "confession" of two "crimes" to her. At first many of these clues may seem surprising, but the reader may find it helpful to reread von Wright's and Malcolm's memoirs alongside her article, for in most cases hers supplements rather than conflicts with theirs. Her essay appeared originally in the *Encounter* issue of August 1973, and it appears here in a revised form, with a few changes Mrs. Pascal wished to add.

Wittgenstein's "Remarks on Frazer's *Golden Bough*" appears here for the first time in a complete English translation. John Beversluis has based his translation on the German text that appeared in *Synthese* in 1967, but it includes several corrections to that text, which are indicated in the footnotes. Rush Rhees originally compiled the text of the "Remarks," extracting it from two distinct sources. Part I of the "Remarks" begins in an entry in one of Wittgenstein's manuscript books, dated 19 June 1931. More remarks were added on this and other topics during the following weeks, and, probably later in the same year, Wittgenstein edited most of this material into a typescript. Rhees has selected the first part of the "Remarks" from sections of this typescript. Part II of the "Remarks" was written much later—certainly no earlier than 1936, and, Rhees estimates, probably after 1948. This section consists of notes written on loose scraps of paper, which Wittgenstein wrote as commentary to certain pages in the one-volume edition of *The*

Golden Bough. Mr. Rhees has graciously supplied the relevant quotations for Wittgenstein's page number references, and they are included as footnotes to the text.

Wittgenstein's "Letters to von Ficker" appears here for the first time in English, translated by Bruce Gillette, and edited by Allan Janik. They originally appeared in German in *Briefe an Ludwig von Ficker,* edited by G. H. von Wright (Salzburg: Otto Müller Verlag, 1969), and the translation is of that text.

G. H. von Wright's two contributions to this volume explain the historical and textual origins of Wittgenstein's two most famous works. The first essay, on the *Tractatus,* appeared originally as a "Historical Introduction" to the Routlege & Kegan Paul/Cornell University Press edition of the *Prototractatus.* It appears here with a few changes in that text. Footnote references to translations of the von Ficker letters are to the translation by Gillette in this volume. In addition to several of these letters, von Wright refers to letters from Wittgenstein to Engelmann, Frege, Keynes, Moore, and Ogden, to trace the publishing history of the *Tractatus.* He explains the relation of the finally published work to its three typescript sources, which he calls the Engelmann-TS, Vienna-TS, and Gmunden-TS, and he discusses Wittgenstein's relations with several would-be publishers of the work. The translation into English by Odgen is discussed, and the article concludes with an explanation of how the originally proposed title of the book, "Philosophical Logic," got changed to its Latin title, with its "Spinozistic ring."

Von Wright's second article appears here for the first time. It is a detailed account of the history of the *Investigations,* which traces it from its beginnings in 1936 through three versions, culminating in the final version of Part I of 1945–1946. All of his references to typescript and manuscript numbers refer to his catalog of the Wittgenstein *Nachlass* in the *Philosophical Review,* Volume 78, 1969. As a result of his investigations which led to this essay, however, some of the information in that catalog now stands corrected here. In addition to containing a discussion of the relation of Part I of the *Investigations* to its various manuscript sources, von Wright's essay also describes the sources of Part II and comments on the publication history of the book, including Wittgenstein's own early plans for publication. Von Wright concludes by stating his own view as to the philosophical relation between Parts I and II of the work: that the former should be seen as a complete work in itself and that Part II is essentially new material. He suggests that it, too, should be read as a whole and that *Zettel* constitutes the third part of what is essentially a trilogy.

Allan Janik's article relates directly to the letters to von Ficker, as he uses them to develop his thesis that the central point of the *Tractatus* has been overlooked, if not neglected, by most readers of the work. This view is, of course, the same as that developed by Janik and Stephen Toulmin in *Wittgenstein's Vienna,* but in this essay Janik not only expands on the significance of the Ficker letters for interpreting the *Tractatus,* but also presents a more complete view of Wittgenstein's place in the turn-of-the-century Austrian cultural milieu. In addition, Janik discusses those letters that provide insights into Wittgenstein's role as a soldier in World War I and role as patron of the arts. Indeed, it is in this latter role that Wittgenstein begins his correspondence with Ficker, for his first letter is a request of Ficker to help him in distributing 100,000 crowns "among Austrian artists who are without means."

In his Preface to the *Tractatus* Wittgenstein had acknowledged two sources of indebtedness: to "Frege's great work and to the writings of my friend Mr. Bertrand Russell for much of the stimulation of my thoughts." In their essays David Pears and P. M. S. Hacker deal with the relation of these philosophers to Wittgenstein's work. Russell is mentioned by name in almost thirty sections of the *Tractatus,* but in only one (4.0031) is he cited for having made a positive contribution to philosophy. Nearly all of the other citations are intended either to distinguish his views from those being developed in the *Tractatus,* or explicitly to criticize them. Pears shows how far-reaching some of the differences between Wittgenstein and Russell are and locates the sources of many of them. He claims that much of the picture theory should be construed as an explicit reaction against particular things Russell had said in an unpublished manuscript of 1913, entitled "Theory of Knowledge." Much of this work, according to

Pears, was a development of certain ideas that had first been presented in "On the Nature of Truth and Falsehood," published in the *Philosophical Essays* of 1910. Wittgenstein had discussed this latter work with him and had criticized it harshly, but Russell's attempts to remedy some of its defects in "Theory and Knowledge" were still thought by Wittgenstein to be wholly misguided. For example, the notion of an abstract object existing in another world, which Russell thought necessary for understanding logical connectives and the forms of propositions, was entirely rejected by Wittgenstein in the *Tractatus* in favor of a more Aristotelian view. Wittgenstein also found it important to account for many of the things Russell's theory did not account for, such as logical truth, and the isomorphism between the (nonlogical) elements of propositions and the elements of the world. It was largely to these ends, Pears claims, that the famous picture theory was developed. Pears's article is therefore valuable not only in presenting some of the main features of Russell's MS for the first time, but also in detailing Wittgenstein's reasons for taking exception to it and his attempts in the *Tractatus* at solving some of the problems he saw in it. The article was written especially for this volume, but was published first in the *Philosophical Review*, Volume 86, 1977.

P. M. S. Hacker discusses Frege's famous dictum that a word has meaning only in the context of a proposition, and he analyzes the influence this dictum had on Wittgenstein throughout his writings. Hacker calls this the "holistic dictum," or the "principle of semantic holism," to distinguish both Frege's and Wittgenstein's views from semantic atomism. He begins by explicating the foundations of the principle in Frege's early thought, indicating how it emerges from the mathematical analysis of language and from the principle that treats the meaning of a sentence as given by its truth conditions, and he points to the constructive use to which the principle is put. Contrary to received opinion, however, he argues that Frege neither abandoned nor repudiated the principle in his later works. With the development of the sense/reference distinction, the dictum was instead transformed so as to apply to the sense of words, and Hacker argues that the Fregean doctrine that sentences are themselves names of truth-values does not, *pace* Dummett, require the repudiation of holism. Hacker goes on to trace Wittgenstein's use of the dictum in both the *Tractatus* and post-*Tractatus* writings, including the "Big Typescript," *Philosophical Remarks,* and *Philosophical Grammar.* His use of it in the *Tractatus* is adjusted to a semantics which employs the sense/reference distinction in a way quite different from that of Frege. In its revised form the dictum becomes an integral part of the picture theory and its related ontology. It is in the post-1929 writings, however, that Wittgenstein shifts the ground for the dictum, while yet retaining it to do important philosophical work. Hacker provides several arguments to show how Wittgenstein's later work led to a repudiation of the Fregean rationale behind the dictum, and how Wittgenstein's new rationale allowed it to develop into the view that a sentence has meaning only in the context of a language. Thus the dictum is traced from its beginnings in Frege's early work on mathematics to some of the most influential passages in the *Investigations,* where it forms part of the discussion of language, language acquisition, and language-games.

Gordon P. Baker has written on part of the "middle period" of Wittgenstein's philosophical life in which he was in close contact with Friedrich Waismann. Baker's research provides much valuable historical data on Wittgenstein's influence (through the medium of Waismann) on the Vienna Circle, and on the nature of Wittgenstein's relation to Waismann's book, *The Principles of Linguistic Philosophy* (*Logik, Sprache, Philosophie*). He shows that the book was written by Waismann in collaboration with Wittgenstein and intended as a systematic presentation of Wittgenstein's philosophical ideas, including both those of the *Tractatus* and some more recent ones. Wittgenstein was the first to realize, however, that his emerging views in the early 1930s could not be reconciled with those of the *Tractatus,* and so the writing of the book, with its numerous revisions and shifts, reflected the ongoing changes in Wittgenstein's philosophy. Baker compares many of these new ideas with ideas in the contemporaneous *Blue and Brown Books* and "Big Typescript" and suggests that the *Principles* in many places illuminates dark passages in those works. Baker's aim is not entirely historical, however, for he uses this material to defend his own thesis about Wittgenstein's later philosophy, that it is, in his words, "obscurantist dogma" to claim that Wittgenstein's remarks against philosophical theorizing should be taken to mean that he was incapable of or opposed to presenting his own philosophical system. Since his collaboration with Waismann was nothing other than an attempt to present his own system, and since this was being done at the same time many of the warnings against philosophical systems were being written, Baker argues that it is perfectly appropriate to inquire about Wittgenstein's own philosophical system, even though it may be one that underwent constant development and one with which Wittgenstein was never completely satisfied.

Kent Linville's essay is on Wittgenstein's treatment of Moore's Paradox, and in it he adverts frequently to passages from Descartes's *Meditations* to show the sorts of considerations that seem to render "It is raining but I don't believe it" meaningful, though absurd to assert. That statement is simply self-contradictory if "I don't believe it is raining" is taken to refer to the rain, rather than to the mental state of the speaker, and so the Paradox depends on its being taken as self-referential. Linville presents three Cartesian considerations in favor of its being self-referential, and then shows how Wittgenstein's notion of "seeing-as" can be used both to defeat the necessity of its being self-referential and to reveal a misinterpretation its intelligibility requires. Thus Linville is able to relate section x of Part II of the *Investigations,* in which the Paradox is discussed, to its more famous successor, section xi, in which Wittgenstein discussed the dawning and seeing of an aspect. Linville concludes by relating this latter section to the theme of philosophical perplexity developed in Part I of the *Investigations,* which theme he takes to be ideally illustrated in Moore's Paradox.

In his article Robert L. Arrington draws heavily from material in the *Philosophical Grammar* to challenge the standard interpretation of Wittgenstein's views toward ostensive definition. He argues that Wittgenstein's position is neither as far-reaching nor as destructive as it has ordinarily been thought to be. Arrington claims that much confusion has resulted from failing to recognize the distinction Wittgenstein makes between ostensive definition and ostensive teaching. Conceived as a *mechanism* for teaching the meaning of words, ostension has no significant limitations placed on it. Conceived as having a role in a *calculus,* or language-game, ostensive definition itself *can* provide grammatical rules that determine the meaning of words. Wittgenstein was, to be sure, concerned with a problem about ambiguity in ostensive definitions. But, Arrington claims, he neither developed an argument to show that that problem rendered all ostensive definitions suspect, as most commentators seem to have thought he did, nor did he ever develop *any* argument to show that they are. His criticisms of ostensive definition are directed rather against certain inadequate *theories* of ostensive definition, chiefly that of Augustine, rather than against ostensive definition itself. Seen in that light, Wittgenstein's own views about ostensive definition do not set limitations upon the possibility of ostension serving a positive role either in teaching or in the analysis of meaning.

Some of the articles in this book have been in my hands for over a year now, and I wish to thank the authors of those articles for their patience and indulgence while others were being completed. Also, I wish to thank Norman Malcolm and Robert Arrington for their help in preparing this volume, and to thank Georgia State University, particularly for providing me with the aid of two graduate assistants, Elsa Sibley and Robert Lee, and two secretaries, Connie White and Patti Tucker. I am indebted to Leila Komara for typing various versions of the papers contained herein. I wish also to express appreciation to the Wittgenstein Literary Executors for their permission to publish the translations of the "Letters to Ludwig von Ficker" and the "Remarks on Frazer's *Golden Bough,*" and to them and the Executors of Waismann's, Neurath's, and Schlick's literary estates for permission to include parts of letters that Baker has included in his article. Thanks are also due to the Editor of *Encounter* for permission to include Fania Pascal's article, to the editors of the *Philosophical Review* for permission to reprint David Pears's article, to Routledge & Kegan Paul Ltd. and Cornell University Press for permission to print a revised version of Georg Henrik von Wright's "Origin of Wittgenstein's *Tractatus*," which originally appeared in *Prototractatus*, and to Peter Smith, Publisher, for permission to include the translation of Georg Trakl's "Grodek" in Allan Janik's article.

1 Wittgenstein: A Personal Memoir

FANIA PASCAL

Nobody can write down personal memories of Wittgenstein without being almost physically aware of his disapproval and scathing glance. He often expressed his conviction that what we would like to pass for interest in other people is first and foremost malice. Yet, just as he might (though an ascetic) now and then enjoy a nice piece of cake, so have I seen him (once or twice) savour a harmless piece of gossip, against his will as it were.

He would above all abhor anybody enquiring into his personal life. This I have not done. The few facts I have found out about his relations with Francis Skinner are and were, surely, part of his public life. Besides, in my recollection the two men were inseparable.

Yet, even allowing for my lack of the experience and habit of writing, was it the consciousness of his condemnation that made me spend nearly three years on these few pages? The time went not so much in improving the material as in halting. But just as surely I would go back to it, taking it up at the sentence, at the word where I had stopped. I had a feeling that in spite of advancing years I was not in a hurry, even that my snail's pace belonged to the nature of my subject.[1]

This essay appeared in slightly different form in *Encounter,* 41, no. 2 (1973) and is reprinted by permission.

1. I found help and incentive in two books that give valuable biographical information: *Ludwig Wittgenstein, A Memoir,* by Norman Malcolm (London and New York: Oxford University Press, 1958), which includes a "biographical sketch" by G. H. von Wright; and *Letters from Ludwig Wittgenstein with a Memoir,* by Paul Engelmann, translated by L. Furtmüller and edited by B. F. McGuinness (Oxford: Blackwell, 1967).

Is Wittgenstein's stock still rising, as it was till recently? The young are certainly amazed when, if his name comes up, I say: "Oh, I taught him Russian." Anecdotes follow. A few years ago a visiting American professor carried the news home and I had an enquiry from a zealous philosopher. I answered his letter, for much the same reasons as I am writing this now, but his further enquiries brought questions such as what "textual or oral evidence" I had of Wittgenstein's attitude to Marx and Engels, or his attitude to Russia, and already my husband Roy and I were being roped into establishing a thesis. We beat a hasty retreat.

I think I should say at the outset that I know next to nothing about Wittgenstein's philosophy. Only the *Tractatus* had been published when I knew him. I tried to read it but soon abandoned the effort. My ignorance was a feather in my cap as far as Wittgenstein was concerned. In the *Philosophical Investigations* I can browse; I can read it as a collection of aphorisms. Some time in our acquaintance—and he must have been in an exceptionally amiable mood for me to ask and for him to answer patiently—I did say: "Why are you so sure your work is no earthly good to me?" He said, as far as I can remember: "Suppose you were trying to draw a chart of the progress of a hospital sister walking round her ward, then of another doing likewise on another floor, and finally, to produce *one* chart which would combine and illustrate their joint progress . . . ?" I cried out: "Oh, I could never grasp it!"

One of the things that pressed upon me and prompted me to answer the American professor's letter in the first place is the absence of references to Francis Skinner in all that is written about Wittgenstein (except that he took down some of the Notebooks at Wittgenstein's dictation). Now I knew him to have been the constant companion of Wittgenstein throughout most of the 1930s, till his early death in 1941. They walked, talked, and worked together, at times sharing rooms over a small general grocer's shop. Together they came to have Russian lessons with me.

I started writing these notes in the autumn of 1969, in Canada; and on returning home I renewed contact with Francis's sister, Mrs. Truscott. What I heard from her deepened my interest in everything to do with this relationship, and revived my flagging resolve to carry on with my task.

Likewise, but in a totally different way, I miss all mention of another intimate friend of Wittgenstein's, Dr. Nicholas Bachtin, earlier a lecturer in Classics in Southampton, then in Birmingham where he was finally Reader in Linguistics. He died a year before Wittgenstein. When just before the war we too moved to Birmingham, where my husband was appointed to the Chair of German, it was when Wittgenstein was visiting the Bachtins (often accompanied by Skinner) that we saw him or both of them. "Wittgenstein loved Bachtin," Constance, Bachtin's widow, told me (she died in 1959 after having been for years disastrously afflicted by multiple sclerosis). From her I heard of the interminable discussions that went on between the two men, and of Wittgenstein's idiosyncrasies.

Nicholas Bachtin, an exile from the Russian Revolution but by the outbreak of the Second World War a fiery communist, was an inspired teacher and lecturer. He had a deep-seated difficulty in writing down his work, and I do not know of any other completed work of his than the few essays and lectures of the memorial volume that Professor Austin Duncan-Jones edited. What I do know and what in itself would call for attention to the friendship is that Wittgenstein indeed loved Bachtin, was unusually happy and gay in his presence, and never dropped him as he easily did others. His was the rare case of Wittgenstein taking a person as he found him. All this in spite of the fact that they were poles apart in outlook and character. Bachtin was given to extremes of passion and an uncontrolled exuberance of feeling and expression. He always seemed on the verge of erupting, like a volcano. He suffered from many irrational fears and obsessions, loved expansiveness, was a great gourmet. Unlike Wittgenstein, Bachtin, though childless, could take delight in children, even in cats. They did however share a kind of childlike innocence, and lacked everything commonplace.

But I should not like it to be understood that I am writing

this solely out of concern for two long-dead friends of Wittgenstein's and ours. To have known him was an experience that gave one an uplift that endures, but that also, in my case, resulted in strife that still rankles. I also wanted to describe Wittgenstein's confession as he made it to me.

In the autumn of 1969 we were packing to go to Canada, where my husband had accepted a visiting professorship. "What will you do with yourself?" a friend asked. "What you want is a project." And I did in fact have too much time on my hands. I found moreover that every schoolchild in Canada was "doing a project", where in old days he would have been doing his homework. This then was to be my project: a memoir of Wittgenstein.

I am bad at dates and exact details. But with the help of a few landmarks in my life, like marriage and the birth of our children, I can put the events of the 1930s into some sort of order. Thus I calculate that it was in 1934 (or maybe late 1933) that Francis Skinner called at our Cambridge house to ask whether I would give him lessons in Russian. He was at the time a post-graduate scholar of Trinity College, an extremely shy, boyish chap. He had a club foot, and the memory of his rapid ascent of the stairs and as rapid noisy rushing down them two or three at a time is vivid in my mind. Though not many years in England and Cambridge, I was already used to this very English phenomenon—the over-shy young sons of the educated middle classes. Was his shyness aggravated by being a cripple? I respected him from the start for the way he paid no attention to his self-consciousness and discussed arrangements looking straight at me. I knew what tricks I would use if I found myself blushing before a stranger. Our sensibilities we should leave in the care of others—some such thought went through my head. I had an impression that the fee I asked, though standard at the time, appeared too high for him. "Could a friend come along to the lessons? But he isn't sure yet. He hasn't made up his mind." "Bring him along. The fee will be the same for two." They seemed to be grateful, for soon they sent me the largest hydrangea I have ever seen. I was quite unprepared to find, when they knocked at the door, that Francis's friend was Dr. Wittgenstein.

I had come to Cambridge in 1930 and used to attend the meetings of the Moral Science Club before my marriage in the summer of 1931. This was the time when, under the impact of Wittgenstein, young men went about saying: "It's absurd to say that 2 is a number—what else could it be?" It was mostly students who came to these gatherings that were presided over by Professor G. E. Moore; and Wittgenstein was the disturbing (perhaps disrupting) centre of these evenings. He would talk for long periods without interruption, using similes and allegories, stalking about the room and gesticulating. He cast a spell. The expression on Moore's face as he listened patiently and attentively was tolerant, impressed, but also questioning. I should doubt the veracity of this ancient memory if television had not brought home to me that a facial expression, a look in the eye, can never be disguised, stands out, and outlives the words of the speaker and all else to do with the occasion. To me this look of Moore's stands for the attitude of educated Cambridge to Wittgenstein at that time.

I had just taken a Ph.D. in philosophy in Berlin, but this was something quite different. I was only just learning to speak English, and much of what was said went over my head. I remember a paper given by Richard Braithwaite which Wittgenstein appeared to tear to pieces only to end up, to the amazement of all, by giving it his approval or maybe just letting it pass. Clarity might not always result from these discussions, but there was always revelation. Once he said: "You cannot love God, for you do not know him," and went on elaborating the theme. Some complaints about his monopolising the discussion led to his abandoning the Moral Science Club. But soon he was begged to come back. All this was in 1930–1931.

When in 1934 he and Francis came for lessons I knew much about him without having met him. He seemed to have been a legend from the start and Cambridge was full of stories about him. First and foremost he was the feared (why feared?) author of the *Tractatus*. Before he became a Fellow of Trinity he had to be asked to leave his private lodgings because he ran the bath in the night. He asked about every single object: "But is it genuine?" He disliked intellectual women and in company literally turned his back on them; a friend of mine, whom he had treated in this rude way, thought it a huge joke. His opinions on most matters were absolute, allowing no argument. At a time when intellectual Cambridge was turning Left he was still an oldtime conservative of the late Austro-Hungarian Empire. But he was charmed to find Mrs. Lettice Ramsey doing some complicated sewing, would watch her at it, and would want to know how it was done. A young friend told me what a delightful experience it had been to go with Wittgenstein to buy a pen-knife. His keenness on and involvement in instruments, material objects, and all skills was something very special—for them he had the patience and tolerance he could never have for human beings. He would often be seen walking in the narrow streets or along the river with some young man or other, talking and gesticulating, keeping a step ahead of his companion so as to turn and face him. In schoolboy language he could be a holy terror and a *Besserwisser*, a know-all. To the early 1930s belongs a poem by Julian Bell (later killed driving an ambulance in Spain) in a student magazine lampooning Wittgenstein for telling everybody off for misusing language while himself doing all the talking. Also for being rude and inconsiderate to others. When the poem appeared the kindest people enjoyed a laugh; it released accumulated tension, resentment, perhaps fear. For no one could ever turn the tables on Wittgenstein and pay him back in kind.

So now, hearing that he was to have Russian lessons with me, one of the kindest people I ever knew, Mrs. Jessie Stewart, said: "So Wittgenstein is to be your pupil? Good. Now you have got him where you want him." Actually he turned out to be a fairly docile as well as an outstanding pupil.

The Student of Russian

His appearance has often been described: small in stature but of concentrated inner energy, neat, with a keen look as of a bird in flight. I never saw him wearing a closed collar or tie. He found it hard to sit still; it seemed as though at any minute he might take off. There was something stern and forbidding, yet naive, in his expression, directed to others but also to himself. He might strike one as a man with a chip on his shoulder. "Satanic pride" I called it, exaggerating as usual. He looked distant except when he relaxed, got absorbed in study, or told a childish joke with a grin. Once he started talking he could hold you in thrall; I don't think he was aware of this gift. The man who was later to make the famous statement: "Philosophy is the struggle against the bewitchment of our mind by means of language" had no inkling how he himself cast a spell whenever he said something, anything. He was altogether a naive man, remarkably unself-conscious. He could be irritable in the extreme, but much (maybe most of it) he could not help—his life was made hard by excessive sensibility, a sensitivity affecting all the senses. More things could drive him mad than would other people. Being irritable myself, though I may have been less so at that time, I cannot think of another person anything like so irascible. His most typical frequent expression was the cry "Intolerable, intolerable," not sounding the first vowel, "*'ntolerable, 'ntolerable,*" throwing back his head and rolling his eyes upwards. It was impossible to doubt the sincerity of this as of everything else he said.

All our talks were in English. It was also English that Wittgenstein spoke in the Moral Science Club and, as far as I know, whenever he lectured. His English was idiomatic, imaged, and expressive, it flowed freely once he got going, and was inspiring to listen to.

His gestures were very expressive: throwing up his arms in despair or (rarely) a gesture to express approval. Bachtin told me years later, "Wittgenstein thinks your *teaching* is good, like this . . . , " punctuating the air with thumb and forefinger joined in imitation of Wittgenstein. "Teaching" was stressed; it was a drop in the ocean of his strictures on things I did and, above all, on my manner of speaking. That was always too flamboyant and imprecise for him. But while we had work to do friction did not obtrude. They came once a week for a two-hour lesson; I think of the experience with pleasure. In a remarkably short time they mastered the grammatical structure (the part I most love teaching) and proceeded to read good Russian prose. Soon I was able to amuse them with a fitting proverb. In later years I was rarely to see them so cheerful again. I cannot recall after how many (or rather how few) weeks it happened that Wittgenstein was ill in bed and sent me a translation he had made of a Grimm's fairy tale from German into Russian. I sat up and realised that although Francis was going ahead extremely well I should have to deal with them separately. How I did it I cannot think now. The period in which both came for lessons could not have been more than three Cambridge terms of eight weeks each. Wittgenstein also came in 1935 by himself for Russian conversation, on the eve of his trip to the USSR.

Francis Skinner reached considerable proficiency and in the vacations would write me letters in Russian that I would send back corrected. Alas, I now can find only a single letter from him in my possession, written in English. It was sent in August 1940 from the Bachtins' house, where he and Wittgenstein were on a visit, to a farm near Pershore where we were picking fruit. Regretting our absence—"Best wishes in this anxious time"—uncertain when we might have another chance to meet—"Dr. Wittgenstein is going back to Cambridge, tomorrow latest, as if anything happened he may not be able to return." It brings back the summer of 1940 when they were indiscriminately rounding up and interning German and Austrian nationals and refugees. (Like Wittgenstein, Francis always wrote on lined pages torn out of a school exercise book.)

Whether the fairy tale Wittgenstein translated was *Rumpelstiltskin* or another I am not sure, but I remember him picking up the volume of Grimm's tales and reading out with awe in his voice:

Ach, wie gut ist dass niemand weiss
Dass ich Rumpelstilzchen heiss.

"Profound, profound," he said. I liked *Rumpelstiltskin*, understood that the strength of the dwarf lay in his name being unknown to humans; but was unable to share Wittgenstein's vision. To watch him in a state of hushed, silent awe, as though looking far beyond what oneself could see, was an experience next only to hearing him talk.

Halfway through the lesson a tray of tea and home-made fruit cake would arrive and be much enjoyed. There would be an occasional set-to, as when Wittgenstein called for more water in his tea. "More, more water," he clamoured, while I told him his cup was already nearly pure water. He then told an anecdote of an Austrian peasant who kept on asking for rum in his coffee (*"Noch einen Schuss"*) and went on until he was drinking it neat. His rare anecdotes would be of this innocent character. Asking for a second slice of cake he said: "You remember a person who has put a good meal before you." I always imagined he was not a born ascetic and could appreciate the "good things" of life, all those things he voluntarily gave up. In 1935 we were moving house and I said I would need new curtains. "I could help you choose," he said. It slipped out and he immediately withdrew his offer, looking scared.

One afternoon my little girl, aged two-and-a-half, burst into the room. When she was removed, I said: "Children disturb you." This called forth his ire, expressed only in a gesture: children are children, they are there to be put up with, what an absurd thing to talk about. Soon after, Francis brought an armful of toys for the little girl, all bought at Woolworth's. This store, where no object at that time cost more than sixpence, had become their favourite shop. There, only questions of utility need arise. Wittgenstein squirmed if you so much as mentioned "taste." Yet years later I was to meet a lady who had been a student in Cambridge before the First World War and who remembered Wittgenstein as an aesthete.

Dostoevsky's *Crime and Punishment* soon became his favourite reading in Russian. More than twenty years later Mrs. Truscott, Skinner's sister, whom I then met for the first time, gave me Wittgenstein's copy of the book that she had found among her brother's things. In it every single accent had been pencilled in. As soon as Wittgenstein assured himself that there are no absolute rules of accentuation in Russian, he put in the lot. I had read some passages with him. It is a feat by any standard to have accented the entire novel, and a learner cannot do it on his own—or rather, if he could, there would be no need for it. Did he have another teacher of Russian or, what is more likely, did he read it with Bachtin? We read no poetry, but once he quoted a Pushkin lyric to me. That he most certainly had from Bachtin, who adored reading Russian poetry out aloud. On the subject of Dostoevsky we quarrelled. I once said, which is a matter of fact, that he learned much from Dickens. Wittgenstein would not have it, and was indignant. "Dickens," he pointed two feet above the floor—"Dostoevsky," his arm went up high.

Wittgenstein and Skinner

I never heard him talk politics, though who can doubt that he was deeply disturbed by the events of those years, and may have been shaken in the conservatism he brought from home. Yet whenever a political issue would come up he would bristle. Once when he said something derogatory about Marxism I turned on him furiously, saying that it was nothing like so discredited as were his own antiquated political opinions. To my astonishment he looked taken aback. He was silenced! In six to seven years' acquaintance it did not happen more than three or four times that he would stop to consider something I said (apart from my teaching), and then his expression would imply: Can it be she knows what she is talking about? I like to recall that honest doubt, as I do the occasion when I spoke of a blunder I had committed, and he weighed it up: "Yes, you lack sagacity."

I had just been elected to the Cambridge Committee of the Friends of the Soviet Union and imparted the good news to the two of them. Wittgenstein told me firmly that political work was the worst possible thing for me to do; it would do me great harm. "What you should do is to be kind to others. Nothing else. Just be kind to others." It was a disturbing experience when he wanted you to do something other than what you were doing. He conjured up a vision of a better you, undermining your confidence. I soon noticed that I could say things to him in Russian that would have infuriated him if said in English. Maybe because spoken Russian (other than political jargon) is freer of clichés, or maybe because he would not have recognised a Russian cliché. By exploding, "making a scene," one also escaped the restrictions that uttering factual statements imposes. He allowed one to have strong feelings, and would accept things said in a temper.

Since I can hardly pretend not to be aware how much one needs credentials to talk of Wittgenstein at all, I am apprehensive that my "project" may read as though it describes a friendship with the man, a thing I have no claim to. All I should be doing is to relate the things I remember of him and my thoughts about him in the years from 1934 to 1941. It must be understood that a lunch at our house or a tea with him in Trinity College were rare, isolated events.

He was the most elusive of men, shrouding his comings and goings in mystery. Once, maybe twice, he called with a rucksack on his back, as if he had just arrived by train, perhaps from abroad; yet you would not ask him where he came from. I would never have dreamed of asking him a personal question (how many people did?), and he never asked me one. He called when he wanted to see you or had some business with you. The latter offered the best basis for some kind of understanding, of getting on with him. He dictated throughout the form of relationship in which people stood to him. Much of his life will remain forever unknown to his closest friends.

I have no doubt that in those years Francis Skinner was the person closest to him. His attitude to Francis is what above all I should like to evaluate. His tone to the so much younger (Francis was twenty-two then, Wittgenstein forty-five) and very shy man was stern, as of a judge, yet Francis was the only one to whom I heard Wittgenstein refer in his absence by his Christian name. Otherwise he used surnames. The stern tone was of course habitual to him, the tone in which he talked philosophy. We and the Bachtins noticed how much gayer and more at ease Francis was when Wittgenstein was not about. There again, how many people were gay and at ease in his presence?

Soon Wittgenstein was to play a decisive role in Francis's life by influencing him to give up mathematics and become an apprentice in the Cambridge Scientific Instrument Company. "Was Wittgenstein good or bad for Skinner?"—this was a question raised in recent years in a talk with me by Francis's sister when I first met her. In a restrained way she told me of the consternation in her family when her brother, a brilliant mathematician and a scholar of Trinity College, decided to give it all up. "Why," she asked, "*why*?" She described how she and their parents would set out from Letchworth to look up Francis in College, and how he would come running down the stairs, hushing them: "I'm busy. I've got Dr. Wittgenstein here. We're working. Come back later." Hushing and repression are connected for me with much I heard about Wittgenstein.

His moral and practical influence on those around him strikes one as at least as significant as his work. Was it his fault that he left an imprint on the character and manner of speech of some, so that a decade after his death Roy and I recognised it in a new acquaintance, a non-philosopher? I left Roy talking to the visitor and went to make some coffee. When I came back I heard them talking about a picture in the National Gallery. The young man was saying: "You mean the one that hangs in room number so-and-so, on the left as you enter the door. Its size about. . . . " We pricked up our ears. Soon it transpired that, yes, he had been a friend of Wittgenstein's. In spite of his stern and difficult character he had innumerable friends in unexpected places.

You recognised a disciple and *some* friends by the way they cautiously threaded their path in conversation, as though stepping on stones across a morass. But then, Wittgenstein would most likely pick people of factual utterance as most congenial to him (Bachtin was an exception). It is hard to imagine Francis Skinner, a fellow of extreme modesty, ever talking in any other way. Yet when Francis sniffed at the sight of a history book lying on the table, you detected bad influence. To my eyes he showed no signs of suffering from dictatorial treatment. Over the years he was noticeably gaining in confidence and maturity, yet preserving unscathed his own innate qualities of kindness and sensitivity to others. With a hard struggle he overcame his terrible shyness. He could be cheerful and liked the company of others. Without guile of any kind, he was incapable of thinking evil of anyone. He could and did learn to be more practical though, alas, he would always be too unselfish, too self-effacing. While his life was immeasurably enriched by Wittgenstein's philosophy and friendship, I think of him as spiritually holding his own. His decision to volunteer for the International Brigade during the Spanish Civil War was entirely independent, free. (That he was not accepted must have been due to his physical disability.)

When Francis became a mechanic in 1935, Wittgenstein, who never justified his actions, said once "He would never be happy in academic life." That was probably true. The working people were kinder, less self-conscious, than his own class. He would go to a party at Pye's, to which he transferred from the Cambridge Scientific Instrument Company, and join in the fun, even dance. Yet the question whether Wittgenstein had a right to influence some young person in such far-reaching practical decisions just because it was given to him to do so, still remains unanswered. I know that to ask this is to talk "nonsense" in Wittgenstein's terms. But it is not nonsense in terms of the problems that arise in the relations between the generations and of the grave responsibilities that devolve on an older generation. What I mean is, how far can and should parents, teachers, and prophets go in directing the young? It is a staggering thought that Wittgenstein almost certainly never asked himself: are there other people close to Francis whose attitude should be taken into account? He would treat Francis as a responsible adult able to take his own decisions, without realising the immense force of his own personality and how inescapably it came into play. On the other hand, one cannot criticise but must admire him for the fact that calculations about status, class, and worldly success never entered his head. What he was concerned with was that people should be true to their own nature; without this they could not be happy.

On our return from Canada I realised how important a part of my "project" Wittgenstein's relations with Skinner constituted. I had already had an intimation of how they looked to Skinner's parents. Might Wittgenstein have appeared as an evil genius to them? Feeling the need for more knowledge I got in touch with Mrs. Truscott, who added some factual information. A former tutor of Trinity College, Professor Harry Sandbach, kindly looked up for me some data concerning Skinner's years there.

In 1925, when Francis was thirteen, he was seriously ill with osteomyelitis, which in the absence of modern antibiotics required that part of the bone was cut away, making him a cripple and subject to renewed dangerous attacks. His physical development was retarded and he could never play games at school. To his family he was always a very delicate though brilliant boy who needed to be treated with exceptional care. In 1930 he went up to Trinity from St. Paul's as a scholar, took mathematics and was a wrangler in 1933. He received prizes and scholarships for another two years of post-graduate work, though by then it would seem that he was totally immersed in Wittgenstein's philosophy and devoted himself to working with him.

Well might it seem to his mother that he was given a studentship by Trinity in order to work with Wittgenstein. According to Professor Sandbach, however, it is unlikely that special conditions were laid down by the college, though his application would probably have stated what he proposed to do. Under Wittgenstein's influence Francis decided to give up mathematics. He talked of taking up medicine (this had been done by another, earlier pupil of Wittgenstein's, Drury); but his parents could not afford to see him through medical studies. There was talk as an alternative of his becoming a mechanic, and later an idea that he might go and settle in Russia (with or without Wittgenstein, Mrs. Truscott is not sure). This plan caused the parents great consternation. He and Wittgenstein spent holidays together, one in Norway, another in Ireland. For the summer of 1935 plans were made for the two to go to the Soviet Union. But at the last moment Francis had a recurrence of his illness and could not travel. Wittgenstein then presumably went on his own (not with the "friend"—who was Francis—as Professor von Wright suggests in his biographical sketch). On Wittgenstein's return from the USSR, as Mrs. Truscott remembers, whatever plans they had had were abandoned. This was also my impression at the time—I will come to it later.

Francis in that year started work at the Cambridge Scientific Instrument Company. He continued to be a close friend of Wittgenstein's until his death; and at weekends they often went for long walks together. During the war he was on war-priority work. Mrs. Truscott says that at the funeral (October 1941) Wittgenstein looked "more desperate than usual." Her parents, she thinks, scarcely made contact with him; and he behaved to ordinary people (in her words) like "a frightened wild animal." He refused to go to the house after the funeral, but she saw him walking round Letchworth afterwards with Dr. Burnaby, the tutor of Trinity, looking "quite wild."

We know that Wittgenstein dictated the Brown Book to Skinner in 1934–1935. But would we not be wrong to assume that Skinner acted only as an amanuensis? Even to an outsider it appeared as if Wittgenstein tested and perfected his thoughts in his endless talks with Francis and a few other young men. They were somehow essential to the formulation of his thought, and perhaps the clue to why he chose to live in England. In them, sons of the English middle class, were combined the two features Wittgenstein required at that time in a disciple: childlike innocence and first-class brains.

The American professor I mentioned at the beginning of my account asked, in answer to my information, "What did Francis Skinner publish?" It was the vulgar-academic reaction. Francis published nothing, never thought of it. But if there is really no sort of record or recognition of his contribution, above all in the years 1933–1935, when he devoted himself entirely to working with Wittgenstein—let that contribution have been only a momentary hesitation on his part during a discussion, his unhappiness over some complex sentence, a mild protest ("Yes, but . . . ")—then something essential has been lost and overlooked, not least an important feature of Wittgenstein's mode of work.

I must pick up the main thread of my account of Wittgenstein. Although there would be continuing contact between us, and business too, until we left Cambridge in 1939, and occasional meetings after then, the easier times of my relationship with him came to an end with the end of the lessons.

I was expecting my second baby in January 1935. With the approach of the Christmas vacation I had to tell them that I should not be able to continue. I was in my eighth month and looked it; it never entered my head that they would not have noticed it. But they were quite ignorant of my condition, assumed I was in bad health, assured me that I would be better after a rest. Their naivety was as of two schoolboys, and it inhibited me from telling them of the coming confinement. I had to leave it till the baby arrived, and told them by letter.

Of the two following years my memory brings back events with some uncertainty as to their exact order. The common factor was that Wittgenstein was working hard, complaining frequently of not being able to concentrate. I think of 1935 as a lighter-coloured period. Extra depression affecting the man is connected for me with the time before he left for Norway in 1936.

Pleasant scenes of the earlier times arise in the memory. Roy and I went to the Tivoli to see Fred Astaire and Ginger Rogers in *Top Hat,* and in the foyer we met Wittgenstein and Skinner; Wittgenstein spoke of their dancing with lively admiration, with enthusiasm, making detailed and quite serious comments on their technique. Later in the darkened cinema we saw them sitting in the front row—a short and tall silhouette; Wittgenstein was very short-sighted but (I was told) refused to wear glasses. On another occasion he told me that he never missed seeing Ruth Draper.

One day, somewhat solemnly, they invited us to tea with them in Trinity. We sat in those famous deckchairs which I found rather uncomfortable for my back. The room was bare, without a flower or a picture. They produced thick tomato sandwiches, saying with pride they were bought at Woolworth's. After tea Wittgenstein talked and we listened. What it was about I don't now know, except that he was transported and so were we. He spoke at us, yet occasionally lost sight of us—Roy and I could exchange a glance. We walked home saying that there was nobody else who could in this way make you feel that your mind was stretched, thrown off its course, forced to look at matters it had never considered before. When we were eating the thick sandwiches Wittgenstein praised Woolworth's merchandise. He had bought a camera there in components each at 6d, total price two shillings—an excellent instrument! It led to his offering to take some snaps of me, and he did so one sunny day in Neville's Court in Trinity. I sat on a bench, and as he knelt on one knee to peer through the lens I had the sensation that I was a material object to him and that he might come up and absentmindedly move my elbow an inch. Francis told me that Wittgenstein would devote hours to shaving off tiny slivers from the small photos he took before he would be satisfied with some kind of balance achieved. Certainly when he gave me my copies they were much reduced from the original size; one was now smaller than an inch square. During the Spanish Civil War, Wittgenstein, seeing in our room an enlarged photograph of John Cornford, who had just been killed in Spain, sniffed: "They think you can just enlarge a photo. Now look. It's all trousers." I looked, and of course, he was right. On the day he photographed me he also showed me round the Fellows' Garden and stood in awe before some plant, saying "You can almost see it grow hourly. . . . " I had my tonsils out and was in the Evelyn Nursing Home feeling sorry for myself. Wittgenstein called. I croaked: "I feel just like a dog that has been run over." He was disgusted: "You don't know what a dog that has been run over feels like."

Visiting Russia and Norway

That summer, preparing for his trip to Russia, he came by himself for Russian conversation. Francis was now working in the factory and did not join in this. Nor was I told that he was included in the plan to visit Russia. The conversation lessons were excruciating. We sat in the garden. With the utmost impatience he rejected any topic I would suggest—everything verbal that a traveller or a simple mortal anywhere might need. To him they were all absurd, all non-topics. Questions that would have come naturally to me—why are you going, what are your plans, etc.—I knew I must not ask. Only if I cried out in Russian—"They could find nothing to talk about and wished each other a good morning"—would he relax and we would have started. It was good, but rare, to get him to laugh at himself. Did he know how much he inhibited others, while his dearest wish was for them to behave in a natural way? His temperament surely was immeasurably more intolerant and exacting than any logical theory could ever demand. He was driven to distraction by the manner in which people spoke.

When he returned from Russia he sent Skinner to give me a report. At least, that was what Francis said: "Dr. Wittgenstein asked me to give you a report." First came some technical details of the journey. He had been well received. He went to Moscow University to call on Mrs. Yanovska, Professor of Mathematics, and sent in his name. He heard her exclaim in astonishment: "What, not the great Wittgenstein?" At this stage I conjectured that he had sent Skinner so as to report truthfully things he could not have spoken of himself. He had been offered a chair of philosophy at Kazan, the university where Tolstoy had studied. He had taken no decisions about his future.

Of Professor Yanovska, Wittgenstein told me later that she was a fine person, with a young son to bring up. Her life was hard, and she suffered from diabetes. Trying to sort out events in my head, I always assumed that Wittgenstein, before going to Norway in 1936, had asked me to send Professor Yanovska some medicine for her complaint. But a letter of his from Norway (dated 4 September 1937) that I unearthed quite recently proves that I was mistaken; a "postscript" to this letter (dated 12 October 1937) confirms my error—though I don't think my other assumption is wrong, namely that he first returned from Norway in the summer of 1937.

The letter, from Skjolden i Sogn, is longer than his usual short business-like notes, and originally enclosed one in Russian from Professor Yanovska in which she asked Wittgenstein to send her some medicine for her illness (Protamine-Zinc-Insulin, Quibbs, New York—this should have been Squibb). He asked me to enquire whether it could be done through Boots in Cambridge, saying he would be prepared to help her if it wouldn't come to more than £10 or £15. He underlined three words in Russian that he could not make out in her letter and asked me to explain them; I was to return the letter to him and not talk of it to anyone, but to ask Roy's advice. His handwriting was of wonderful energy and gives me a thrill even now; he wrote on lined pages from a school exercise book. The end of the letter is missing; "annoyed" is spelt "anoied." I carried out his request, and Boots did the sending. The postscript I referred to is on the back of two small pictures of Bergen. It says that he had arranged through a London friend "who acts as my banker" to send me a cheque for £3. "If your expences (sic) are more we shall arrange things at Xmas or before, when I come to Cambridge." Of this I have no recollection. His anxiety about the money was due to the fact that at the time he was no longer a Fellow of Trinity and had no regular income.

While still on matters to do with his trip to Russia in 1935, I should like to repeat what I said earlier: that my impression was that on returning he had decided almost at once against going to settle there, though the idea of Russia as a spiritual refuge was to recur in his last letter to Engelmann of 21 June 1937, an echo of a desire expressed in a much earlier letter to the same friend of September 1922: "It still goes round in my head—an eventual flight to Russia. . . . " I think these give a clue to his attitude to Russia, a matter to which I shall return. Suggestions of a second Russian visit in 1939 rest only on remote hearsay and are clearly mistaken.

I return to the year 1936 and Wittgenstein's departure for Norway. Is it hindsight on my part, a trick of memory, that I think of that year as one in which his spirits were more than usually oppressed by anxiety and uncertainty, driving him to cut himself entirely off from people? When he came back to Cambridge a year later his mind still appeared unrelieved of the extra burden, and the confession seems to have been the outcome of a long period of crisis. Certainly no lighter-coloured memories as of the previous year come to mind. Yet there is reason for caution in trying to evaluate the mental state of a person who in some manner was always given to despair.

Before leaving for Norway he made a tour of Brittany by car with (as he told me) a newly acquired friend who knew the area well and was an excellent driver. Wittgenstein had evidently enjoyed the trip. "My friend is a cripple," he added, "lame in one leg." I remember this detail of a second lame friend, for it struck me as odd. Saying goodbye he asked me to send him regularly an English weekly to Skjolden. Which one? The *Illustrated London News*! His expression—anticipating my astonishment, yet forbidding comment as trivial and superfluous—was only too familiar. Francis visited Wittgenstein in Norway, and on his return gave me a description of what it was like. It was a life of total isolation and solitude. You had to row across in a boat to buy bread; it was difficult to get housecleaning done.

A letter of Wittgenstein's from Norway caused the greatest explosion of fury on my part, a fury that rankled the more since I would not dare to express it to him and I could only vent it when talking to one or two friends. I had been doing a little teaching and political work, but was longing for more things that would take me out of the house. So I was happy when I was asked to take a W.E.A. course on current events. Looking back thirty-five years I can see that it was idiotic of me, knowing Wittgenstein, not to anticipate how he would react to these tidings. Yet, I still think, my stupidity does not justify or excuse the harsh and hectoring letter I had from him. To think too that it was to be the only personal letter of any length that he ever wrote me, as though stern duty impelled him to do it!

Nowadays, when I no longer lecture or teach, I still cannot recall this letter calmly. He had a great capacity to wound. The wholeness of his character makes partial criticism of him appear carping, but I could never look on his ability to find out the weak spots of another human being and to hit out hard as anything but a flaw. The knowledge that he was at the same time a man of great purity and innocence cannot alter my feeling.

What he wrote was that I must on no account give that course, it was wrong for me, it was evil and damaging. I quote from memory of its impact, as in a fury I tore up the letter. Though there was never any danger that his strictures would divert me from what I was doing, yet here I am, still feeling hot under the collar at the memory; and I draw from this the conclusion that his influence was bad for me, and maybe for others like me. Though he was a shrewd judge of character and free of self-righteousness, he applied to others the stern standards he applied to himself. If you had committed a murder, if your marriage was breaking up, or if you were about to change your faith, he would be the best man to consult. He would never refuse to give practical help. But if you suffered from fears, insecurity, were badly adjusted, he would be a dangerous man, and one to be kept away from. He would not be sympathetic to common troubles, and his remedies would be all too drastic, surgical. He would treat you for original sin. The passage in an early letter to Engelmann (11 October 1920) is quite ghoulish: "I simply had to chop off a limb or two, those that remain are the healthier for it. . . . " The manner of his confession also throws light on this tendency. You would have to fight hard not to acquire a new brand of guilt—looking over your shoulder, what would Wittgenstein say to your doing this, saying that, reading some book or other? It would mean a conflict, for you well knew that you could learn from him more than from anyone else (and I do not mean logic or philosophy). If only he had been less imperious, less ready with prohibitions, more patient with another person's character and thought. Alas, he was no pedagogue.

It may seem that I am making sweeping statements because Wittgenstein wrote me a harsh letter. But I am fully aware of the very personal nature of my own reaction, just as I am of the fact that he disliked professional women and that his treatment of people varied greatly. If I generalise it is because I am thinking of the position he occupied in Cambridge at the time. People to whom you spoke of him showed great tolerance, taking for granted that he himself was and could not help being intolerant, irascible, idiosyncratic. Such was the reaction of a younger friend of ours, Alister Watson, a mathematician, who with his wife Susan was also good friends with Wittgenstein. To him I complained of Wittgenstein's letter; and he, only about half Wittgenstein's age and not yet settled in a profession, shrugged, smiling ever so wisely: "Well, he is like that. . . . "

If by a sense of humour we mean the capacity to see ourselves in the very act of dealing with others, then Wittgenstein lacked it entirely. He could not possibly have been aware of the harshness, amounting to cruelty, with which he hit out, never pulling his punches.[2] Nor would he know of the fear he inspired in people. A less inhibited man, one more given to wrath and quick anger, it is hard to imagine. I was talking of these things to an intelligent young woman I got to know in Canada. "Much good it is criticising Wittgenstein," I said, disgusted with myself. Her answer: "Perhaps it is no good, but might it not help, through these memories, to describe the man? If you were only carping, you would try to make up for it by extolling him." "Intolerable, intolerable," I cried, in the way I remember him doing. I thought it clever of her to sug-

2. Dr. F. R. Leavis told my husband of a typical case that occurred in his presence, and on this occasion, not uncharacteristically, Wittgenstein readily accepted Dr. Leavis's criticism of his behavior.

gest tentatively that an excess of sensibility might itself account for diminished sensitivity to the feelings of others.

When Wittgenstein said to Professor Norman Malcolm (as he reports in his biographical sketch) that he lacked affection though he was in need of it, I think he may well have been wrong. He certainly often expressed and showed gratitude; he sent the Bachtins and us Carlsbad plums one Christmas, might post a picture-postcard from Vienna with birdies wishing one "*Fröhliche Ostern.*" Constance Bachtin told me that when staying with them he would struggle in, carrying and spilling over the floor a dozen little packages of coffee, small so that they should not go stale. I remember the delicacy with which he sent me the news of Francis's death, enclosing it in a letter addressed to Roy.

The Confession

I always wanted to write down Wittgenstein's confession as I remember it since I find it revealing about him and something to learn from; also because it might help me to overcome a feeling of guilt, for I felt at the time and feel now that I was unkind to him on this occasion. It was embarrassing to find that it remained a taboo subject long after his death. Engelmann in his edition of Wittgenstein's letters to him (1967) omits the one that contained the confession, though there is in another letter an explicit reference to it. The years were going by, and one by one the people died who I knew had heard it, until only two Englishmen in this category are alive (now I fear maybe only one). I felt I must hurry and write it down, for I could hardly expect an Englishman to come out with a matter told him in confidence.

It happened on Wittgenstein's return from Norway in the summer of 1937.[3] He rang one morning to ask whether he

3. I have probably made a mistake in the date of this visit, and may have been influenced by the fact that Wittgenstein's letter to Engelmann that refers to the confession is dated June 1937. But from the book Ludwig Wittgenstein, *Letters to Russell, Keynes, and Moore*, ed. G. H. von Wright (Ithaca, N.Y.: Cornell University Press, and Oxford: Basil Blackwell, 1974), I see that Wittgenstein visited Cambridge round the New Year 1937 and then talked to friends about personal matters—"He referred to these talks as 'confessions' " (p. 170). This then must have been the time when he came to see me.

could come and see me; and it put me into a temper to be told firmly, when I asked whether it was urgent (I believe one of the children was not well), that it was urgent and could not wait. "If ever a thing could wait," I thought facing him across the table, "it is a confession of this kind and made in this manner." How often does a mental attitude appear in the memory bearing physical attributes—I could swear to it now that he kept his mackintosh on throughout, buttoned up, sitting up very straight and forbiddingly. Can I even separate my attitude to him then from the much modified view of the event that by degrees I came to adopt?

"I have come to make a confession." He had just been to Professor Moore for the same purpose. "What did Professor Moore say?" He smiled. "He said, 'You are an impatient man, Wittgenstein'. . . . " "Well, did you not know you were?" Wittgenstein, with disdain: "I did not know." I can remember two "crimes" to which he confessed: the first had to do with his being Jewish in origin, the second with a wrong he committed when he was a teacher in a village school in Austria.

On the first issue he said that he understood that most people who knew him, including his friends, took him to be three-quarters Aryan and one-quarter Jewish. In fact the proportion was the reverse, and he had done nothing to prevent this misapprehension.

I cannot be sure, but in his precise way he may have used the terms Aryan, non-Aryan throughout, not Jewish or non-Jewish, a very significant difference in his case and at that time. Mistakenly I took it for granted at the time that his words implied that he had three Jewish grandparents, in the sense that they were members of the Jewish community. I continued in this belief till 1969, in fact till I read the introductory note by Dr. B. F. McGuinness to Engelmann's *Letters from Wittgenstein,* from which I discovered that one of the grandparents was a gentile, two were Jews baptised as children, and one was baptised on marriage. "Some Jew," my grandmother would have said.

Leaving all argument aside as to whether an assimilated family like the Wittgensteins can be described, as I have seen it done, as "a typical Viennese Jewish family" (for what in heaven's name should we then call families like the Schnitzlers or the Freuds who did not repudiate the old faith and the Jewish community?), it would appear nevertheless that when Wittgenstein came to England before the First World War and again in the late 1920s he had no need to designate himself a Jew, and perhaps never even thought of himself as one.

On the other hand, it may be due to the fact that I misunderstood the meaning of his words that the idea of three Jewish grandparents became firmly fixed in my mind, so that the actual terms used by him can never now be dug out and restored to my memory. I had no idea whether he knew that I was a Jewish girl from the Ukraine, who had been through pogroms during the Civil War, whose childhood was darkened, branded by the anti-Semitism of Tsarist Russia. I understood too well the agony a Jew might endure if he was taken for a gentile. The "Jewish problem"—what is it for many but what it feels like to be a Jew? I can talk to any purpose on the subject (rarely and sparingly) only with my sister. My reaction to Wittgenstein raising it could only be one of great unwillingness, of longing to get it over quickly.

To make a confession must have appealed to Wittgenstein as the most radical way of relieving his mind of an oppressive burden of guilt. He did not ask for an emotional response. His manner forbade it. He was willing to answer questions, and left it to his hearer to react according to his or her nature. He was brought up as a Catholic: was this the accepted, normal form for him? It was not so for me! In later years, whenever I blamed myself for feeling somehow antagonistic, I excused it by thinking: if you come from Russia you cannot cope with a confession made with composure, prepared as it were beforehand; you could if someone came to you with "gnashing of teeth." I know I did say to him: "I am Jewish, and I have often missed the chance to come out with it in time to stop others from revealing their profound dislike of Jews in general. Anyhow, the English are shrewd. I assume they know about me, they probably know about you. . . . " I was moved to see that he looked up hopefully.

When I ask myself now what makes me so absolutely sure that Wittgenstein never made a false statement about his racial origins—and that if he was taken for something other than he was, it could only have been due to omission, conscious or unconscious, on his part—I say firstly: I have never met anyone more incapable of telling a lie, and secondly (and this seems to me to be more concrete evidence) where are the people who were on such terms with him as to ask him pertinent, straightforward questions to do with his family in Vienna, his past, his friends? Whatever people in England assumed about his background they did not enquire from him, and he told no untruth. Before Hitler came to power in 1933 the matter may not have impinged on his mind.

I think he talked for quite a while and certainly said many things I do not now remember. At one stage I cried out: "What is it? You want to be perfect?" And he pulled himself up proudly, saying: "Of *course* I want to be perfect." This memory alone would make me burst with the wish to describe the scene.

I have seen it said that people making personal statements about Wittgenstein are likely to drag him down to their own level. I do not think, however, there are many so mad as to compare themselves in some way, in any way, with him. It would always be obvious that he formed a class, a category of his own. The danger is that he may appear altogether inhuman to future generations. Those who knew him could never see him in this light. The more that is recorded of him, including any faults and frailties, the better, it seems to me. Do not writers on Milton, like Tillyard, still struggle to prove that he was not entirely lacking in amiability?

The most painful part of the confession came at the end, a traumatic experience to re-live and own up to. I recall well that at this stage he had to keep a firmer control on himself, telling in a clipped way of the cowardly and shameful manner in which he had behaved. During the short period when he was teaching at a village school in Austria, he hit a little girl in his class and hurt her (my memory is, without details, of a physically violent act). When she ran to the headmaster to complain, Wittgenstein denied he had done it. The event stood out as a crisis of his early manhood. It may have been this that made him give up teaching, perhaps made him realise that he ought to live as a solitary. On this occasion he did tell a lie, burdening his conscience for ever. How like Rousseau's youthful crime against the young servant girl, how like something many of us carry about with us. Wittgenstein was, after all, a man amongst men. Yet the confession also illustrates his own very extreme and drastic way of dealing with a condition when guilt caught up with him, when it became an obstacle to work, very different in character from difficulties inherent in the work itself, to which he wanted nothing better than to devote himself heart and soul.

One may make a guess that the non-Aryan issue having become oppressive for him with the existence of Nazi Germany, other painful memories of wrongs done by him associated themselves naturally, incapacitating him and demanding drastic surgery—a package-deal would be very much in line with his radical nature. He continued, as he spoke, to be so remote as to make it impossible for me to react in sympathy. Did he sense that my feelings were far from kind? They were very unlike those of the two above-mentioned Englishmen who (I know without being told) listened patiently, said little, but showed friendly participation, implying by manner and look that there was no need for him to make this confession, but if he thought he should, well and good, so be it. At the risk of being thought fanciful, I should like to add, I can imagine Bachtin, if put in such a position, pacing up and down like a tiger, gesticulating and muttering. And Francis? He would have sat transfixed, profoundly affected, his eyes undeviatingly on Wittgenstein.

I have always blamed myself for my coldness and for being at a loss what to say. Thirty-five years later I think I should have tried to probe why that old memory became so oppressive for him at that time, whether there was something he could do in a practical way to relieve the burden. These are idle speculations. Yet the question seems relevant: should he not have realised that many people live with a constant feeling of guilt? But his temperament was cast in an unchangeable mould. Just as the great modifications in his own philosophical thought did not make him put up more willingly with the manner in which people spoke, so this crisis in his life, so far as I know, did not make him any more tolerant.

A Lunch and Other Incidents

One never dreamt of asking him to a meal with other people. It was hard to foretell what his reactions might be on meeting a stranger.

I clearly remember his having lunch with us on one occasion. Only Roy and I were there, our little girl, and a young nursemaid who looked after her. There was tension, and silence. Wittgenstein glared. We were eating lamb. I seized the chance to break the silence, and said that with English children being so encouraged by books and nursery rhymes to love pets like chicks and lambs, it was awkward to say in a child's presence that it was lamb we were eating. Wittgenstein woke as from a trance. He turned upon me: "Nonsense, there is no problem in this, no problem at all." He was always genuinely cross when I "invented problems" where he could see none, as though I would be adding to his burden by gratuitously increasing their number.

I came in from shopping and the daily help said: "A man has just called with a large rucksack on his back." I ran to the gate and saw Wittgenstein walking off in the direction of the grocery shop over which Skinner had lodgings which Wittgenstein occasionally shared. The heavy metal-frame rucksack was half his height. For all I knew he might just have arrived from abroad.

I caught up with him at the corner of East Road and Hills Road and we both stood looking on while five or six soldiers were digging shallow trenches on the green; they were about three or four inches in depth. It was the days before Munich;

Mr. Neville Chamberlain was making a stand, acting as though the country was preparing for war. We looked on in silence at the diggers' efforts. I turned to Wittgenstein to protest, to cry out that it's all a sham, that we are lost, but he silenced me by raising his hand forbiddingly. He said: "I am as much ashamed of what is happening as you are. But we must not talk of it." As often, when he stopped you from saying something he looked as though by speaking you would inflict a wound.

This, by the way, is one of the few statements of a political nature for which I can quote him verbatim.

Early after the outbreak of war I had my appendix out. Soon our little girls were evacuated with their school to Shropshire, to be brought back to Birmingham in the summer of 1940, just in time for the "Battle of Britain" and the bombing of Coventry and Birmingham.

In the early spring of 1940, before Hitler's offensive in the West, I was staying in Cambridge with my sister, who was herself at that time a visitor at the house of Francis Cornford in Madingley Road. Wittgenstein rang me there and arranged to call. I walked out along the Madingley Road towards the Observatory to meet him. It must have been exceptionally warm for the time of year, for I remember wearing a light dress, and we did not go indoors, but walked up and down the garden. I told him the children had been evacuated. He may have commiserated with me. I cried out: "What are the Government up to? Not a shot has been fired. There is no war." (It was the time of the phoney war.) I prefer to think that on this occasion he looked more sorrowful than stern. But he reproved me all the same. "Some people," he said, "feel disgusted because birds feed on grubs." One of the rare sayings, profound I think, that have stuck in my memory.

If he spoke of himself at this meeting, it would be most likely to say he could not work, a recurrent theme with him.

He got ready to go. I said: "Come in and have a cup of tea. Meet my sister." He looked scared: "I mustn't. No. I can't." I was furious, yet I still saw him down the long drive. What an enslaver the man was! Was he reluctant because of some fear of meeting a new person? Unwilling to walk into Professor Cornford's house? Or just disinclined to comply, accustomed as he was to act entirely according to his own wishes?

On the way he asked (and it could only have been then and at no other time, for another opportunity of mentioning my sister never recurred): "What does your sister do?" "She's trying to write down her childhood memories." He enquired her age and hearing that she was forty, said very firmly: "It is too soon." My sister always thought it a wise remark.

A later memory, with the war no longer phoney but all-too-real and at a very grim stage, is of Wittgenstein walking up and down in our sitting room in Birmingham. At the time he was a medical orderly in a London hospital—his very characteristic contribution to the war effort.

I asked him about his accommodation. He answered in a hushed voice which was expressive of the horror of the experience that his room was below the one into which women in labour were moved. *Intolerable, intolerable*!

Finally, a trifling example of his naivety in some practical matters. This was in the 1930s, in peacetime.

He asked me whether I would put up a friend of his, Drury, when he next visited him in Cambridge. I promised to do so. Weeks passed. One evening the door-bell rang—we were not expecting anyone. A youngish man stood there with a small suitcase. "I am Drury. Dr. Wittgenstein said you would put me up. . . . " Wittgenstein had my promise and never imagined it was advisable to confirm it.

Attitudes to England and Russia

On Wittgenstein's attitude to England and to Russia, complex questions that go beyond mere memories and impressions, I should have been wise to keep quiet. But I am urged on by the lack of common sense of much that has been said on this subject. I hope it will emerge why I treat them as one theme.

Engelmann's *Letters from Wittgenstein with a Memoir* are a fund of information about Wittgenstein during the First World

War and up to 1925. It is here that we find some clue to his state of mind when the idea of a "flight" to Russia occurred to him: once in a letter of 14 September 1922, and then in that last letter of June 1937 that I have already mentioned. In the two instances, separated by fifteen years, his state of mind would appear to have been one of despair—in the earlier letter at the prospect of teaching in a school where he detested the people around, in the latter because of general doubt: "God knows what will become of me, perhaps I shall go to Russia." There is also a letter of February 1925 when, on hearing of Engelmann's plans to go to Palestine, Wittgenstein writes, again in a mood of despair: "I might want to join you—would you take me with you?"

In the circumstances it seems naive and contradictory of Engelmann to say in his memoir (p. 60, under the heading "Wittgenstein in Olmütz") that Wittgenstein did not care particularly where he lived and accepted the most primitive material conditions and the lowliest social milieu. Precisely; these he did accept. But from the conditions into which he was born and where he "naturally" found himself, from these he was in constant flight—an attitude he shared with many contemporary intellectuals of Central Europe, except that in his case it assumed an extreme form. When Wittgenstein wished to flee from civilisation, no place was remote or lonely enough.

Yet the over-riding need to do his work always won in the end, and being at heart a rational man with good horse-sense, he could and did put up with a place that served this purpose. This place was England.

Those who say that Wittgenstein did not care for English ways of life possibly form their opinion from the harsh words he did use about some aspects of English life. But why expect strangers to go about praising the country of their adoption? It must be remembered that Wittgenstein was not a refugee who came to England asking for asylum and who would feel in some special way indebted to the country. He came of his free choice. Also, he knew better than to go about praising England; he might think it indecorous. And, even if it had not been the decade of Stanley Baldwin and Neville Chamberlain, of economic crisis and political disarray, surely he had no more reason to laud Britain than had many Englishmen of his day (the English do not expect all their compatriots to do anything so odd).

But when we start from the other end, so to say, and ask why did he choose England, he who fought hard to arrange his entire life so as to have more freedom than any other man or scholar, freedom which for him meant in the end the minimum conditions in which he could go on with his work, then we have the answer: for this he chose England as the most suitable place. True, his choice became more restricted as time went on, but he had made it when many options were open.

Perhaps we should not say "England" but Cambridge (and particularly Trinity College)—a university that unobtrusively gave help and made only the slightest demands on him. And these institutions expressed something in the English cast of mind and manner of speech (not that he would allow such generalisations) that appealed to him. The work of English philosophers could serve as a basis for him to measure his work against, with less rancour attending the process than elsewhere. We must also keep in mind the importance to Wittgenstein of his disciples. These had to be, as I have suggested, of childlike innocence and excellent brain. Where else could he have found them? And, in the general social environment (as my Canadian friend said), nowhere else would he have met with such tolerance.

All this goes quite well with his detestation and denunciation of many things English, and with his continuing great love and nostalgia for old Vienna.

One could be misled by Wittgenstein since, as a solitary, he appeared to live at a distance from the life lived by the rest of mankind, while in fact everything essential did reach him and he had, at all times, a shrewd idea of what was going on about him in the wider world. One thinks of the economic crisis and unemployment, commercialism and vulgarisation, and above all the imminence of war, as matters that were familiarly present to his mind in these years. But he would not react to their impact as others might. He would not quote things said by Lenin or Stalin, and it is inane to affix any political label to him.[4]

Mrs. Truscott says that her parents knew of a tentative plan for her brother Francis to settle in the USSR, talk of which was abandoned after Wittgenstein's return. It seems to have been a joint plan which had not yet taken any definite form, and Wittgenstein's visit was of an exploratory nature. But Wittgenstein had a soft spot for Russia long before 1935, even while he was still what we might call a conservative. The two letters to Engelmann already referred to mention Russia as a place offering a refuge when he was beset by difficulties or maybe when his desire to flee from civilised life gained the upper hand. This idealisation of Russia he shared with many Central European intellectuals of his time, to some of whom she was still "Mother Russia," "Holy Russia" (as she was to Rilke or Barlach). It must be a matter of comfort for some of us that, however unusual and autonomous a man he was, Wittgenstein still belonged to his time and place.

To my mind, his feelings for Russia would have had at all times more to do with Tolstoy's moral teachings, with Dostoevsky's spiritual insights, than with any political or social matters. He would view the latter, which certainly were not indif-

4. My notes on Wittgenstein's attitude to Russia were overtaken by an article by J. Moran on this very theme in the May-June issue (no. 73) of the *New Left Review*, 1972. Mr. Moran reports two items new to me. Until his publication of Wittgenstein's 1935 letter to Keynes there was, to my knowledge, no authoritative statement available from Wittgenstein himself as to the purpose of his visit to the USSR in the summer of that year. Even so, no clear plan emerges; he speaks of "good and bad reasons" for wanting to go to Russia, with a view to settling there later (perhaps having first trained in England to become a medical doctor). As always with Wittgenstein, it is a highly personal statement and difficult to classify. Nevertheless it would seem that his attitude to the Soviet regime at that time was more positive than most knew or assumed. To me it came as more of a surprise to read that Wittgenstein had read Marx (Moran quotes a statement by Rush Rhees), but it is unclear how much he read and whether he made any political sense of it. For this information we are thankful to Mr. Moran. His own comments however show a total misunderstanding of the type of man Wittgenstein was, and that he was above all a person in search of spiritual salvation. The various evidence Mr. Moran quotes would have appeared less motley and contradictory if he had had a clue to the man's character.

ferent to him, in terms of the former. His rarely expressed political opinions might be naive. Alister Watson told me in the middle '30s of a talk he had had with Wittgenstein on the subject of the Russian Revolution. According to Alister, Wittgenstein had said that a Revolution is gradual too. He had also said that Lenin had grabbed the wheel of a runaway car; this was no more than a cliché of those times.

It has been suggested that Wittgenstein was attracted to Russia by the more liberal atmosphere created by Stalin's promise of a new Constitution. It is more than possible that news of a more hopeful prospect did reach Wittgenstein. But when we ask why the USSR reached a high-water mark of popularity among the intelligentsia of the West in those years after 1933 (the years of the Webbs' *Soviet Russia—a New Civilisation*), we find other, perhaps weightier reasons for it than the political development within the USSR. Hitler's coming to power and the approach of war—the shameful behaviour of Western statesman—Litvinov at the League of Nations—turned the hopes of the European intelligentsia towards Russia. Yes, Wittgenstein might, perhaps, have been able to quote Litvinov on peace being indivisible if he had seen any purpose in doing so.

It has also been said that Wittgenstein changed his plan of settling in the Soviet Union because of "harshening political conditions" there. His last letter to Engelmann seems to contradict this. It was written in the summer of 1937 at the peak of Stalin's Purges and two years after his visit. Was he, anyhow, the kind of man who would rush to conclusions about the general conditions of a strange country hard to get to know after a first short stay there? In any case, political and material conditions were in these years never other than harsh in the extreme. They were the times of the immense upheaval of industrialisation, following the collectivisation of the peasants. Nineteen thirty-five was the year of the trial of the Metro-Vickers engineers, the year when the Soviet Government began to tighten regulations affecting scientists who had settled there as refugees from Nazi Germany, some of whom were already being forced out and were arriving in Britain. All I want to say it that there is (so far) no evidence to show what Wittgenstein thought of these gigantic matters or how they affected his plans. One might suggest that the material hardships, hardly conceivable in the West, and the fact that throughout that decade Russia was living under a siege economy, *might* even have appealed to Wittgenstein's ascetic nature, particularly since the hardships still went hand in hand with a certain equality of opportunity and rewards. I am not implying that political repression had any appeal for him, nor that he was indifferent to it.

On the essential matter that was of immediate concern to himself, he could and very likely did form a clear opinion, short though his visit was, and that was whether he could continue his work there or live there; possible too whether it would be a suitable place where Francis might settle.

I am a thoughtless woman, for only at this stage do I ask myself, what would have happened if Wittgenstein had settled in the Soviet Union? A hypothetical question that implies many assumptions: but the answer is straightforward. It would have been a catastrophe. He avoided it thanks to his foresight and to Providence—and by the latter I mean nothing more than a conjunction of factors, including some outside the will and character of the person, which prevented him from making a disastrous choice, and allowed him to continue on the course least uncongenial to his nature.

Wittgenstein's Freedom

Though showing signs of great strains and stresses which he must have undergone in childhood, Wittgenstein in the 1930s was the least neurotic of men. His single-mindedness, resoluteness, and will-power make him stand out as a prophet, a kind of general in battle, not just a philosopher. With this went great artistic sensibility and mechanical skill. He was never at loggerheads with material things. And except for the crisis of his confession he did not appear to be at loggerheads with himself, though making the sternest demands on himself.

He never questioned his motives. He did not suffer from

irrational fears and insecurity, and was entirely unself-conscious. He was not inhibited in his relations with other people, provided these people were of his choice and his relations with them on his terms. It would be absurd to call him a perfectionist in the neurotic sense of the word.

He was contemplative, yet would anybody call him an introvert? Thinking was action to him. He was not intrigued or amused by human nature. Always a puritan, he was sure this nature was evil; and his attitude to it was one of despair. He excepted the lofty achievements of a few in religion, mysticism, and art, but these achievements he declared to be unfathomable, indeed ineffable.

We can understand his cavalier attitude towards Freud (as it emerges in his discussions with Rush Rhees and others), once we realise that he himself felt he had no need of Freud. I am reluctant to use Freudian terminology, but cannot put it more clearly and briefly than by saying that there was in him no perceptible split between the ego and the super-ego. For that matter, no split of any kind.

He was an aggressive and explosive man, but this too in a very peculiar, naive way of his own. At forty-eight he did not know the simplest thing about himself, namely, that he was impatient. I have several times mentioned the forbidding severity he directed at himself. But he never saw himself through the eyes of others, and he had no other standards than his own.

The awe in which he was held by those who knew him was due to this freedom of his, and to the means he used to become free and assure his freedom. He simply gave up everything in which mental troubles and complexes breed and flourish: wealth, family, community, and closer national ties. He gave up trying to fit in, except in the most perfunctory form, with existing ways of life, customs, trends. He discarded everything inessential and trivial, all the material things that make for comfort or relief, all pretence and adaptation (though he would allow himself an occasional visit to a "flick," or might read a crime story).

He became the freest of men, certainly with full freedom of

choice where to live, and with whom to consort. Yet he had to do his work unremittingly, and for this he depended on a small, select band of pupils and disciples: this was the only tie that bound him and this he accepted. If it should be asked, was that tie in any form or manner a homosexual one (a question much in fashion nowadays), I can only say that to my husband and myself, and as far as I know to all others who knew him, Wittgenstein always appeared a person of unforced chastity. There was in fact something of *noli me tangere* about him, so that one cannot imagine anyone who would ever dare as much as to pat him on the back, nor can one imagine him in need of the normal physical expressions of affection. In him everything was sublimated to an extraordinary degree.

Recently I was reminded by Professor George Thomson that Wittgenstein often despaired of philosophy as well as of his own work, and repeatedly said so. Also, his long-standing desire to take up manual labour was, in Professor Thomson's opinion, among the motivations of his wish to go to Russia; this would be entirely consonant with his admiration for the moral teachings of Tolstoy.[5] He detested many aspects of academic life and what it did to those who lived it. He was in this respect vulnerable and impressionable, so that after a visit to a friend in a mental home (in the '30s) he wanted to devote himself to the care of the mentally sick. But still, when we consider his completed life, surely we are right to say that he did throughout what he believed needed doing, and that he was the man he wanted to be.

When I asked my husband what he had learned from his conversations with Wittgenstein, he thought it over and summed it up in this way. He could learn little that was specific from a man whose opinions were so much his very own and sometimes so idiosyncratic. Indeed, the famous dictum

5. George Thomson, at that time a Fellow of King's College, got to know Wittgenstein when the latter came to Cambridge in 1929, and became a close friend of his. After his marriage, Wittgenstein used to have a weekly session with Mrs. Thomson, on Thursdays, when he would whistle Schubert Lieder to her accompaniment on the piano.

from the *Tractatus*: "What can be said at all can be said clearly, and we should keep silence on what we cannot talk about," seemed to him detestably wrong. But in another sense he learned something decisive: that is, that only those thoughts and opinions should be entertained to which you are entirely pledged. It was this that made all Wittgenstein's views and even occasional remarks memorable. Thus he remains a moral presence—oddly enough, not forbidding or admonishing, but benign and encouraging, perhaps because one thinks of him as always engaged in struggle.

As for me, looking back, I see him bulldozing, year in year out, clearing away the rubble that could only continue to accumulate. I know his life to have been one of fulfilment, yet he seems to me a tragic character.

2 Remarks on Frazer's *Golden Bough*

LUDWIG WITTGENSTEIN
Translated by John Beversluis

I

One must start out with error and convert it into truth.

That is, one must reveal the source of error, otherwise hearing the truth won't do any good. The truth cannot force its way in when something else is occupying its place.

To convince someone of the truth, it is not enough to state it, but rather one must find the *path* from error to truth.

I must plunge into the water of doubt again and again.

Frazer's account of the magical and religious views of mankind is unsatisfactory: it makes these views look like *errors*.

Was Augustine in error, then, when he called upon God on every page of the *Confessions*?

But—one might say—if he was not in error, surely the Buddhist holy man was—or anyone else—whose religion gives expression to completely different views. But *neither* of them was in error, except when he set forth a theory.

The very idea of wanting to explain a practice—for example, the killing of the priest-king—seems wrong to me. All that Frazer does is to make them plausible to people who think as he does. It is very remarkable that in the final analysis all these practices are presented as, so to speak, pieces of stupidity.

But it will never be plausible to say that mankind does all that out of sheer stupidity.

When, for example, he explains to us that the king must be killed in his prime, because the savages believe that otherwise his soul would not be kept fresh, all one can say is: where that practice and these views occur together, the practice does not spring from the view, but they are both just there.

It can indeed happen, and often does today, that a person will give up a practice after he has recognized an error on which it was based. But this happens only when calling someone's attention to his error is enough to turn him from his way of behaving. But this is not the case with the religious practices of a people and *therefore* there is *no* question of an error.[1]

Frazer says that it is very hard to discover the error in magic—and that is why it has lasted so long—because, for example, an incantation that is supposed to bring rain certainly seems efficacious sooner or later.[2] But then it is surely remarkable that people don't realize earlier that sooner or later it's going to rain anyhow.

I believe that the attempt to explain is certainly wrong, because one must only correctly piece together what one *knows,*

1. See Sir James George Frazer, *The Golden Bough,* one-vol., abridged ed. (New York and London: Macmillan, 1922), p. 264: "But reflection and enquiry should satisfy us that to our predecessors we are indebted for much of what we thought most our own, and that their errors were not wilful extravagances or the ravings of insanity, but simply hypotheses, justifiable as such at the time when they were propounded, but which a fuller experience has proved to be inadequate. It is only by the successive testing of hypotheses and rejection of the false that truth is at last elicited. After all, what we call truth is only the hypothesis which is found to work best. Therefore in reviewing the opinions and practices of ruder ages and races we shall do well to look with leniency upon their errors as inevitable slips made in the search for truth, and to give them the benefit of that indulgence which we ourselves may one day stand in need of: *cum excusatione itaque veteres audiendi sunt*". All footnotes to *The Golden Bough* refer to the one-volume edition of Frazer's work. The original manuscript refers only to page numbers in this edition, and does not include quotations. They have been supplied by Mr. Rush Rhees, with the exception of footnote 24 [ed.].

2. See Frazer, p. 59: "A ceremony intended to make the wind blow or the rain fall, or to work the death of an enemy, will always be followed, sooner or later, by the occurrence it is meant to bring to pass; and primitive man may be excused for regarding the occurrence as a direct result of the ceremony, and the best possible proof of its efficacy."

without adding anything, and the satisfaction being sought through the explanation follows of itself.

And the explanation isn't what satisfies us here at all. When Frazer begins by telling us the story of the King of the Wood of Nemi, he does this in a tone which shows[3] that he feels, and wants us to feel, that something strange and dreadful is happening. But the question "why does this happen?" is properly answered by saying: Because it is dreadful. That is, the same thing that accounts for the fact that this incident strikes us as dreadful, magnificent, horrible, tragic, etc., as anything but trivial and insignificant, it is *that* which has called this incident to life.

Here one can only *describe* and say: this is what human life is like.

Compared with the impression which the description makes on us, the explanation is too uncertain.

Every explanation is an hypothesis.

But an hypothetical explanation will be of little help to someone, say, who is upset because of love.—It will not calm him.

The crowd of thoughts which does not come out, because they all want to rush forward and thus get stuck in the exit.

If one compares the phrase "the majesty of death" with the tale of the priest-king of Nemi, one sees that they are the same.

The life of the priest-king shows what is meant by that phrase.

Someone who is affected by the majesty of death can also give expression to this through such a life.—This, of course, is

3. Insert *"dass er fühlt und uns fühlen lassen will"* [tr.].

also no explanation, but merely substitutes one symbol for another. Or: one ceremony for another.

No *opinion* serves as the foundation for a religious symbol. And only an opinion can involve an error.

One would like to say: This and that incident have taken place; laugh, if you can.

The religious actions, or the religious life, of the priest-king are no different in kind from any genuinely religious action of today, for example, a confession of sins. This, too, admits of being *'explained'* and not explained.

Burning in effigy. Kissing the picture of one's beloved. That is *obviously not* based on the belief that it will have some specific effect on the object which the picture represents. It aims at satisfaction and achieves it. Or rather: it *aims* at nothing at all; we just[4] behave this way and then we feel satisfied.

One could also kiss the name of one's beloved, and here it would be clear that the name was being used as a substitute.

The same savage, who stabs the picture of his enemy apparently in order to kill him, really builds his hut out of wood and carves his arrow skillfully and not in effigy.

The idea that one can summon an inanimate object to oneself as one can summon a person. Here the principle is that of personification.

And magic is always based on the idea of symbolism and language.

The representation of a wish is, *eo ipso*, the representation of its realization.

4. Insert *"eben"* [tr.].

But magic brings a wish to representation; it expresses a wish.

Baptism as washing.—An error arises only when magic is interpreted scientifically.

If the adoption of a child proceeds in such a way that the mother draws it from under her clothes,[5] it is surely insane to believe that an *error* is present and that she believes the child has been born.

Operations which depend on a false, overly simple idea of things and processes are to be distinguished from magical operations. For example, if one says that the illness is moving from one part of the body to another, or takes precautions to divert the illness as if it were a liquid or a condition of warmth. One is then creating a false picture for oneself, which, in this case, means a groundless one.

What a narrow spiritual life on Frazer's part! As a result: how impossible it was for him to conceive of a life different from that of the England of his time!

Frazer cannot imagine a priest who is not basically a present-day English parson with the same stupidity and dullness.

Why shouldn't it be possible for a person to regard his name as sacred? It is certainly, on the one hand, the most important instrument which is given to him, and, on the other, like a piece of jewelry hung around his neck at birth.

One sees how misleading Frazer's explanations are—I believe—by noting that one could very easily invent primitive practices oneself, and it would be pure luck if they were not actually found somewhere. That is, the principle according to which these practices are arranged (*geordnet*) is a much more general one than in Frazer's explanation and it is present in

5. See Frazer, p. 15: " . . . in Bulgaria and among the Bosnian Turks . . . a woman will take a boy whom she intends to adopt and push or pull him through her clothes; ever afterwards he is regarded as her very son, and inherits the whole property of his adoptive parents."

our own minds, so that we ourselves could think up all the possibilities.—We can easily imagine, for example, that the king of a tribe is kept[6] hidden from everyone, but also that every man in the tribe must see him. Certainly, then, the latter will not be left to happen in some more or less chance manner, but he will be *shown* to the people. Perhaps no one will be allowed to touch him, but perhaps everyone[7] *must* touch him. Recall that after Schubert's death his brother cut some of Schubert's scores into small pieces and gave such pieces, consisting of a few bars, to his favorite pupils. This act, as a sign of piety, is *just as* understandable to us as the different one of keeping the scores untouched, accessible to no one. And if Schubert's brother had burned the scores, that too would be understandable as a sign of piety.

The ceremonial (hot or cold) as opposed to the haphazard (lukewarm) characterizes piety.

Indeed, if Frazer's explanations did not in the final analysis appeal to a tendency in ourselves, they would not really be explanations.

There are dangers connected with eating and drinking, not only for savages, but also for us; nothing is more natural than the desire to protect oneself from these; and now we could devise such preventative measures ourselves.—But according to what principle are we to invent them? Obviously, according to the one by which all dangers are reduced to the form of a few very simple ones which are immediately evident to man. Hence the same principle according to which uneducated people among us say that the illness is moving from the head into the chest, etc., etc. Personification will, of course, play a large role in these simple pictures, for, as everyone knows, men (hence spirits) can become dangerous to mankind.

It goes without saying that a man's shadow, which looks like him, or his mirror-image, the rain, thunderstorms, the phases of the moon, the changing of the seasons, the way in which animals are similar to and different from one another and in relation to man, the phenomena of death, birth, and

6. Insert "*bewahrt*" [tr.].
7. Insert "*jeder*" [tr.].

sexual life, in short, everything we observe around us year in and year out, interconnected in so many different ways, will play a part in his thinking (his philosophy) and in his practices, or is precisely what we really know and find interesting.

How could fire or the similarity of fire to the sun have failed to make an impression on the awakening mind of man? But not "because he can't explain it" (the foolish superstition of our time)—for will an 'explanation' make it less impressive?—

The magic in *Alice in Wonderland*: of drying out by reading the driest thing there is.[8]

With the magical healing of an illness, one *directs* the illness to leave the patient.

After the description of any such magical cure, one always wants to say: If the illness doesn't understand *that*, I don't know *how* one should tell it to leave.

I don't mean that just *fire* must make an impression on everyone. Fire no more than any other phenomenon, and one thing will impress this person and another that. For no phenomenon is in itself particularly mysterious, but any of them can become so to us, and the characteristic feature of the awakening mind of man is precisely the fact that a phenomenon comes to have meaning for him. One could almost say that man is a ceremonial animal. That is, no doubt, partly wrong and partly nonsensical, but there is also something right about it.

That is, one could begin a book on anthropology by saying: When one examines the life and behavior of mankind throughout the world, one sees that, except for what might be called animal activities, such an ingestion, etc., etc., etc., men also perform actions which bear a characteristic peculiar to themselves, and these could be called ritualistic actions.

But then it is nonsense for one to go on to say that the characteristic feature of *these* actions is the fact that they arise from faulty views about the physics of things. (Frazer does this when he says that magic is essentially false physics or, as the case may be, false medicine, technology, etc.)

8. Lewis Carroll, *Alice in Wonderland*, chap. III [tr.].

Rather, the characteristic feature of ritualistic action is in no sense a view, an opinion, whether true or false, although an opinion—a belief—can itself be ritualistic or part of a rite.

If one holds it as self-evident that people delight in their imagination, one should bear in mind that this imagination is not like a painted portrait or plastic model, but a complicated pattern made up of heterogeneous elements: words and pictures. One will then no longer place operating with written and phonetic symbols in opposition to operating with 'mental images' of events.

We must plow through the whole of language.

Frazer: " . . . That these observances are dictated by fear of the ghost of the slain seems certain; . . . "[9] But why then does Frazer use the word 'ghost'? He thus understands this superstition very well, since he explains it to us with a superstitious word he is familiar with. Or rather, this might have enabled him to see that there is also something in us which speaks in favor of those savages' behavior.—If I, a person who does not believe that there are human-superhuman beings somewhere which one can call gods—if I say: "I fear the wrath of the gods," that shows that I can mean something by this, or can give expression to a feeling which is not necessarily connected with that belief.

Frazer would be capable of believing that a savage dies because of an error. In books used in primary schools it is said that Attila had undertaken his great military campaigns because he believed that he possessed the sword of the god of thunder.

Frazer is much more savage than most of his savages, for they are not as far removed from the understanding of a spiritual matter as a twentieth-century Englishman. *His* explana-

9. See Frazer, p. 212.

tions of primitive practices are much cruder than the meaning of these practices themselves.

The historical explanation, the explanation as an hypothesis of development, is only *one* way of assembling the data—of their synopsis. It is just as possible to see the data in their relation to one another and to embrace them in a general picture without putting it in the form of an hypothesis about temporal development.

Identifying one's own gods with the gods of other peoples. One convinces oneself that the names have the same meaning.

"And so the chorus points to a secret law" one feels like saying to Frazer's collection of facts. I *can* represent this law, this idea, by means of an evolutionary hypothesis, or also, analogously to the schema of a plant, by means of the schema of a religious ceremony, but also by means of the arrangement of its factual content alone, in a *'perspicuous'* representation.

The concept of perspicuous representation is of fundamental importance for us. It denotes the form of our representation, the way we see things. (A similar kind of *'Weltanschauung'* is apparently typical of our time. Spengler.)

This perspicuous representation brings about the understanding which consists precisely in the fact that we "see the connections". Hence the importance of finding *connecting links*.

But an hypothetical connecting link should in this case do nothing but direct the attention to the similarity, the relatedness, of the *facts*. As one might illustrate an internal relation of a circle to an ellipse by gradually converting an ellipse into a circle; *but not in order to assert that a certain ellipse actually, historically, had originated from a circle* (evolutionary hypothesis), but only in order to sharpen our eye for a formal connection.

But I can also see the evolutionary hypothesis as nothing more, as the clothing of a formal connection.

* * *

[The following remarks do not accompany the foregoing ones in the typescript:]

I should like to say: nothing shows our kinship to those savages better than the fact that Frazer has on hand a word as familiar to himself and to us as 'ghost' or 'shade' in order to describe the views of these people.

(That is certainly something different than if he, for example, described the savages as imagining that their heads will fall off when they have killed an enemy. Here *our description* would contain nothing superstitious or magical in itself.)

Indeed, this peculiarity relates[10] not only to the expressions 'ghost' and 'shade', and much too little is made of the fact that we count the words 'soul' and 'spirit' as part of our educated vocabulary. Compared with this, the fact that we do not believe that our soul eats and drinks is a trifling matter.

An entire mythology is stored within our language.

To drive out or slay death; but on the other hand it is represented as a skeleton, as itself dead in a certain sense. "As dead as death." "Nothing is as dead as death; nothing is as beautiful as beauty itself." The picture in terms of which one conceives of reality here is such that beauty, death, etc. are the pure (concentrated) substances, while they are present in a beautiful object as an admixture.—And do I not recognize here my own observations about 'object' and 'complex'?

In the ancient rites we have the use of an extremely developed gesture-language.

And when I read Frazer, I continually would like to say: We still have all these processes, these changes of meaning, before us in our verbal language. When what hides in the last sheaf of corn is called the 'Corn-wolf', but also this sheaf itself as

10. Insert "*bezieht*" [tr.].

well as the man who binds it, we recognize herein a familiar linguistic occurrence.[11]. . . . .

I could imagine that I had had the choice of picking a creature of the earth as the dwelling place for my soul, and that my spirit had chosen this unattractive creature as its residence and vantage point. Perhaps because a beautiful residence would be an exception, and would be repugnant to it. One's spirit would certainly have to be very sure of itself to do this.

One could say "every view has its charm", but that would be false. The correct thing to say is that every view is significant for the one who sees it as significant (but that does not mean, sees it other than it is). Indeed, in this sense, every view is equally significant.

It is indeed important that I must also make my own the contempt that anyone may have for me, as an essential and significant part of the world as seen by me.

If a man were given the choice to be born in one tree of a forest, there would be some who would seek out the most beautiful or the highest tree, some who would choose an average or below average tree, and I certainly do not mean out of philistinism, but rather for exactly the same reason, or kind of reason, that the other had chosen the highest. That the feeling which we have for our lives is comparable to that of such a being who could choose for himself his viewpoint in the world underlies, I believe, the myth—or the belief—that we had chosen our bodies before birth. . . . .

I believe that the characteristic feature of primitive man is that he does not act from *opinions* (contrary to Frazer).

I read, among many similar examples, of a Rain-King in Africa to whom the people pray for rain *when the rainy period*

11. See Frazer, p. 449: "In various parts of Mecklenburg, where the belief in the Corn-wolf is particularly prevalent, every one fears to cut the last corn, because they say that the Wolf is sitting in it; . . . the last bunch of standing corn is itself commonly called the Wolf, and the man who reaps it . . . is himself called Wolf. . . . "

comes.[12] But surely that means that they do not really believe that he can make it rain, otherwise they would make it rain in the dry periods of the year in which the land is "a parched and arid desert". For if one assumes that the people formerly instituted this office of Rain-King out of stupidity, it is nevertheless certainly clear that they had previously experienced that the rains begin in March, and then they would have had the Rain-King function for the other part of the year. Or again: toward morning, when the sun is about to rise, rites of daybreak are celebrated by the people, but not during the night, when they simply burn lamps.[13]

When I am furious about something, I sometimes beat the ground or a tree with my walking stick. But I certainly do not believe that the ground is to blame or that my beating can help anything. "I am venting my anger". And all rites are of this kind. Such actions may be called Instinct-actions.—And an historical explanation, say, that I or my ancestors previously believed that beating the ground does help is shadow-boxing, for it is a superfluous assumption that explains *nothing*. The similarity of the action to an act of punishment is important, but nothing more than this similarity can be asserted.

Once such a phenomenon is brought into connection with an instinct which I myself possess, this is precisely the explanation wished for; that is, the explanation which resolves this particular difficulty. And a further investigation about the history of my instinct moves on another track.

It was not a trivial reason, for really there can have been no *reason*, that prompted certain races of mankind to venerate the

12. See ibid., p. 107; " . . . the Kings of the Rain, *Mata Kodou*, who are credited with the power of giving rain at the proper time, that is, the rainy season. Before the rains begin to fall at the end of March the country is a parched and arid desert; and the cattle, which form the people's chief wealth, perish for lack of grass. So, when the end of March draws on, each householder betakes himself to the King of the Rain and offers him a cow that he may make the blessed waters of heaven to drip on the brown and withered pastures."

13. Ibid., pp. 78–79.

oak tree, but only the fact that they and the oak were united in a community of life, and therefore it was not by choice that they arose together, but rather like the flea and the dog. (If fleas developed a rite, it would be based on the dog.)

One could say that it was not their union (the oak and man) that has given rise to these rites, but in a certain sense their separation. For the awakening of the intellect occurs with a separation from the original *soil,* the original basis of life. (The origin of *choice.*)

The form of the awakening spirit is veneration of objects.

II

P. 168.[14] It is, of course, not so that the people believe that the ruler has these powers, and the ruler knows very well that he doesn't have them, or can only fail to know it if he is an imbecile or a fool. But the notion of his power is, of course, adapted in such a way that it can harmonize with experience—the people's as well as his own. That some hypocrisy thereby plays a role is true only insofar as it is close to what people, for the most part, really do.

P. 169.[15] When a man laughs too much in our company (or at least in mine), I half-involuntarily compress my lips, as if I believed I could thereby keep his closed.

P. 170.[16] The nonsense here is that Frazer represents these people as if they had a completely false (even insane) idea of

14. Ibid., p. 168: "At a certain stage of early society the king or priest is often thought to be endowed with supernatural powers or to be an incarnation of a diety, and consistently with this belief the course of nature is supposed to be more or less under his control. . . . "

15. Ibid., p. 169: "In ancient times, he was obliged to sit on the throne for some hours every morning, with the imperial crown on his head, but to sit altogether like a statue, without stirring either hands or feet, head or eyes, nor indeed any part of his body, because, by this means, it was thought that he could preserve peace and tranquillity in his empire. . . . "

16. Ibid., p. 170: "The power of giving or witholding rain is ascribed to him, and he is the lord of the winds. . . . "

the course of nature, whereas they only possess a peculiar interpretation of the phenomena. That is, if they were to write it down, their knowledge of nature would not differ *fundamentally* from ours. Only their *magic* is different.

P. 171.[17] That is true and false. Certainly not the dignity of protection of the person, but perhaps—so to speak—the natural sanctity of the divinity in him.

As simple as it sounds: the distinction between magic and science can be expressed by saying that in science there is progress, but in magic there isn't. Magic has no tendency within itself to develop.

P. 179.[18] How much more truth there is in this view, which ascribes the same multiplicity to the soul as to the body, than in a modern watered-down theory.

Frazer doesn't notice that we have before us the teaching of Plato and Schopenhauer.

We find every childlike (infantile) theory again in today's philosophy, only not with the winning ways of the childlike.

P. 614.[19] Besides these similarities, what seems to me to be most striking is the dissimilarity of all these rites. It is a multiplicity of faces with common features which continually emerges here and there. And one would like to draw lines connecting these common ingredients. But then one part of our account would still be missing, namely, that which brings this picture into connection with our own feelings and thoughts. This part gives the account its depth.

In all these practices one, of course, sees something that is similar to the association of ideas and related to it. One could speak of an association of practices.

17. Ibid., p. 171: " . . . a network of prohibitions and observances, of which the intention is not to contribute to his dignity. . . . "

18. Ibid., p. 179: "The Malays conceive the human soul as a little man . . . who corresponds . . . to the man in whose body he resides. . . . "

19. In Chapter LXII: The Fire Festivals of Europe.

P. 618.[20] Nothing accounts for why the fire should be encircled by such a nimbus. And, how strange, what does it really mean "it had the appearance of being derived from heaven"? from which heaven? No, it is not at all self-evident that fire is looked at in this way—but that's just how it is looked at.

Here the hypothesis seems to give the matter depth for the first time. And one can recall the explanation of the strange relationship between Siegfried and Brunhilde in our *Niebelungenlied.* Namely, that Siegfried seems to have already seen Brunhilde before. It is now clear that what gives this practice depth is its *connection* with the burning of a man.[21] If it were the custom at some festival for the men to ride on one another (as in the game of horse and rider), we would see nothing in this but a form of carrying which reminds us of men riding horseback;—but if we knew that among many peoples it had been the custom, say, to employ slaves as riding animals and, so mounted, to celebrate certain festivals, we would now see something deeper and less harmless in the harmless practice of our time. The question is: does the sinister, as we may call it, attach to the practice of the Beltane Fire Festival in itself, as it was carried on one hundred years ago, or is the Festival sinister only if the hypothesis of its origin turns out to be true? I believe it is clearly the inner nature of the modern practice itself which seems sinister to us, and the familiar facts of human sacrifice only indicate the lines along which we should view the practice. When I speak of the inner nature of the

20. Frazer, p. 618: " . . . As soon as any sparks were emitted by means of the violent friction, they applied a species of agaric which grows on old birch trees, and is very combustible. This fire had the appearance of being immediately derived from heaven, and manifold were the virtues ascribed to it. . . . "

21. Ibid., p. 618: " . . . the person who officiated as master of the feast produced a large cake baked with eggs and scalloped round the edge, called *am bonnach beal-tine—i.e.,* the Beltane cake. It was divided into a number of pieces, and distributed in great form to the company. There was one particular piece which whoever got was called *cailleach beal-tine—i.e.,* the Beltane *carline,* a term of great reproach. Upon his being known, part of the company laid hold of him and made a show of putting him into the fire . . . And while the feast was fresh in people's memory, they affected to speak of the *cailleach beal-tine* as dead."

practice, I mean all circumstances under which it is carried out and which are not included in a report of such a festival, since they consist not so much in specific actions which characterize the festival as in what one might call the spirit of the festival; such things as would be included in one's description, for example, of the kind of people who take part in it, their behavior at other times, that is, their character, the kind of games which they otherwise play. And one would then see that the sinister quality lies in the character of these people themselves.

P. 619.[22] We see something here that looks like the last vestige of drawing lots. And, through this aspect, it suddenly gains depth. If we were to learn that the cake with the knobs had, in a particular case, originally been baked, say, in honor of a button-maker on his birthday and that this practice had been preserved in the region, this practice would in fact lose all 'depth', unless it was embedded in its present form itself. But in such a case one often says: "this practice is obviously ancient". How does one know that? Is it only because one has historical evidence about ancient practices of this kind? Or does it have yet another reason which one arrives at through interpretation? But even if both the prehistoric origin of the practice and its derivation from an earlier practice are proven historically, it is nevertheless possible that the practice has *nothing whatever* sinister about it today, that nothing of the prehistoric horror remains attached to it. Perhaps today it is engaged in only by children who compete in baking cakes and decorating[23] them with knobs. Then the depth lies only in thinking about that derivation. But this can still be very uncertain and one would like to say: "Why worry about so uncertain a matter?" (like a backwards-looking clever Elsie). But it is not that kind of worry.—Above all: where do we get the certainty that such a practice must be ancient (what are our data,

22. Ibid., p. 619: " . . . They put all the bits of the cake into a bonnet. Every one, blindfold, draws out a portion. He who holds the bonnet, is entitled to the last bit. Whoever draws the black bit, is the *devoted* person who is to be sacrificed to *Baal*. . . . "

23. Reading *"Verzieren"* for *"Verzehren"* [tr.].

what is the verification)? But are we certain then? might we not be mistaken and convicted of our mistake by history? Certainly, but then there always remains something of which we are certain. We would then say: "Good, the origin may be different in this case, but in general it is surely prehistoric." Whatever we regard as *evidence* for this must comprise the depth of this assumption. And this evidence is again non-hypothetical, psychological. That is, when I say: the depth in this practice lies in its origin *if* it did come about in this way, then the depth lies either in the thought of such an origin, or the depth is itself hypothetical, and one can only say: *If* it happened that way then it was a deep and sinister business. I want to say: The deep, the sinister, do not depend on the history of the practice having been like this, for perhaps it was not like this at all; nor on the fact that it was perhaps or probably like this, but rather on that which gives me grounds for assuming this. Indeed, how is it that in general human sacrifice is so deep and sinister? For is it only the suffering of the victim that makes this impression on us? There are illnesses of all kinds which are connected with just as much suffering, *nevertheless* they do not call forth this impression. No, the deep and the sinister do not become apparent merely by our coming to know the history of the external action, rather it is *we* who ascribe them from an experience of our own.

The fact that the lots are drawn by the use of a cake is particularly horrible (almost like betrayal with a kiss), and that it strikes us this way is of fundamental importance for the investigation of such practices.

When I see such a practice, or hear of it, it is like seeing a man speaking harshly to someone else over a trivial matter, and noticing from his tone of voice and facial expression that this man can on occasion be frightening. The impression that I receive here can be much deeper and extraordinarily more serious.

The *background* of a way of acting.

In any case, a conviction serves as the basis for the assumptions about the origin of, for example, the Beltane Festival;

namely, that such festivals are not made up by one person, so to speak, at random, but rather need an infinitely broader basis if they are to be preserved. If I wanted to make up a festival, it would die out very quickly or be modified in such a manner that it corresponds to a general inclination of the people.

But what prevents us from assuming that the Beltane Festival has always been celebrated in its present (or very recent) form? One would like to say: it's too foolish for it to have been invented in this form. Isn't that like my seeing a ruin and saying: that must have been a house at one time, for nobody would have put up such a heap of hewn and irregular stones? And if I were asked: How do you know that? I could only say: from my experience with people. Indeed, even in places where people actually build ruins, they take the form of collapsed houses.

One might also put it this way: Anyone who wanted to make an impression on us with the story of the Beltane Festival need not advance the hypothesis of its origin in any case, he need only lay before us the material (which leads to this hypothesis) and say nothing further. One might now perhaps like to say: "Of course, because the listener or reader will draw the conclusion himself!" But must he draw this conclusion explicitly? therefore, draw it at all? And what kind of conclusion is it? That this or that is *probable*?! And if he can draw the conclusion himself, how is the conclusion to make an impression on him? Whatever makes an impression on him must surely be something that he has not made. Is he impressed for the first time by hearing the hypothesis expressed (whether by himself or someone else), or already by the material that leads to it? But couldn't I just as well ask: If I see someone being killed,—is what makes an impression on me simply what I see, or is it the later hypothesis that here a man is being killed?

But it is not simply the thought of the possible origin of the Beltane Festival that carries with it the impression, but rather what is called the enormous *probability* of this thought. As that which is derived from the material.

As it has come down to us, the Beltane Festival is indeed a game, and is similar to children playing robbers. But surely not. For although it has been prearranged that the party who rescues the victim wins, nevertheless what takes place still has an addition of temperament which the mere dramatic presentation does not have. But even if it were merely a question of a wholly cool performance, we would still uneasily ask ourselves: What about this presentation, what is its *meaning*?! And it could then make us uneasy owing to its peculiar meaninglessness, irrespective of any interpretation. (Which shows the kind of basis such uneasiness can have.) Suppose now, for example, that a harmless interpretation were given: They simply cast lots so that they would have the pleasure of threatening someone with being thrown into the fire, which is not pleasant; in this way the Beltane Festival becomes much more like one of those amusements where one of the company has to endure certain forms of cruelty which, such as they are, satisfy a need. By means of such an explanation, the Beltane Festival would also lose all of its mysterious character if it did not itself deviate from such ordinary games of robbers, etc. in its action and mood.

Just as the fact that on certain days children burn a strawman could make us uneasy, even if no explanation for it were given. Strange that they should burn *a man* as part of the festivities! I want to say: the solution is no more disturbing than the riddle.

But why shouldn't it really be only (or certainly in part) the *thought* (*Gedanke*) which gives me the impression? For aren't ideas (*Vorstellungen*) frightening? Can't I be horrified by the thought that the cake with the knobs has at one time served to select by lot the sacrificial victim? Doesn't the *thought* have something frightening about it?—Yes, but what I see in those stories is nevertheless acquired through the evidence, as well as through such things as do not appear to be directly connected with it,—through the thoughts of man and his past, through all the strange things I see, and have seen and heard about, in myself and others.

P. 640.[24] One can very well imagine that—and perhaps the reason given might have been that the patron saints would otherwise pull against one another, and that only one could direct the matter. But this too would only be a later extension of instinct.

All these *different* practices show that it is not a question of the derivation of one from the other, but of a common spirit. And one could invent (devise) all these ceremonies oneself. And precisely that spirit from which one invented them would be their common spirit.

P. 641.[25] The connection between illness and dirt. "To cleanse of an illness."

It affords a simple, childlike theory of illness, that it is dirt which can be washed off.

Just as there are 'infantile theories of sex', so there are infantile theories in general. But that doesn't mean that everything a child does has arisen *out of* an infantile theory as its basis.

The correct and interesting thing to say is not: this has arisen from that, but: it could have arisen this way.

P. 643.[26] That fire was used for purification is clear. But nothing can be more probable than the fact that later on thinking people brought purification ceremonies into connection with the sun, even where the ceremonies had originally been thought of only as purificatory. When one thought forces itself

24. See p. 640: "Various rules were also laid down as to the kind of persons who might or should make the need-fire. Sometimes it was said that the two persons who pulled the rope which twirled the roller should always be brothers or at least bear the same baptismal name . . ." [ed.].
25. Ibid., pp. 640–641: " . . . as soon as the fire on the domestic hearth had been rekindled from the need-fire, a pot full of water was set on it, and the water thus heated was afterwards sprinkled upon the people infected with the plague or upon the cattle that were tainted by the murrain."
26. Ibid., p. 643: " . . . Dr. Westermarck has argued powerfully in favour of the purificatory theory alone. . . . However, the case is not so clear as to justify us in dismissing the solar theory without discussion. . . . "

upon one person (fire-purification) and a different thought upon another (fire-sun), what can be more probable than the fact that both thoughts will force themselves upon a single person. The learned who would always like to have *a* theory!!!

That fire destroys things *completely,* unlike battering or tearing them to pieces, must have astonished men.

Even if one didn't know that the thoughts purification and sun had been connected, one could assume this to have arisen somewhere.

P. 680.[27] 'Soul-stone.' Here one sees how such an hypothesis works.

P. 681.[28] That would point to the fact that here truth rather than superstition lies at the basis. (Of course, it is easy to fall into the spirit of contradiction when face to face with the stupid scientist.) But it may very well be the case that the completely shaved body induces us in some sense to lose our self-respect. (Brothers Karamazov.) There is no doubt whatever that a mutilation which makes us appear unworthy or ridiculous in our own eyes can completely deprive us of the will to defend ourselves. How embarrassed we sometimes become—or at least many people (I)—by our physical or aesthetic inferiority.

27. Ibid., p. 680: " . . . in New Britain there is a secret society. . . . On his entrance into it every man receives a stone in the shape either of a human being or of an animal, and henceforth his soul is believed to be knit up in a manner with the stone."

28. Ibid., p. 680–681: " . . . it used to be thought that the maleficent powers of witches and wizards resided in their hair, and that nothing could make any impression on the miscreants so long as they kept their hair on. Hence in France it was customary to shave the whole bodies of persons charged with sorcery before handing them over to the torturer."

3 Letters to Ludwig von Ficker

LUDWIG WITTGENSTEIN
Translated by Bruce Gillette
Edited by Allan Janik

A Note on the Translation

Although Wittgenstein's letters to Ludwig von Ficker are written in a conversational tone, the dated Austrian colloquialisms and expressions deriving from the Habsburg monarchy and its military terminology, in particular, present problems for the translator. Wittgenstein's reference to a *Krampus* in the postscript to Letter 26, for example, is drawn from Austrian folklore, in which a *Krampus* or devilish person is associated with St. Nicholas and represented in the procession celebrating his feast day, 6 December, the day following the date of writing. The word which we have rendered "babbling" in Letters 22 and 23 (which Wittgenstein contrasts with the silence of the *Tractatus*) is *schwefeln*. In Viennese dialect it is a synonym for *schwatzen*, to chatter or gossip, and *lügen*, to lie. It is etymologically related to *schwafeln*, to talk silly or drivel, and *schwabeln*, to speak incomprehensibly (in the manner of the Swabians). The equivalent of this word in most south German dialects is *bappeln*, a cognate of our babble.

The abbreviation *k.u.k.* was used in the Austro-Hungarian state to denote things public in much the same way as we use "U.S." It stands for *kaiserlich und königlich* and emphasizes the unity of the emperor of Austria (more precisely, "of the lands represented in the *Reichsrat*") and the king of Hungary in the person of the Habsburg monarch. We have chosen to render it "I & R" for Imperial and Royal. We have rendered military terms by their American equivalents. So *technischer Beamter*, literally, technical-official, becomes "warrant officer" in Letter 13.

Wittgenstein's spelling, especially of proper names, is occasionally inaccurate. We have corrected it to conform to standard usage. We have written out the month where Wittgenstein used numerals to avoid confusion between European and American usage. Wittgenstein's emphasis in the text corresponds to the standard method for transferring underscoring to the printed page: one underlining is indicated by italics, two by small capitals, three by large capitals.

This translation has been prepared from Wittgenstein's *Briefe an Ludwig von Ficker* edited by G. H. von Wright with the aid of Walter Methlagl (Brenner Studien, I; Salzburg: Otto Müller, 1969). We are pleased to acknowledge Dr. Methlagl's assistance in the preparation of this translation. Professor Rush Rhees also read the translation and provided valuable suggestions for its improvement. They bear no responsibility for its shortcomings.

Bruce Gillette
Allan Janik

1.

Hochreit
Hohenberg, Lower Austria
14 July 1914

Dear Sir:
Forgive me for asking you for a big favor. I should like to transfer a sum of 100,000 crowns to you with the request that you distribute this sum, at your own discretion, among Austrian artists who are without means. I am turning to you in this matter since I assume that you are acquainted with many of our best talents and know which of them are most in need of support. Should you care to fulfill my request, please write to me at the above address, but in any event, please keep this matter secret for the time being.

Very truly yours,
Ludwig Wittgenstein, Jr.

2.

Hochreit, Hohenberg, L.A.
19 July 1914

Dear Sir:
In order to convince you that I am sincere in my offer, I can probably do nothing better than actually transfer the sum of money to you; and this will happen the next time I come to Vienna—in the course of the next two weeks. I want to inform you briefly now what moved me to my plan. I inherited a large fortune through my father's death a year and a half ago. It is a custom in such cases to donate a sum to charitable causes. So much for the exterior motive. As agent of my own affairs, I chose you because of what Kraus wrote about you and your journal in the *Fackel,* and because of what you wrote about Kraus. Your friendly letter has increased my trust in you even more. I should like to close now. Perhaps I may meet you and talk with you sometime? *I hope so very much.*
Please accept my warmest thanks for your help.

Most respectfully yours,
Ludwig Wittgenstein, Jr.

3.

Vienna XVII
Neuwaldeggerstraße 38
1 August 1914

Dear Mr. von Ficker:
Many thanks for your friendly letter and for Dallago's which you included. (I do not know whether you still have any use for it, but I am returning it anyway.) Thanks once more for your visit and also for introducing me to Loos. It makes me *very* happy to have been able to meet him. My address for the time being is the above since we have moved to Vienna on account of the war. With best regards.

Yours very truly,
Ludwig Wittgenstein

4. Postcard

(postmarked) Kraków
14 August 1914

Dear Mr. von Ficker:
Forgive me for writing to you in pencil; I do not have any ink here. I should only like to inform you that I have volunteered for military service and that my address, for correspondence purposes, now is: Fortress Artillery Regiment No. 2, 2nd Cadre, Kraków. With the very best regards

Yours very truly,
L. Wittgenstein

5. Military Postcard

Military Headquarters
Kraków
H.M.S. Goplana
(undated)

Just a line so that you do not forget me!

Ludwig Wittgenstein

6. Military Postcard

Military Headquarters
Kraków
Military Post Office No. 186
(undated)

Dear Mr. von Ficker:
I just received both of your friendly letters today. Many thanks. I was aboard a Vistula ship in Russia for four weeks and just returned to Kraków today. I am, of course, in complete agreement with your last proposal concerning Rilke. *Please* see to it that he receives his amount as quicky as possible. My address is on the other side. The *sincerest* thanks for your friendliness and *sincerest* regards.

Very truly yours,
Ludwig Wittgenstein

7. Military Postcard

Military Headquarters
Kraków
Military Post Office No. 186
(undated)

Dear Mr. von Ficker:
This is only a P.S. to a card which I sent you this morning. I forgot to say that I am in complete agreement with all of your proposals.—So, Trakl is also in the war! It is perhaps foolish to think that we might be able to meet, but I should like that very much. I wish you the very best.

Very truly yours,
Ludwig Wittgenstein

8. Military Postcard

Military Headquarters
Kraków
H.M.S. Goplana
(undated)

Dear Mr. von Ficker:
Many thanks for your kind card and Rilke's letter. He writes that the war is tearing people away from their work—and, just imagine, *I* have been working in the last six weeks as seldom before! May it be with many as it has been with me! I am also looking forward to seeing you, hopefully, soon.

Very truly yours,
Ludwig Wittgenstein

9. Military Postcard

Military Headquarters
Kraków
H.M.S. Goplana
(undated)

Dear Mr. von Ficker:
Many thanks for your card. At the same time a letter from Lieutenant Molé came in which he wrote me that you had

inquired about me. What a pity that we were not able to meet!!—I pity poor Trakl very much, perhaps I shall still be able to see him when I return to Kraków again. Kindest regards

Yours,
Ludwig Wittgenstein

10. Military Postcard

Military Headquarters
Kraków
H.M.S. Goplana
(postmarked) 9 November 1914

Dear Mr. von Ficker:
I arrived here last night and received the news of Trakl's death this morning at the garrison hospital. I am deeply moved although I did not know him! May I only be allowed to see you here once more!

Sincerely yours,
Ludwig Wittgenstein

11.

16 November 1914

Dear Mr. von Ficker:
Thank you for your card of the ninth. The only information I have learned of poor Trakl's end is this: Three days before my arrival he died of a heart attack.—I was reluctant to inquire further about the circumstances since all that mattered had already been said. On 30 October I had received a card from Trakl asking me to visit him. I answered immediately: I hoped to arrive in Kraków within the next few days and then would go to him right away. May the good spirit not forsake you! And also not

Yours sincerely,
Ludwig Wittgenstein

12. Military Postcard

Military Headquarters
Kraków
H.M.S. Goplana
(postmarked) 28 November 1914

Dear Mr. von Ficker:
Thank you for sending Trakl's poems. I do not understand them, but their *tone* makes me happy. It is the tone of the true genius. How much I should like to see you and speak my mind about some things! With kindest regards,

Yours,
Ludwig Wittgenstein

13. Military Postcard

Imperial and Royal Workshop of
the Fortress Kraków
Artillery Motor Detachment
(undated)

Dear Mr. von Ficker:
A short time ago I was transferred from the Vistula ship, *Goplana,* and am now a warrant officer with the Artillery Motor Detachment (exact address on the other side).
With kindest regards

Sincerely yours,
Ludwig Wittgenstein

14. Military Postcard

Artillery Motor Detachment
First Lt. Gürth
Military Post Office No. 186
(postmarked) 17 January 1915

Dear Mr. von Ficker:
Today I received your card of 10 January. It is addressed quite correctly and its being sent back can only be attributed to the

workings of our postal service. However, the address on the back of this card is the safest way.

Kindest regards,

Sincerely yours,
Ludwig Wittgenstein

15. Military Postcard

I & R Artillery Workship of the
Fortress Kraków
Military Post Office No. 186
(postmarked) 1 February 1915

Dear Mr. von Ficker:
Unfortunately I have not yet received the letter you mentioned. One is truly "cut off from the world by the Military Postal Service." It would be wonderful if you could come here sometime. In any event try to force some news through. With kindest regards,

Yours sincerely,
Ludwig Wittgenstein

16.

I & R Artillery Workshop of the
Fortress Kraków
Military Post Office No. 186
9 February 1915

Dear Mr. von Ficker:
I just received Trakl's book. Many thanks. I am now in a sterile period and have no desire to assimilate foreign thoughts. I have this only during a decline of productivity, not when it has *completely* ceased. However—UNFORTUNATELY I now feel completely burnt out. One just has to be patient. How much I should like to see you now!

Sincerely yours,
Ludwig Wittgenstein

P.S. I still have not received the letter you mentioned.

17.

I & R Artillery Workshop of the
Fortress Kraków
Military Post Office No. 186
13 February 1915

Dear Mr. von Ficker:

Many thanks for your kind letter of 21 December 1914. Enclosed are the documents which I am returning, with exception of the lines which Hauer wrote to me and Rilke's kind, noble letter. I would not have needed the other letters as documents; as thanks they were—to be frank—for the most part highly distasteful to me. A certain degrading, *almost* swindling tone—etc.

Rilke's letter to you both moved and deeply gladdened me. The affection of any noble human being is a support in the unsteady balance of my life. I am totally unworthy of the splendid present which I carry over my heart as a sign and remembrance of this affection. If you could only convey my deepest thanks and my faithful *devotion* to Rilke.

Trakl's grave has the file number 3570 and the notation: Group XXIII. Row 13 Grave No. 45.

May your military activity be pleasing to you.

How wonderful it would be if it brought us together!

Kindest regards.

Sincerely yours,
Ludwig Wittgenstein

18.

I & R Artillery Workshop of the
Fortress Kraków
Military Post Office No. 186
(postmarked) 24 July 1915

Dear Mr. von Ficker:

A week ago I received your letter of the 11th. The same day I suffered a nervous shock and a few light injuries through an explosion in the workshop, therefore could not answer right away. I am writing this in the hospital. I did not receive your letter from Brixen. I understand your sad news all too well. You are living, as it were, in the dark and have not found the saving word. And if I, who am essentially so different from you, should offer some advice, it might seem asinine. However, I am going to venture it anyway. Are you acquainted with Tolstoi's *The Gospel in Brief*? At its time, this book virtually kept me alive. Would you buy this book and read it?! If you are not acquainted with it, then you cannot imagine what an effect it can have upon a person. If you were here, then I should like to say a lot. In a week I shall probably go to Vienna for fourteen days. Do write me again.

Sincerely yours,
Ludwig Wittgenstein

19.

I & R Artillery Maintenance Platoon 1
Military Post Office No. 12
(Undated)

Dear Mr. von Ficker:

My address is now:

I & R Arty. Maintenance Platoon 1.
Military Post Office No. 12.

How are you?? I hope Fate allows me to see you again.

Sincerely yours,
Ludwig Wittgenstein

20. Military Postcard

I & R Arty. Maint. Plat. 1
Military Post Office No. 12
(postmarked) 12 September 1915

Dear Mr. von Ficker:

I do not know whether I have already given you my new address:

I & R Artillery Maintenance Platoon 1
Military Post Office No. 12
Please write soon how you are. God be with you!

Sincerely yours,
L. Wittgenstein

21. Military Postcard

I & R Arty. Maintenance Platoon 1
Military Post Office 12
2 November 1915

Dear Mr. von Ficker:

It has been many months since the last time I heard from you. How are you? When one does not hear from his friends, this terrible period seems to last forever. One is often almost overcome by disgust. God be with you!

Faithfully yours,
L. Wittgenstein

22.

(Undated)

Dear Mr. von Ficker:

It is an odd coincidence that I received your letter today, just as I was about to go to Mr. Loos to get your address, since I wanted to write to you. The reason is that I have decided to ask you for something, and I want to come right out with it: but I must ask you above all to maintain complete silence about the entire matter and *everything which has anything to do with it*. And something else: I have no idea whether my request can even be fulfilled, if it cannot, please do not think that I am impudent and answer with a simple no.—And now: About a year ago, just before being captured, I finished a philosophical work on which I had worked for the previous seven years. It is quite strictly speaking the presentation of a system. And this presentation is *extremely* compressed since I have only retained in it that which really occurred to me—and how it occurred to me. Immediately after finishing the work, when I was on leave in Vienna, I wanted to find a publisher.

And therein lies a great difficulty: the work is very small, only about sixty pages long. Who writes sixty-page brochures about philosophical matters? The works of the great philosophers are all about 1,000 pages long, and the works of the philosophy professors are also approximately of this size: the only ones who write philosophical works of fifty to one hundred pages are those certain, totally hopeless hacks who neither have the mind of the great, nor the erudition of the professors, and yet would like to have something printed at any price. Therefore such products are usually printed privately. But I simply cannot mix my life's work—for that is what it is—among these writings. Therefore I thought of an isolated publisher like Jahoda & Siegel. However, he rejected it, presumably because of technical difficulties. Having returned from captivity, and having already become somewhat weary, I turned to the publishing house of Braumüller. (I thought of him because he published Weininger.) He is so gracious as to think—after I had provided him with a very warm recommendation from a friend, Prof. Russell of Cambridge—that he might be disposed to take over the publishing, if I would pay for the printing and paper myself. (Of course, I told him quite frankly that he would not make any money with my book since no one will read it, even less understand it.) I have to make a comment concerning this matter: first, I do not have the money to pay the publisher of my work myself, because I have disposed of my entire estate (*how* I shall tell you sometime. The matter is, by the way, STRICTLY secret!) Second, I could get the money, but I do not *want* to, for I consider it to be indecent to force a work upon the world—to which the publisher belongs—in this way. The writing was *my* affair; but the world must accept it in the normal manner.

Finally I turned to a professor in Germany who knows the publisher of a sort of philosophical journal. From him I received the promise to take over the work if I would mutilate it from beginning to end and, in a word, make another work out of it. Finally it occurred to me whether *you* might be inclined to take the poor thing into your protection. And *that* is what I should like to ask you for. I shall only send you the manuscript if you think its acceptance in the *Brenner* is conceivable. Until then I should only like to say this about it: The work is strictly philosophical and, at the same time, literary, but there is no babbling in it. And now please consider the matter and write me as soon as possible. My address is: Vienna III. Untere Viaduktgasse 9, c/o Mrs. Waniceck. I am going to the Teacher's College now since I want to become a teacher. Whether I can survive the, for me, unusually great difficulties of the training period, is yet to be seen. I have much to do and cannot even think of leaving Vienna. But perhaps you will come here sometime, and then I could tell you a lot.

For now the best regards.

Sincerely,
Ludwig Wittgenstein

23.

(Undated)

Dear Mr. Ficker:

I am sending the manuscript to you together with this letter. Why didn't I *immediately* think of you? Believe me, I *did* think of you right away; however, at a time when the book could not yet be published because it wasn't finished yet. When it had come to that point, however, we were at war, and it wasn't possible to think of your help. Now, however, I am pinning my hopes on you. And it will probably be helpful for you if I write a few words about my book: For you won't—I really believe—get too much out of reading it. Because you won't understand it; the content will seem quite strange to you. In reality, it isn't strange to you, for the point of the book is ethical. I once wanted to give a few words in the foreword which now actually are not in it, which, however, I'll write to you now because they might be a key for you: I wanted to write that my work consists of two parts: of the one which is here, and of everything which I have *not* written. And precisely this second part is the important one. For the Ethical is delimited from within, as it were, by my book; and I'm convinced that, *strictly* speaking, it can ONLY be delimited in this way. In brief, I think: All of that which *many* are *babbling* today, I have defined in my book by remaining silent about it. Therefore the book will, unless I'm quite wrong, have much to say which you want to say yourself, but perhaps you won't notice that it is said in it. For the time being, I'd recommend that you read the *foreword* and the *conclusion* since these express the point most directly.—

The MS which I'm sending you now isn't the corrected version, but only a hastily corrected copy, which will, however, suffice for your orientation. The corrected copy has been thoroughly revised; presently, however, it is in England with my friend Russell, to whom I sent it while in captivity. He will be sending it back to me shortly, however. And thus I wish myself a lot of luck for the time being.

With kind regards,

Sincerely yours,
Ludwig Wittgenstein

My present address is: XIII. St. Veitgasse 17 c/o Mrs. Sjögren.

24.

22 November 1919

Dear Mr. Ficker:

Your letter, naturally, wasn't pleasant for me, although I wasn't really surprised by your answer. I don't know where I can get my work accepted either. If I myself were only somewhere else than in this lousy world!—

As far as I am concerned you can show the manuscript to the philosophy professor (although showing a philosophical work to a professor of philosophy is like casting pearls . . .). At any rate he won't understand a word of it.

And now, only *one* more request: Make it short and sweet with me. Tell me 'no' quickly, rather than too slowly; that is Austrian sensitivity which my nerves are not strong enough to withstand, at the moment.

Sincerely yours,
Ludwig Wittgenstein

25.

4 December 1919

Dear Mr. Ficker:

It was very kind of you to answer my threatening letter with such a friendly telegram. Indeed, I would prefer that you accept my book because you consider it to be worth it, rather than just doing me a favor. And how can I recommend my own work to you?—I think in all such cases it is so: A book, even when it is written completely honestly, is always worthless from *one* standpoint: for no one would really need to write a book because there are quite different things to do in this world. On the other hand, I think I can say that if you print Dallago, Haecker, etc., *then* you can also print *my* book. And that is also everything that I can say as justification of my wish, because if one measures my book with an absolute measure, then God only knows where it will come to be.

With best regards I am,

Sincerely yours,
Ludwig Wittgenstein

26.

5 December 1919

Dear Mr. Ficker:

I had hardly sent off my answer to your telegram yesterday when your kind letter of 28 November arrived. The sacrifice which you want to chance for me, if everything goes wrong, I can, of course, not accept. I couldn't accept the responsibility of a person's (whoever's) livelihood being placed in jeopardy by publishing my book.—However, I don't quite understand it all, because people have often written books which didn't agree with the common jargon, and these books were published and the publishers weren't ruined by them. (On the contrary.)—You are in no way deceiving my trust, for my trust, or rather, simply my hope, was only directed to your perspicacity that the treatise is not junk—unless I am deceiving myself—but not to the fact that you would accept it, without thinking something of it, just *out of kindness toward me and against your interests.* Briefly then, I will be *very* grateful to you if you can attain something for me through Rilke; if that isn't possible, we can just forget about it.—(By the way, the decimals will have to be printed along with the sentences because they alone give the book lucidity and clarity and it would be an incomprehensible jumble without this numeration.)

And now farewell, and don't worry yourself on my account. Everything will turn out all right.

Sincerely yours,
Ludwig Wittgenstein

6 December 1919. à propos: is there a *Krampus* who fetches evil publishers?

27.

Vienna XIII
St. Veitgasse 17, c/o Mrs. Sjögren
28 December 1919

Dear Mr. Ficker:

The day before yesterday I returned from Holland where I met Prof. Russell and spoke with him about my book. In case I can't get it published in Austria or Germany, then Russell will have it printed in England. (He wants to translate it.) Of course, I should consider this as the *ultima ratio.* This is how things stand now: Russell wants to write an introduction to my treatise, and I have agreed to this. This introduction is supposed to be half the size of the treatise itself and explain the most difficult points of the work. With this introduction the book is now a much smaller risk for a publisher, or perhaps even none at all, since Russell's name is very well known and ensures a quite special group of readers for the book. By this I naturally don't mean to say that it will thus come into the right hands; but, at any rate, favorable circumstances are less excluded.

Please write to me as soon as possible what you think of the matter since I must let Russell know.

Best regards,

Yours,
Ludwig Wittgenstein

28.

Vienna XIII
St. Veitgasse 17
c/o Mrs. Sjögren
19 January 1920

Dear Mr. Ficker:

Please be so kind as to send me my manuscript immediately, because I have to send it to Reclam in Leipzig who in all probability will be inclined to publish my book. I am curious how many years it's still going to take until it appears. I hope it's before I die.

Yours,
Ludwig Wittgenstein

29.

26 January 1920

Dear Mr. Ficker:

It is sad to hear that you are having such trouble with the *Brenner*. I'm convinced that it isn't pusillanimity on your part, that you aren't taking my book. I wrote you several days ago and asked you for immediate return of my manuscript since I must send it to Reclam who will probably take over the work. What kind of profession will you take up then? It would make me happy if it would somehow bring us together again. Please let me know what you intend to do.

Yours,
Ludwig Wittgenstein

P.S. I too am struggling against great adversities now.

4 The Origin of Wittgenstein's *Tractatus*

GEORG HENRIK VON WRIGHT

This is not an account of the origin and sources of the ideas contained in Wittgenstein's book, but of the origin and publishing history of the book itself.

As will be plain from the account, many points in this history remain obscure. Some of them may still become clarified through the discovery of documents which have not been available or known to me when working on this essay.[1]

1

In September 1965 I found in Vienna a hitherto unknown manuscript in Wittgenstein's hand. It contains an early, but essentially complete, version of his *Logisch-Philosophische Abhandlung*. The manuscript is written in pencil in a hard-cover notebook measuring 20 × 24½ cm.

An examination of the manuscript shows that it consists of two parts and a Preface. The first, and by far the longer, part is by itself a complete work; this is the early version, mentioned above, of the *Tractatus*. For the sake of convenience, I shall henceforth refer to it by the label "Prototractatus."

This essay is adapted from a version that appeared in *Prototractatus: An Early Version of Tractatus Logico-Philosophicus,* edited by B.F. McGuinness, T. Nyberg, and G. H. von Wright (London: Routledge & Kegan Paul; Ithaca, N.Y.: Cornell University Press, 1971).

1. Preliminary versions of this essay were read by various persons, and the author is greatly indebted to them for their comments and corrections. In particular he would like to express his thanks to Mr. Brian McGuinness. The author will gratefully receive and record any further information concerning the connexions which he is here trying to unravel. The German passages in this essay have been translated by Mr. McGuinness except for the letters to Engelmann, which were translated by Dr. L. Furtmüller.

The second part has the character of additions to and further elucidations of the thoughts contained in the "Prototractatus". With few exceptions the remarks[2] in this part have the same number as the corresponding remark in the *Tractatus*. In most cases there is also complete identity of formulation; the differences which there are are insignificant.

At the very end of the manuscript there is a Preface (Vorwort). It differs from the preface of the *Tractatus* only in not giving any date and place (nor the author's initials) *and* in containing an additional paragraph at the very end. This paragraph reads: "Meinem Onkel, Herrn Paul Wittgenstein, und meinem Freund Herrn Bertrand Russell danke ich für die liebevolle Aufmunterung die sie mir haben zuteil werden lassen."[3]

Since the Vorwort must have been written after the second part of the manuscript, it cannot be regarded as a preface specifically for the "Prototractatus".

There are in the "Prototractatus" 30 remarks and 6 'loose' or unnumbered paragraphs which do not occur in the *Tractatus*. There is also one loose paragraph which does. In approximately 400 places the actual wording of the text of the "Prototractatus" differs from the corresponding place in the text of the *Tractatus*. Often, however, the difference is insignificant. In addition to differences of formulation there are also differences in the arrangement of the thoughts. These last are probably the most interesting differences between the two works.

2

The manuscript thus discovered begins with a page which reads: "Zwischen diese Sätze werden alle guten Sätze meiner anderen Manuskripte gefügt. Die Nummern zeigen die Reihenfolge und die Wichtigkeit der Sätze an. So folgt 5.04101 auf 5.041 und auf jenen 5.0411 welcher Satz wichtiger ist als 5.04101."[4]

2. By a 'remark' I here understand a paragraph, or section consisting of several paragraphs, with a number—either in the "Prototractatus" or in the *Tractatus*.

3. "I wish to thank my uncle Mr. Paul Wittgenstein and my friend Mr. Bertrand Russell for the kind encouragement they have extended to me."

4. "In between these sentences are inserted all the good sentences from my other manuscripts. The numbers indicate the order and the importance of the

Then follows the page with the title, the page with the motto and the dedication, and the first page of the text, which lists the six principal 'theses' of the work and some of the main 'sub-theses' under them.[5]

A student of the manuscript is struck by the use of the *accusative* in "Zwischen diese Sätze" and by the phrase "werden alle guten Sätze . . . gefügt". The question arises which are the sentences, of which it is said that in between them all the good sentences of Wittgenstein's other notes will be inserted. My conjecture is that they are the sentences listed on the first text-page, or possibly first few text-pages. Perhaps the note at the very beginning was written after Wittgenstein had on the first text-page written down the remarks which so to speak constitute the backbone of the entire work.

It is, unfortunately, no longer possible to tell exactly which were the manuscripts from which the remarks which constitute the "Prototractatus" were selected.

Of Wittgenstein's writings prior to the completion of the *Tractatus* the following items, in addition to the present manuscript, have been preserved:

Three notebooks from the time of the first Great War. The first two are continuous and cover the period from 9 August 1914 to 11 June 1915; the third covers from 15 April 1916 to 10 January 1917. These notebooks also contain a diary written for the most part in code. In 1952, when I first saw them, the notebooks were in the house of Wittgenstein's youngest sister, Mrs. M. Stonborough, at Gmunden. I shall here call them the Gmunden notebooks. The philosophic content of the notebooks was, with a few slight omissions, edited by Miss Anscombe and me and published in 1961.

There are further "Notes on Logic" of September 1913 which Wittgenstein sent to Bertrand Russell. There exist two versions of the notes, possibly both by Wittgenstein himself. The more

sentences. Thus 5.04101 follows after 5.041, and 5.0411 follows after and is more important than 5.04101."

5. Thesis 7 is found on page 71 of the manuscript.

final version was published as an Appendix to the 1914–1916 Notebooks.

Finally, there are the notes dictated to G. E. Moore on the occasion of Moore's visit to Wittgenstein in Norway in April 1914. They, too, are printed as an Appendix to the 1914–1916 Notebooks.

Fifty-seven letters from Wittgenstein to Russell from the years 1912–1921 have been preserved.[6] There are also, from the pre-*Tractatus* period, letters from Wittgenstein to his friend, the architect Paul Engelmann,[7] to Ludwig von Ficker, editor of *Der Brenner*,[8] to J. M. Keynes,[9] G. E. Moore[10] and C. K. Ogden[11] and to a few other persons.

Wittgenstein's last visit to Vienna before his death was from December 1949 to March 1950. Miss Anscombe, who saw him in Vienna, testifies that Wittgenstein had then ordered several notebooks which still existed from the time of germination of the *Tractatus* to be destroyed. (She thinks it was only by accident that the notebooks at Gmunden were preserved.) I have not been able to confirm that the order was carried into effect, but there seems no strong reason for doubting that it was.

In a letter, dated 23 April 1953, to Professor F. A. Hayek, giving biographic information about Wittgenstein, the late Mr. Paul Engelmann writes: "Seine Manuskriptbücher waren große, in schwarz und grün gestreiftes Leinen gebundene Geschäftsbücher, wie man sie in Österreich als Hauptbücher

6. Now in the Library of McMaster University. Published in *Ludwig Wittgenstein: Letters to Russell, Keynes, and Moore,* ed. G. H. von Wright with the assistance of B. F. McGuinness (Oxford: Basil Blackwell; Ithaca, N.Y.: Cornell University Press, 1974). Hereafter abbreviated as *R.*

7. Published in German with an English translation in Paul Engelmann, *Letters from Ludwig Wittgenstein with a Memoir,* trans. L. Furtmüller, ed. B. F. McGuinness (Oxford: Basil Blackwell, 1967).

8. Ludwig Wittgenstein, *Briefe an Ludwig von Ficker,* ed. G. H. von Wright (Brenner Studien, I: Salzburg: Verlag Otto Müller, 1969). (These letters have been translated by Mr. Bruce Gillette, and appear as the third section of this volume [ed.])

9. Deposited in King's College Library, Cambridge.

10. In the possession of Mrs. D. Moore.

11. In the possession of the executors of C. K. Ogden.

verwendete. . . . Der Tractatus ist der endgültige Extrakt aus 7 solchen Büchern, die er nach dem Erscheinen des Buches vernichtet hat."[12]

This report gives rise to many questions. Were the three Gmunden notebooks among the seven to which Engelmann refers—in which case it would not be true that they were all destroyed?[13] The Gmunden notebooks were composed at an average speed of one notebook in six months. Between the second and the third there is a gap of a little less than a year. Assuming that the final composition of the *Tractatus* took place in the summer of 1918, there is a gap of a year and a half between the third notebook and this final stage. Assuming further the same 'writing speed' throughout the whole war period, it is reasonable to suppose that there existed at least four wartime notebooks which are now lost and which were of a similar character to the three which we have.

In a letter without date, which Russell received in January 1915, Wittgenstein writes: "Sollte ich in diesem Krieg umkommen, so wird Dir mein Manuskript, welches ich damals Moore zeigte, zugeschickt werden; nebst einem, welches ich jetzt während des Krieges geschrieben habe."[14]

From this it is evident that Wittgenstein already in April 1914, when Moore came to visit him in Norway, had 'a manuscript'. The other manuscript to which he refers and of which he says that it has been written during the war is probably the first (or first two) of the Gmunden notebooks. The way he speaks of the two manuscripts would indicate that they were

12. "His manuscript volumes were large office-books bound in black and green striped cloth, of the kind used in Austria as ledgers. . . . The *Tractatus* is the final selection from seven books of this kind, which he destroyed after the appearance of the book."

13. In a later letter to Hayek (12 June 1953), Engelmann says that he saw the manuscript-books only at Olmütz and not later in Vienna. Engelmann's friendship with Wittgenstein dates from the autumn of 1916, when Wittgenstein was in an officers' training school at Olmütz. Wittgenstein also visited Olmütz later in the war when on leave from the army. But we have no evidence that he came to Olmütz to visit Engelmann after his return from captivity in Italy after the end of the war.

14. "If I should not survive the present war, my manuscript, which I showed Moore in the past, will be sent to you along with another which I have now written, during the war."

of a roughly similar character, i.e., that the second was a continuation of, rather than superseded, the first.

The above letter is a reply to a letter from Russell, which is dated 28 July 1914 but which reached Wittgenstein only much later. It seems that Russell had complained that Moore had not been able to explain to him Wittgenstein's ideas. "Daß Moore meine Ideen Dir nicht hat erklären können, ist mir unbegreiflich. Hast Du aus seinen Notizen irgend etwas entnehmen können?? Ich fürchte, Nein."[15]

On 22 May 1915 Wittgenstein wrote to Russell in reply to a letter dated 10 May:

> Daß Du Moores Aufschreibungen nicht hast verstehen können tut mir außerordentlich leid. Ich fürchte, daß sie ohne weitere Erklärung sehr schwer verständlich sind, aber ich halte sie doch im Wesentlichen für endgültig. Was ich in der letzten Zeit geschrieben habe wird nun, wie ich fürchte, noch unverständlicher sein; und, wenn ich das Ende dieses Krieges nicht mehr erlebe, so muß ich mich darauf gefaßt machen, daß meine ganze Arbeit verloren geht.—Dann soll mein Manuskript gedruckt werden, ob es irgend einer versteht, oder nicht.[16]

At the time when Wittgenstein wrote this letter, he had nearly completed the second of the Gmunden notebooks. What he *here* calls 'my manuscript' is, I conjecture, the manuscript he had shown to Moore *and* the first two wartime (Gmunden) notebooks.

On 22 October the same year Wittgenstein wrote again to Russell. He now says:

> Ich habe in der letzten Zeit sehr viel gearbeitet und, wie ich glaube, mit gutem Erfolg. Ich bin jetzt dabei das Ganze zusammenzufassen

15. "I find it inconceivable that Moore has not been able to explain my ideas to you. Have you been able to understand anything at all from his notes? I am afraid the answer is: no."

16. "I am extremely sorry that you weren't able to understand the notes that Moore took down. I am afraid they are very hard to understand without further explanation; yet I consider them essentially as definitive. And now I'm afraid that what I've written recently will be still more incomprehensible and if I don't live to see the end of the present war I must be prepared for all my work to go for nothing—in that case my MS must be printed whether anyone understands it or not." (The notes are evidently those published with the 1914–1916 Notebooks.)

und in Form einer Abhandlung niederzuschreiben. Ich werde nun keinesfalls etwas veröffentlichen, ehe Du es gesehen hast. Das kann aber natürlich erst nach dem Kriege geschehen. Aber, wer weiß, ob ich das erleben werde. Falls ich es nicht mehr erlebe, so laß Dir von meinen Leuten meine ganzen Manuskripte schicken, darunter befindet sich auch die letzte Zusammenfassung mit Bleistift auf losen Blättern geschrieben. Es wird Dir vielleicht einige Mühe machen alles zu verstehen, aber laß Dich dadurch nicht abschrecken.[17]

Here Wittgenstein evidently is referring to something which is *not* of the same character as the notebooks but which is a '*Zusammenfassung*' of their content—to something like the "Prototractatus" in fact. Could it be the "Prototractatus" itself? An affirmative answer is excluded if only by the fact that the "Prototractatus" also contains remarks from the third Gmunden notebook which was written in 1916. The letter, moreover, speaks of a 'letzte Zusammenfassung' on loose sheets. It does not, in my opinion, follow that there must at that time have existed *two 'Zusammenfassungen'*. The '*Zusammenfassung*' to which Wittgenstein refers with the words "Ich bin dabei das Ganze zusammenzufassen" can be the same as the one on loose sheets. But we may safely conclude that the "Prototractatus" had *at least one* predecessor.[18]

It is thus certain that, in addition to the manuscripts which have been preserved, there existed at least one manuscript from the time before the war (spring 1914), probably of the same nature as the Gmunden notebooks, and at least one '*Zusammenfassung*' from the autumn of 1915, perhaps of similar character to the "Prototractatus". This is all we know for cer-

17. "I have recently done a great deal of work and, I think, quite successfully. I'm now in the process of summarizing it all and writing it down in the form of a treatise. Now whatever happens I won't publish anything before you've seen it. But of course that can't happen until after the war. But who knows whether I shall survive it. If I don't survive, get my people to send you all my manuscripts: among them you'll find the final summary written in pencil on loose sheets of paper. It will probably cost you some trouble to understand it all, but don't be put off by that."

18. Dr. Heinrich Groag, who knew Wittgenstein during the first war, remembers a manuscript lent to him in the winter of 1917–1918 which was written in pencil on loose sheets with numbered propositions. It is not unlikely that this manuscript was another 'predecessor' of the "Prototractatus". (I am indebted to Mr. B. F. McGuinness for this item of information.)

tain. But it seems to me a reasonable conjecture that there also existed one or two notebooks from the period June 1915–April 1916, and two or three notebooks from the time January 1917–August 1918 which have been lost. If this is right, there once existed 7–9 notebooks in all, from which the content of the *Tractatus* is an extract. This squares relatively well with the information in Engelmann's letter to Hayek.

We also know[19] that when Wittgenstein in the autumn of 1913 left Cambridge and moved to Norway, he deposited with a furniture dealer (Jolly) a number of things, including some books, diaries and manuscripts. The diaries and manuscripts Wittgenstein ordered to be burnt and the other things to be sold. Russell writes in his *Autobiography*[20] that he himself bought the books and furniture; of the fate of the manuscripts nothing is said. The money from the sale was evidently used to finance Wittgenstein's visit to Holland and meeting with Russell in December 1919.

When was the "Prototractatus" and the rest of the manuscript-book in which it appears written?

In a postcard to Russell, dated 9 February 1919, from Cassino in Italy, Wittgenstein says that he has been a prisoner in Italy since November (1918) and that he hopes to be able to communicate with Russell "after three years" interruption.[21] He adds: "I have done lots of logical work which I am dying to let you know before publishing it."

On 10 March Wittgenstein again wrote a postcard—in reply to a card from Russell which had reached him in the meantime. Here he says: "I've written a book which will be published as soon as I get home." And he adds: "I think I have solved our problems finally."

Later in March Wittgenstein sent a letter to Russell from the prison-camp. In it he describes more fully the work he had done:

19. *R* 40.

20. *The Autobiography of Bertrand Russell: 1914–1944*, p. 100.

21. There seems to have been no communication between the two friends in the time 22 October 1915–9 February 1919.

I've written a book called "Logisch-philosophische Abhandlung" containing all my work of the last six years. I believe I've solved our problems finally. This may sound arrogant but I can't help believing it. I finished the book in August 1918 and two months after was made Prigioniere. I've got the manuscript here with me. I wish I could copy it out for you; but it's pretty long and I would have no safe way of sending it to you. . . . I will publish it as soon as I get home.

Soon after, however, Wittgenstein was able to send his work to Russell. In his next letter, Cassino 12 June 1919, we read: 'Vor einigen Tagen schickte ich Dir mein Manuscript durch Keynes's Vermittelung. . . . Es ist das einzige korrigierte Exemplar, welches ich besitze und die Arbeit meines Lebens. Mehr als je brenne ich jetzt darauf es gedruckt zu sehen."[22]

The next letter is the last one written in the prison-camp. Its date is 19 August 1919. Here Wittgenstein repeats a wish which he had already earlier expressed that Russell and he should meet and discuss the work. As a possible meeting-place he suggests Holland or Switzerland. "Please write to Vienna IV, Alleegasse 16. As to my MS, please send it to the same address; but only if there is an absolutely safe way of sending it. Otherwise please keep it. I should be very glad though, to get it soon, as it's the only corrected copy I've got."

Wittgenstein continues: "I also sent my MS to Frege. He wrote me a week ago and I gather that he doesn't understand a word of it all." Then in a long postscript to the letter he proceeds to answer a number of questions concerning his work which Russell had raised.[23]

The only date which is significant for the dating of Wittgenstein's work and which is mentioned in the correspondence with Russell from the prison-camp is that he finished the book in *August* 1918.

At the beginning of the second part of the manuscript there is a puzzling footnote. It says that the numbers of the remarks in this part are the numbers in the *'Korrektur'*. The word *'Kor-*

22. "Some days ago I sent you my manuscript through Keynes's intermediacy. It is the only corrected copy that I possess and is my life's work. I long more than ever to see it printed."

23. *R* 37.

rektur' could mean the proofs of a printed text. It is internally extremely unlikely that this is what they mean here. The earliest possible printed proofs would have been those of the publication in Ostwald's *Annalen* in 1921; and we have no evidence that Wittgenstein ever saw these proofs. What the word *'Korrektur'* probably refers to is a corrected MS- or TS-copy of the *Tractatus* or "Prototractatus".

I here make the following conjecture: After having written down in the manuscript-book all the remarks which constitute the "Prototractatus", Wittgenstein did to the manuscript the same thing as we have done to it here, viz. he copied it out, or had it copied out, with the remarks arranged in their proper number-order. Probably either this copy was a typescript or a typescript copy of it was made (see p. 109). Then he worked with this text (the *'Korrektur'*) changing the formulations, grouping remarks which carried separate numbers under one single number, rearranging the order in places. Having done this (or when doing this) he also made some additions. These additional entries he noted down in handwriting in the same notebook as the "Prototractatus". When he had finished with the additions, he wrote the *Vorwort,* and probably transferred it too to the *'Korrektur'*. Another possibility is that the *'Korrektur'* simply was the copy of the work which he sent to Russell from Cassino and of which he said that it was "the only corrected copy". (Cf. above, p. 107.)

If the above reconstruction of what took place is correct, it still does not answer the question, when the "Prototractatus" was composed. We know that Wittgenstein was on a longish leave in the summer of 1918. He spent it, partly at the family estate Hochreit, partly, it seems, with his uncle (the Paul Wittgenstein referred to in the Vorwort at the back of the "Prototractatus" notebook) at Hallein near Salzburg, and partly in Vienna. Did he do *all* the work of finishing the book then, beginning with the extracting of the "Prototractatus" from the earlier notes? Or did he start then with the composition of the 'Korrektur', having already extracted the "Prototractatus"—perhaps in the winter and spring of that same year?

Engelmann, in his letter to Professor Hayek of 12 June

1953, says: "Vor seinem Abgang an die italienische Front hat er sein Manuskript in die Maschine diktiert."[24] Wittgenstein was transferred to the Italian front in March 1918. It is not certain, however, that this dictation for the typewriter took place before Wittgenstein went there for the first time. Nor is it certain that the manuscript referred to by Engelmann was the "Prototractatus".

The dedication to the memory of David Pinsent is already in the "Prototractatus". There seems no reason to think that it had been added to the MS later. Pinsent was killed in the war on 8 May 1918. News could hardly have reached Wittgenstein until a month or so later. The most likely conjecture seems to me to be that work on the "Prototractatus" immediately preceded the final composition of the book in the summer of 1918.

3

Three different typescripts of the *Tractatus* are known to exist, or to have existed. One later belonged to Wittgenstein's friend Engelmann, who died in Tel Aviv early in 1965. It is now in the Bodleian Library at Oxford. Another typescript, from which the last page is missing, I found in Vienna in 1965. A third, to which was also attached a typescript of Russell's "Introduction", I saw in 1952 at Gmunden. This typescript is now missing. Attempts to find it have so far proved unsuccessful. I shall refer to these typescripts as the Engelmann-TS, the Vienna-TS, and the Gmunden-TS respectively.

Engelmann, to whom Wittgenstein had given the typescript as a gift, believed that his was the copy from which the book had actually been printed. On grounds, partly of annotations on the typescript and partly of the correspondence which took place between Wittgenstein and C.K. Ogden in 1922, it seems certain that the printing of the book in Ostwald's *Annalen* was from this typescript. But the subsequent printing of the book by Kegan Paul in London evidently was from (an off-print of) the publication with Ostwald (see below, p. 132).

24. "Before going to the Italian front he dictated his manuscript for the typewriter."

The Gmunden-TS, as I remember it, contained a great number of corrections and marks in pencil. I cannot recall whether Russell's "Introduction" was a part of the *same* typescript—nor even whether it was in English or German. I listed it among my notes, at the time when it was shown to me, as a "typescript (with corrections) of the whole *Tractatus* with Russell's Introduction".[25]

The Vienna-TS is, surprisingly, not a carbon copy of the Engelmann-TS. It contains relatively few corrections in pencil, and no substantial additions. It does not, for example, contain the remark 6.1203, which has been added to the Engelmann-TS in handwriting on a separate sheet. I have found one difference in substance between it and the Engelmann-TS. This is the remark 6.241 which in the Engelmann-TS and the printed text is a proof of the proposition that $2 \times 2 = 4$ but which in the Vienna-TS is the much simpler proof that $2 + 2 = 4$.

There is at present no way of telling whether the Gmunden-TS is a second copy of either the Engelmann- or the Vienna-TS, or whether it is a third typescript 'original'.

As we have seen, Wittgenstein in his letters from Cassino to Russell speaks of his work as a 'manuscript'. This, however, cannot be taken as proof that it was, in fact, a *manu*script and not a *type*script. There is good evidence for thinking that it was the latter. Thus Ludwig Hänsel, who was with Wittgenstein in the prison-camp at Cassino and remained a close friend of Wittgenstein's ever after, writes in a letter to Hayek of 28 January 1953: "Er hatte ein maschingeschriebenes fertiges Exemplar in seinem Rucksack bereits mit. (Er hat es mir damals zu lesen gegeben, auch mit mir sehr ausführlich besprochen.) Hinzugefügt hat er in der Gefangenschaft nur einige Stellen, so die Schemata von 6.1203."[26]

25. In 1952 there also existed, at Gmunden, a handwritten version, dated November-December 1936, of the first 189 sections of the *Philosophische Untersuchungen* and a manuscript and a typescript of the Lecture on Ethics. These are now missing.

26. "He already had a complete typescript copy with him in his rucksack. (He gave it to me to read at the time and also discussed it with me in great detail.) He added only a few passages while a prisoner, as, for example, the schemata in 6.1203."

In[27] his first letter (after the two postcards) to Russell from Cassino Wittgenstein says he wishes he could copy the thing out for Russell. This speaks in favor of thinking that he had only *one copy* of it with him. In the next letter, dated 12 June 1919, Wittgenstein says that the 'manuscript' which he had just sent to Russell was his only *corrected* copy. In the letter after that (19 August 1919) he says that he had also sent a copy to Frege and that he now has no copy with him at Cassino.

The copy to Frege had in fact been sent already in December 1918, i.e. nearly half a year before he sent his only corrected copy to Russell. We know this from records of communications to Frege from one of Wittgenstein's sisters. (See below p. 114.) The copy had been sent by this sister and not 'directly' by Wittgenstein. Perhaps it was a copy which Wittgenstein had left behind at home when going back to the front. We know, moreover, from the same records that, when Frege received the copy, one page was missing from it. This may be regarded as slight evidence for thinking that the copy in question was in fact the Vienna-TS. The missing page, however, was later, in March 1919, sent separately to Frege. Whether it was eventually returned with the typescript we do not know. Nor do we know when the typescript was sent back. But we know that Wittgenstein had a copy of his work in Vienna on his return from captivity in the middle of August 1919. (Cf. p. 112, letter to Russell 20 August 1919.) Perhaps this was a third typescript—possibly the Gmunden-TS.

The remark 6.1203 and the diagrams mentioned in the letter by Hänsel quoted above are missing from the Vienna-TS. They have been added to the Engelmann-TS, as it now exists, in handwriting. The fact that the remark had not been added to the Vienna-TS is additional evidence that Wittgenstein had only *one* copy, probably the Engelmann-TS, with him at Cassino and that two other copies, probably the Vienna- and Gmunden-TS, had been left by him in Austria.

27. The passage from here to the end of the section has been rewritten on the basis of additional information relating to the Wittgenstein-Frege correspondence which I received in 1975 from Professor Gottfried Gabriel, Konstanz.

4

Towards the end of the summer 1918, when still on leave from the army, Wittgenstein had offered his book to the Viennese publisher Jahoda & Siegel for publication.[28] When back in the army, he was impatiently waiting for an answer.[29] He got it on 25 October, a few days before the end of the war. The answer was negative. Wittgenstein wrote to his friend Paul Engelmann: "Heute erhielt ich von Jahoda die Mitteilung, daß er meine Arbeit nicht drucken kann. Angeblich aus technischen Gründen. Ich wüßte aber gar zu gern, was Kraus zu ihr gesagt hat. Wenn Sie Gelegenheit hätten es zu erfahren, so würde ich mich sehr freuen. Vielleicht weiss Loos etwas. Schreiben Sie mir."[30]

The letter may be taken as an indication that Karl Kraus, the satirist, and Adolf Loos, the architect, had been involved in this first effort to find a publisher for Wittgenstein's book.

With the Jahoda episode we enter the long and troubled history of the publication of the *Tractatus*. It is obvious that Wittgenstein was very anxious to publish his book. The many difficulties and obstacles must have depressed him deeply.

On 20 August 1919, only a few days after his return from captivity, Wittgenstein wrote to Russell:

Ich bin jetzt mit einer Kopie meines MS zu einem Verleger gegangen, um den Druck endlich in die Wege zu leiten. Der Verleger, der natürlich weder meinen Namen kennt, noch etwas von Philosophie versteht, verlangt das Urteil irgendeines Fachmanns, um sicher zu sein, daß das Buch wirklich wert ist, gedruckt zu werden. Er wollte sich deshalb an einen seiner Vertrauensmänner hier wenden (wahrscheinlich an einen Philosophie-Professor). Ich sagte ihm, nun, daß hier niemand das Buch beurteilen könnte, daß *Du* aber vielleicht so gut sein würdest, ihm ein kurzes Urteil über den Wert der Arbeit zu schreiben; was, wenn es günstig ausfällt, ihm genügen wird um den Verlag zu übernehmen. Die Adresse des Verlegers ist: Wilhelm

28. See the letters to Engelmann of 14 July, 9 October, 22 October, and 25 October 1918.

29. Letters to Engelmann of 9 October and 22 October.

30. "Today I received notification from Jahoda that he cannot publish my treatise. Allegedly for technical reasons. But I would dearly like to know what Kraus said about it. If there were an opportunity for you to find out, I should be very glad. Perhaps Loos knows something about it. Do write to me."

Braumüller. XI. Servitengasse 5 Wien. Ich bitte Dich nun, dorthin ein paar Worte, so viel Du vor Deinem Gewissen verantworten kannst, zu schreiben.[31]

Wilhelm Braumüller was the publisher of the work of Otto Weininger, which Wittgenstein much admired. In a letter to Ludwig von Ficker written later that autumn Wittgenstein says it was this fact which induced him to approach Braumüller.[32] The copy of the work mentioned in the letter to Russell was neither the typescript which he had sent to Russell, nor the one which he had sent to Frege. For these typescripts had not by then been returned to the author (see below, pp. 115, 116f.). It could have been the typescript which, a year earlier, he had given to Jahoda.

From Wittgenstein's next letter to Russell (6 October 1919) we learn that Braumüller had received a letter of recommendation from Russell, but had not yet made up his mind whether to publish the book. Soon after, however, this effort to get the book published came to an end. Braumüller made the publication conditional upon the author's paying for the paper and the printing. This humiliating condition Wittgenstein could not accept. He explains his attitude in the above-mentioned letter to Ficker as follows:

Erstens habe ich nicht das Geld, um den Verlag meiner Arbeit selbst zu zahlen, weil ich mich meines gesamten Vermögens entledigt habe. . . . Zweitens aber könnte ich mir zwar das Geld dazu verschaffen, will es aber nicht; denn ich halte es für bürgerlich unanständig ein Werk der Welt—zu welcher der Verleger gehört—in

31. "I have now been to a publisher with a copy of my manuscript in order to get its printing finally under way. The publisher, who naturally neither knows my name nor understands anything about philosophy, required the judgement of some expert in order to be sure that the work is really worth printing. For this purpose he wanted to apply to one of the people that he relies on here, probably a Professor of Philosophy. So I told him that no one here would be able to form a judgement on the book—but that *you* would probably be kind enough to write him a brief assessment of the value of the work, and if this happened to be favourable that would be enough to induce him to publish it. The publisher's address is: Willhelm Braumüller, XI Servitengasse 5, Vienna. Now please write him a few words, as much as your conscience will allow you to." (See also letter to Engelmann of 2 September 1919.)

32. Cf. "Letters to Ludwig von Ficker," #22, this volume, p. 93 [ed.].

dieser Weise aufzudrängen: Das Schreiben war *meine* Sache; annehmen muß es aber die Welt auf die normale Art und Weise.[33]

Wittgenstein then, the letter continues, had turned to "a professor in Germany", who knew the editor of a philosophical periodical. "Von diesem erhielt ich die Zusage die Arbeit zu übernehmen, wenn ich sie vom Anfang bis zum Ende verstümmeln, und mit einem Wort eine andere Arbeit daraus machen, wollte."[34]

The professor in Germany must have been Frege and the periodical *Beiträge zur Philosophie des deutschen Idealismus* in which Frege had himself published. This can be verified from a lapidary annotation by the late Professor Heinrich Scholz to a list of Wittgenstein's letters to Frege. The letters were kept in the Frege-*Archiv* which Heinrich Scholz had collected and deposited at Münster in Germany. The collection was destroyed in the bombings during the 1939–1945 war. No copies of the letters had been taken or none were rescued. But a, probably incomplete, list of the correspondence has been preserved.[35] It mentions three letters by Wittgenstein from the time before the First World War, four postcards by him from the time of the 1914–1918 war, three postcards and one letter from Cassino, and four letters from the autumn of 1919. It must have been in reference to these last letters that Wittgenstein wrote in the letter to Russell of 6 October: "Mit Frege stehe ich in Briefwechsel. Er versteht kein Wort von meiner Arbeit und ich bin schon ganz erschöpft vor lauter Erklärungen."[36]

The annotation by Scholz refers to a letter of 16 September 1919 and goes as follows: "Brief W. an Fr. vom 16.9.1919. Inhalt: Dank für 'Der Gedanke', kritische Bemerkungen dazu. Bitte um Verwendung für Druck seiner Abh. in den BPhDI."[37]

33. Cf. p. 93 this volume [ed.].

34. *Ibid.* [ed.].

35. For information concerning the Frege-Wittgenstein correspondence I am indebted to Professor Dr. W. Kambartel and Professor Gottfried Gabriel.

36. "I'm in correspondence with Frege. He doesn't understand a single word of my work and I'm thoroughly exhausted by giving what are purely and simply explanations."

37. "Letter from W. to Fr. dated 16 September 1919. Content: thanks for 'The Thought': critical observations thereon. Request for assistance towards the printing of his *Tractatus* in BPhDI."

'Der Gedanke' is a paper by Frege which was published in 1919 in the *Beiträge zur Philosophie des deutschen Idealismus.* Frege had evidently sent Wittgenstein a copy of his paper.

It was when the efforts to get his book published through Frege had failed that Wittgenstein turned to Ludwig von Ficker. He did this in the letter from which we have already quoted. The letter is undated. To judge by existing evidence, I should say it was written some time in the middle of October 1919. After having told of his adversities with Jahoda, Braumüller, and Frege, Wittgenstein continues:

> Da fiel mir endlich ein ob *Sie* nicht geneigt sein könnten, das arme Wesen in Ihren Schutz zu nehmen. Und *darum* möchte ich Sie eben bitten: Das Manuscript würde ich Ihnen erst schicken wenn Sie glauben daß überhaupt an eine Aufnahme in den Brenner zu denken ist: Bis dahin möchte ich nur soviel sagen: Die Arbeit ist streng philosophisch und zugleich literarisch, es wird aber doch nicht darin geschwefelt. Und nun bitte überlegen Sie sich die Sache und schreiben Sie mir möglichst bald.[38]

Ludwig von Ficker (1880–1967), who lived at Innsbruck, was editor of *Der Brenner,* a kind of cultural periodical, and head of a small publishing firm. The two men had met in Vienna on the eve of the outbreak of the war. Wittgenstein had arranged for the distribution through Ficker of a considerable sum of money to some Austrian writers and artists, among them Rilke, Trakl, and Oscar Kokoschka. During the war they had some correspondence. Wittgenstein's letters and postcards to Ficker, 29 in all and from the time 14 July 1914 to 26 January 1920, are now in the *Brenner-Archiv* of Innsbruck University.[39] Ficker's letters to Wittgenstein seem to be lost.

Ficker's first reaction to Wittgenstein's request was apparently a friendly letter, in which he asked for the manuscript and expressed mild surprise that Wittgenstein had not approached him in the matter at once. Wittgenstein's reply is extremely interesting because of the information it contains of

38. Cf. pp. 93–94, this volume [ed.].
39. I am much indebted to Dr. Walter Methlagl for access to materials in the *Archiv* and for information about Ficker and *Der Brenner.* See also above, n. 8.

how Wittgenstein viewed his work. The letter, which is undated, too, is here reproduced in toto:

Lieber Herr Ficker!

Zugleich mit diesem Brief geht das Manuscript an Sie ab. Warum ich nicht *gleich* an Sie dachte? Ja, denken Sie, ich *habe* gleich an Sie gedacht, allerdings zu einer Zeit, wo das Buch noch gar nicht verlegt werden konnte, weil es nicht fertig war. Wie es aber dann so weit war, da hatten wir ja Krieg und da war wieder an Ihre Hilfe nicht zu denken. Jetzt aber hoffe ich auf Sie. Und da ist es Ihnen vielleicht eine Hilfe, wenn ich Ihnen ein paar Worte über mein Buch schreibe: Von seiner Lektüre werden Sie nämlich—wie ich bestimmt glaube—nicht allzuviel haben. Denn Sie werden es nicht verstehen; der Stoff wird Ihnen ganz fremd erscheinen. In Wirklichkeit ist er Ihnen nicht fremd, denn der Sinn des Buches ist ein Ethischer. Ich wollte einmal in das Vorwort einen Satz geben, der nun tatsächlich nicht darin steht, den ich Ihnen aber jetzt schreibe, weil er Ihnen vielleicht ein Schlüssel sein wird: Ich wollte nämlich schreiben, mein Werk bestehe aus zwei Teilen: aus dem, der heir vorliegt, und aus alledem, was ich *nicht* geschrieben habe. Und gerade dieser zweite Teil ist der Wichtige. Es wird nämlich das Ethische durch mein Buch gleichsam von Innen her begrenzt; und ich bin überzeugt, daß es, *streng,* NUR so zu begrenzen ist. Kurz ich glaube: Alles das, was *viele* heute *schwefeln,* habe ich in meinem Buch festgelegt, indem ich darüber schweige. Und darum wird das Buch, wenn ich mich nicht sehr irre, vieles sagen, was Sie selbst sagen wollen, aber Sie werden vielleicht nicht sehen, daß es darin gesagt ist. Ich würde Ihnen nun empfehlen, das *Vorwort* und den *Schluß zu lesen, da diese den Sinn am unmittelbarsten zum Ausdruck bringen.*

Das M.S., das ich Ihnen jetzt sende, ist nicht das eigentliche Druckmanuscript, sondern eine von mir nur flüchtig durchgesehene Kopie, die aber zu Ihrer Orientierung genügen wird. Das Druck M.S. ist genau durchgesehen; es befindet sich aber augenblicklich in England bei meinem Freund Russell, dem ich es aus der Gefangenschaft geschickt habe. Er wird es mir aber in der nächsten Zeit zurückschicken. Und so wünsche ich mir einstweilen viel Glück.

Seien Sie herzlich gegrüßt von Ihrem ergebenen
Ludwig Wittgenstein[40]

As was noted above (p. 107), Wittgenstein had shortly before his release from the prison-camp begged Russell to return the manuscript to Vienna. The request was repeated in the autumn, but it was not until 21 November that Wittgenstein

40. Cf. pp. 94–95, this volume [ed.].

could, in a letter to Russell, acknowledge safe receipt of the only corrected and complete copy then in existence of his work.

It was probably on the same day that Wittgenstein received from Ficker the unpleasant news that Ficker too was hesitant to publish the book. In the letter to Russell of the 21st he does not mention this; but in a letter one week later (27 November) he complains: "Ich habe jetzt erneute Schwierigkeiten wegen meines Buches. Niemand will es verlegen."[41] And on the 22nd he had written to Ficker:

Lieber Herr Ficker!
Ihr Brief hat mich natürlich nicht angenehm berührt, obwohl ich mir ja Ihre Antwort ungefähr denken konnte. Ja, wo meine Arbeit untergebracht werden kann, das weiß ich selbst nicht. Wenn ich nur selbst schon wo anders untergebracht wäre als auf dieser beschissenen Welt.—Von mir aus können Sie das Manuscript dem Philosophie-Professor zeigen (wenn auch eine philosophische Arbeit einem Philosophie-Professor vorzulegen heißt, Perlen . . .). Verstehen wird er übrigens kein Wort. Und jetzt nur noch *eine* Bitte: Machen Sie's kurz mit mir und schmerzlos. Sagen Sie mir lieber ein rasches Nein als ein gar so langsames; das ist österreichisches Zartgefühl, welches auszuhalten meine Nerven momentan nicht ganz stark genug sind.
Ihr ergebener
Ludwig Wittgenstein.[42]

The highly emotional tone of the letter alarmed Ficker and he sent the author a soothing telegram. On 4 December Wittgenstein replied:

Lieber Herr Ficker!
Es war sehr schön von Ihnen, daß Sie mir auf meinen Brandbrief mit einem so freundlichen Telegramm geantwortet haben. Freilich, lieber wäre es mir Sie nähmen mein Buch, weil Sie etwas darauf halten als, um mir einen Gefallen zu tun. Und wie kann ich Ihnen mein eigenes Werk anempfehlen?—Ich glaube, es verhält sich damit in allen solchen Fällen so. Ein Buch, auch wenn es ganz und gar ehrlich geschrieben ist, ist immer von *einem* Standpunkte aus wertlos: denn eigentlich brauchte niemand ein Buch schreiben, weil es auf der Welt ganz andere Dinge zu tun gibt. Andererseits glaube ich sagen

41. "The difficulties over my book have started up again. No one wants to publish it."
42. Cf. p. 95, this volume [ed.].

zu können: Wenn Sie den Dallago, den Haecker, u.s.w. drucken, *dann* können Sie auch *mein* Buch drucken. Und das ist auch alles, was ich zur Rechtfertigung meines Wunsches sagen kann, denn, wenn man mein Buch mit einem *absoluten* Maßstab mißt, dann weiß Gott wo es zu stehen kommt.
Mit vielen Grüßen bin ich Ihr ergebener
Ludwig Wittgenstein[43]

On the same day as this letter was written Wittgenstein also received a letter from Ficker, to which he replied the day after:

Lieber Herr Ficker!
Kaum hatte ich gestern meine Antwort auf Ihr Telegramm abgeschickt, als Ihr lieber Brief vom 28.11. eintraf. Das Opfer, daß Sie mir, wenn alle Stricke reißen, bringen wollen, kann ich natürlich nicht annehmen. Ich könnte es nicht vor mir verantworten, wenn die Existenz eines Menschen (wessen immer) durch die Herausgabe meines Buches in Frage gestellt würde. So ganz verstehe ich es freilich nicht. Denn es haben ja schon oft Menschen Bücher geschrieben, die mit dem allgemeinen Jargon nicht zusammenfielen, und diese Bücher sind verlegt worden und die Verleger sind nicht an ihnen zu Grunde gegangen. (Im Gegenteil.)—Mein Vertrauen täuschen Sie durchaus nicht, denn mein Vertrauen, oder vielmehr bloß meine Hoffnung, bezog sich doch nur darauf, es möchte Ihnen vielleicht Ihr Spürsinn sagen, daß die Abhandlung kein Mist sei—wenn ich mich hierin nicht vielleicht selbst täusche—aber doch nicht darauf, Sie möchten sie, ohne etwas von ihr zu halten, aus Güte gegen mich und gegen Ihr Interesse annehmen.—Kurz, ich bin Ihnen *sehr* dankbar, wenn Sie in meiner Sache durch Rilke etwas erreichen können; geht das aber nicht, so lassen wir Gras darüber wachsen.—(Nebenbei bemerkt, müssen die Dezimalnummern meiner Sätze unbedingt mitgedruckt werden, weil sie allein dem Buch Übersichtlichkeit und Klarheit geben und es ohne diese Numerierung ein unverständlicher Wust wäre.)
Und nun leben Sie wohl und machen Sie sich meinetwegen keine Sorgen. Es wird schon alles in Ordnung kommen.
Ihr Ergebener
Ludwig Wittgenstein
6.12.19 à propos: giebt es einen Krampus, der die schlimmen Verleger holt?[44]

In the letter there is a reference to the poet Rainer Maria Rilke. The background to Rilke's entering the stage of the publication history of the *Tractatus* is as follows:

43. Cf. p. 96, this volume [ed.].
44. Cf. pp. 96–97, this volume [ed.].

In order to help the author in his efforts to find a publisher, Ficker had written to Rilke. Apparently without disclosing to Rilke the identity of the anonymous donor of 1914 he asked whether Rilke could find a publisher for that donor's "Logisch-philosophische Abhandlung". Rilke replied with the question whether Ficker thought the Insel-Verlag (Rilke's own publisher) suitable and with a request for names of German publishers to whom he might write. Rilke's reply to Ficker is dated 12 November 1919. He said he had received Ficker's letter the day before. There is no indication that either Ficker or Rilke did anything further to pursue this line.

In the letters to Russell during that autumn we can see how the plans (first mentioned in the letter from Cassino in April 1918) for a meeting of the two friends made progress. They eventually met in the Hague in the middle of December 1919, probably from the 13th to the 20th. On the 15th Wittgenstein wrote from Holland to Engelmann: "Russell will meine Abhandlung drucken und zwar vielleicht deutsch und englisch (er wird sie selbst übersetzen und eine Einleitung zu ihr schreiben, was mir ganz recht ist)."[45]

The tone of the last letter is quite euphoric. Wittgenstein obviously was very pleased with the meeting. In his first letter to Russell after his return to Vienna (8 January 1920) he says: "Ich habe unser Beisammensein *sehr* genossen und ich habe das Gefühl, daß wir in dieser Woche sehr viel wirklich gearbeitet haben. (Du nicht auch?)"[46] And in a letter to Engelmann, dated 29 December, he says: "Mein Zusammensein mit Russell war sehr genußreich."[47]

From the meeting with Russell in the Hague Wittgenstein also wrote to Frege, announcing a visit on the way home to Austria.[48] The visit, however, had to be cancelled, because

45. "Russell wants to print my treatise, possibly in both German and English (he will translate it himself and write an introduction, which suits me)."

46. "I enjoyed our time together *very* much and I have the feeling (haven't you too?) that we did a great deal of real work during the week."

47. "My meeting with Russell was most enjoyable."

48. Annotation by Scholz: "Brief an Fr. vom . . . Zeit des Treffens mit Russell mit der Unterschrift R's Ankündigung des Besuchs von W." ("Letter to Fr. of . . . time of meeting with Russell, with Russell's signature, notice of a visit by W.")

Wittgenstein's companion on the journey to Holland, Mr. Arvid Sjögren, had fallen seriously ill. Wittgenstein arrived back from the meeting with Russell on 26 or 27 December.

It was thus at the meeting in the Hague that the plan came up that Russell should write an Introduction to the book. Wittgenstein was quite optimistic that with this authoritative support his book would find a publisher. He wrote to Engelmann (29 December 1919): "Mit einer Einleitung von Russell ist das Buch für einen Verleger gewiß ein sehr geringes Risiko da Russell sehr bekannt ist."[49] He also wrote about the forthcoming Introduction to the publishers whom he had contacted. In a letter to Russell of 8 January 1920 he writes: "Von meinen vorhabenden Verlegern habe ich noch keine Antwort auf die Mitteilung, daß Du meinem Buch mit einer Einleitung nachhelfen willst."[50]

The publishers (in the plural) to whom Wittgenstein is here referring were Ficker and, perhaps, Braumüller and/or Reclam. To Ficker he wrote (28 December):

> Lieber Herr Ficker!
>
> Vorgestern bin ich aus Holland zurückgekommen, wo ich Prof. Russell traf und mit ihm über mein Buch sprach. Falls ich es nicht in Österreich oder Deutschland verlegen kann, so wird Russell es in England drucken lassen. (Er will es übersetzen.) Dies würde ich natürlich als die ultima ratio ansehen. Nun steht die Sache aber so: Russell will zu meiner Abhandlung eine Einleitung schreiben und damit habe ich mich einverstanden erklärt. Diese Einleitung soll ungefähr den halben Umfang der Abhandlung selbst haben und die schwierigsten Punkte der Arbeit erläutern. Mit dieser Einleitung nun ist das Buch für einen Verleger ein viel geringeres Risiko, oder vielleicht gar keines mehr, da Russells Name sehr bekannt ist und dem Buch einen ganz bestimmten Leserkreis sichert. Damit will ich natürlich nicht sagen, daß es so in die rechten Hände kommt, aber immerhin ist dadurch ein güngstiger Zufall weniger ausgeschlossen.

49. "Surely, with an introduction by Russell, the book will be a very small risk for a publisher, as Russell is very well known."

50. "I've not yet had any answer from my prospective publishers to the notification that you are willing to give my book a helping hand with an introduction."

Schreiben Sie mir bitte so bald als irgend möglich, was Sie von der Sache halten, da ich Russell Bescheid geben muss.
Besten Gruss
Ihr
Ludwig Wittgenstein[51]

We do not know whether Ficker had replied to this letter, when suddenly a new prospective publisher appeared in the picture. This was the well-known German publishing house Reclam in Leipzig. It seems to have been Engelmann who had suggested this new possibility to Wittgenstein.[52] Engelmann evidently made some inquiries on the author's behalf. It must be with a reference to these inquiries that Wittgenstein on 19 January 1920 wrote to Russell: "Heute erhielt ich die Nachricht, daß der Verlag von Reklam in Leipzig aller Wahrscheinlichkeit nach mein Buch nehmen will. Ich werde also mein MS aus Innsbruck kommen lassen und es an Reklam schicken. Wann aber kommt Deine Einleitung?! Denn ohne sie kann ja der Druck nicht beginnen."[53]

Wittgenstein wrote to Ficker the very same day:

Lieber Herr Ficker!
Bitte seien Sie so gut mir umgehend mein Manuscript zu schicken, da ich es an Reklam in Leipzig senden muß, der aller Wahrscheinlichkeit nach gewillt sein dürfte, mein Buch zu verlegen. Ich bin neugierig, wieviele Jahre es noch dauern wird, bis es erscheint. Hoffentlich geht es noch vor meinem Tod.
Ihr
Ludwig Wittgenstein[54]

One week later, when the book had not yet arrived, he wrote another letter, a last one, to Ficker:

Lieber Herr Ficker!
Es ist traurig zu hören, daß es Ihnen mit dem Brenner so schlecht

51. Cf. pp. 97–98, this volume [ed.].
52. See Wittgenstein's letter to Engelmann of 29 December 1919.
53. "I have had word today that the publisher Reclam in Leipzig is in all probability prepared to take my book. So I will get my manuscript from Innsbruck and send it to Reclam. But when is your Introduction going to arrive?! Because the printing can't begin without it."
54. Cf. p. 98, this volume [ed.].

geht. Ich bin davon überzeugt, daß es nicht Kleinmut Ihrerseits ist, daß Sie mein Buch nicht nehmen. Ich schrieb Ihnen vor einigen Tagen und bat Sie um umgehende Rücksendung meines Manuscripts, da ich es an Reklam schicken muß, der die Arbeit wahrscheinlich übernehmen wird. Welche Art von Beruf werden Sie dann ergreifen? Es würde mich freuen, wenn er uns irgendwie wiederum zusammenführte. Benachrichtigen Sie mich bitte davon, was Sie zu tun gedenken.
Ihr
Ludwig Wittgenstein
P.S. Auch ich kämpfe jetzt mit großen Widerwärtigkeiten.[55]

As this letter shows, Wittgenstein must have received a letter from Ficker, in which Ficker had complained of financial difficulties with the *Brenner* and evidently also expressed some uneasiness at his refusal to print Wittgenstein's book. Thus ended this chapter in the publication history of the *Tractatus.* But thirty-four years later, in the final issue of *Der Brenner,* Ficker wrote an epilogue to the story which must also be mentioned.

Ficker's essay is called "Rilke und der unbekannte Freund. In memoriam Ludwig Wittgenstein."[56] In it we are told that Wittgenstein in the autumn of 1919 had come to visit Ficker in Innsbruck. It is not quite clear whether the author of the essay has in mind one or several visits. For he also says that Wittgenstein came to see him on his way back to Austria from the meeting with Russell in Holland. He says, moreover, that Wittgenstein had taken the route via Hamburg in Germany, where he ran short of money and had to spend the night in a Salvation Army hostel ('Nachtasyl') in the harbour. It was on the occasion of this visit on the way home that he allegedly brought with him and left with Ficker a typed copy ('Durchschlag') of his book. Ficker never saw Wittgenstein again, he says.

There is nothing in the letters to Ficker which would confirm this story. Some details are easily shown to be false. We know, for example, that the manuscript was sent to Ficker before the meeting with Russell in Holland in December—and that Ficker's request to Rilke for assistance with the publishing

55. Cf. p. 98, this volume [ed.].
56. "Rilke and the unknown friend: in memory of Ludwig Wittgenstein."

was made in November. But there are several details of the story, as told by Ficker, which make it highly improbable that it is unconscious invention. Such details concern, for example, the way Wittgenstein was dressed and how he declined Ficker's hospitality for the night. I think the truth in the matter is as follows:

Wittgenstein, on all reliable evidence we have, did *not* visit Ficker in the autumn of 1919, nor on his way back from the meeting with Russell in Holland in December. Their only contact during this period was by letter. But some two and a half years later, in August 1922, Wittgenstein and Russell met at Innsbruck (see below, p. 134). In a letter to Engelmann (10 August 1922) Wittgenstein tells about the meeting and also mentions that he had seen Ficker on the same occasion. My conjecture is that Ficker, when writing down his recollections of Wittgenstein more than thirty years later, was not relying exclusively on the letters but also on defective memory—thus conflating his correspondence with Wittgenstein in 1919–1920 concerning the publication of the *Tractatus* with the author's actual visit to him some years later, when the book was already on the point of being published by Kegan Paul in England.[57] The Hamburg episode again belongs to a journey to Norway which Wittgenstein undertook in the summer of 1921 in the company of Arvid Sjögren.

Ficker eventually returned the typescript, but Russell's Introduction was not yet there. Somewhat impatiently Wittgenstein wrote to Russell on 19 March 1920: "Wie steht's mit der Einleitung? Ist sie schon fertig?"[58] And at the very end of the letter: "Schreib mir bald einmal und schicke auch Deine Einleitung."[59]

By the beginning of April the Introduction was there. Letter of 9 April:

57. It must be mentioned, however, that Ficker in a letter to F. A. Hayek of 4 December 1953 expressly says that Wittgenstein's visit was in *October* 1919 and that he knows nothing of a visit to Innsbruck a few years later and a meeting there with Russell.

58. "How are things with the Introduction? Is it ready yet?"

59. "Do write to me soon, and also send me your Introduction."

Besten Dank für Dein Manuskript. Ich bin mit so manchem darin nicht ganz einverstanden; sowohl dort, wo Du mich kritisierst, als auch dort, wo Du bloß meine Ansicht klarlegen willst. Das macht aber nichts. Die Zukunft wird über uns urteilen.—Die Einleitung wird jetzt übersetzt und geht dann mit der Abhandlung zum Verleger. Hoffentlich nimmt er sie![60]

Wittgenstein's satisfaction with Russell's Introduction did not last long, however. Letter of 5 May 1920:

Deine Einleitung wird nicht gedruckt und infolgedessen wahrscheinlich auch mein Buch nicht.—Als ich nämlich die deutsche Übersetzung der Einleitung vor mir hatte, da konnte ich mich doch nicht entschließen sie mit meiner Arbeit drucken zu lassen. Die Feinheit Deines englischen Stils war nämlich in der Übersetzung—selbstverständlich—verloren gegangen und was übrig blieb war Oberflächlichkeit und Mißverständnis. Ich schickte nun die Abhandlung und Deine Einleitung an Reclam und schrieb ihm, ich wünschte nicht daß die Einleitung gedruckt würde, sondern sie solle ihm nur zur Orientierung über meine Arbeit dienen. Es ist nun höchst wahrscheinlich, daß Reclam meine Arbeit daraufhin nicht nimmt (obwohl ich noch keine Antwort von ihm habe). . . . Und nun sei nicht bös! Es war auch vielleicht undankbar von mir, aber ich konnte nicht anders.[61]

Wittgenstein's misgivings were justified. Reclam did not accept the book. To judge from a letter to Engelmann, dated 30 May 1920, Wittgenstein had by then received the negative

60. "Thank you very much for your manuscript. There's so much of it that I'm not quite in agreement with—both where you are critical of me and also where you are simply trying to elucidate my views. But that doesn't matter. The future will pass judgment on us. The Introduction is in the course of being translated, and will then go with the treatise to the publisher. I hope he will accept them!"

61. "Your Introduction is not being printed and consequently it's probable that my book won't be either.—You see, when I actually saw the German translation of the Introduction, I couldn't bring myself to let it be printed with my work. All the refinement of your English style was, obviously, lost in the translation and what remained was superficiality and misunderstanding. Well, I sent your Introduction to Reclam and wrote saying that I didn't want it printed: it was to serve only for his own orientation in relation to my work. It is now highly probable that Reclam will not accept my work (though I haven't had an answer from him yet). . . . And now, don't be angry with me. Perhaps it was ungrateful of me, but I couldn't do anything else."

news from the publisher. But it was not until some six weeks later, on 8 July or the very day when he received his diploma from the teachers' training college (*Lehrerbildungsanstalt*) which he had attended, that he wrote about this to Russell (8 July 1920): "Reclam hat mein Buch natürlich nicht genommen und ich werde vorläufig keine weitere Schritte tun, um es zu publizieren. Hast Du aber Lust es drucken zu lassen, so steht es Dir ganz zu Verfügung und *Du kannst damit machen, was Du willst.* (Nur wenn Du am Text etwas änderst, so *gib an, daß die Änderung von Dir ist.*)"[62]

Wittgenstein's efforts to find a publisher for his book had thus come to an end. He withdrew from Vienna and became a schoolmaster in the country. Exactly how he disposed of the typescripts and manuscripts at that time, we do not know. At least one typescript must have been in the hands of Bertrand Russell. This evidently was the same one which Russell had received through Keynes from Cassino and of which Wittgenstein had then said that it was his only corrected copy.

5

In the autumn of 1920 Russell went to China and he did not return until the end of August in the following year. Before leaving England he gave the typescript of Wittgenstein's work to Miss Dorothy Wrinch and asked her to try to get it published.[63] She offered the book to the Cambridge University Press. The Syndics of the Press, at their meeting on 14 January 1921, declined the offer.[64]

62. "Reclam has, naturally, not accepted my book and for the present I won't take any further steps to have it published. But if you feel like getting it printed, it is entirely at your disposition and *you can do what you like with it.* (Only, if you change anything in the text, *indicate that the change was made by you.*)"

63. I am indebted to Miss Wrinch for information relating to this stage of the publishing history of the *Tractatus*. In his *Autobiography: 1914–1944*, pp. 99–100, Russell says that he had been discussing the book with Miss Wrinch and the French philosopher Jean Nicod (probably in the autumn of 1919).

64. The Secretary of the Syndics, Mr. R. W. David, tells me in a letter that he thinks, on the evidence of the minutes of the meeting for 14 January 1921, that the work had been offered to the Press *without* the Introduction by Russell.

After the Cambridge Press had refused to publish the book, Miss Wrinch wrote to three German periodicals offering them the book and, evidently, Russell's introduction as well. All three editors replied during February.[65] F. Schumann of the *Zeitschrift für Psychologie und Physiologie der Sinnesorgane* said that he could not take the work unless it were psychological rather than philosophical in content. Ludwig Stein of the *Archiv für systematische Philosophie* was quite willing to publish work by a pupil of Russell's but said there would be some delay in printing and asked Miss Wrinch to write to him again in May before sending the manuscript. These two letters are dated 12 February 1921. The date of the letter from Wilhelm Ostwald is not perfectly clear[66] but must have been about the same time. He wrote:

> In jedem anderen Falle würde ich auf die Aufnahme des Aufsatzes verzichtet haben. Ich schätze aber Herrn Bertrand Russell so ungewöhnlich hoch als Forscher und als Persönlichkeit, dass ich den Aufsatz von Herrn Wittgenstein gern in meinen *Annalen der Naturphilosophie* veröffentlichen werde: die Einleitung von Herrn Bertrand Russell wird besonders willkommen sein.[67]

He went on to say that the next issue of the periodical would not be for a couple of months but that, if it were not too expensive, off-prints could be produced earlier. Miss Wrinch sent off the manuscripts on 24 February and in a postcard postmarked 10 March 21 Ostwald acknowledged the receipt of the *Tractatus* and his intention to publish it. It did in fact duly appear in the final issue of *Annalen der Naturphilosophie*[68] and, as will be seen, some off-prints were available.

65. Their replies are in the Russell Archives at McMaster University, Hamilton, Ontario.

66. It appears to be 52 21 (for 5.2.21?) but he apologizes for his delay in replying. 15.2.21 or 21.2.21 (the 52nd day of the year) would fit in better with the date of despatch of the manuscript, see below.

67. "In any other case I should have declined to accept the article. But I have such an extremely high regard for Mr. Bertrand Russell, both for his researches and for his personality, that I will gladly publish Mr. Wittgenstein's article in my *Annalen der Naturphilosophie*: Mr. Bertrand Russell's Introduction will be particularly welcome."

68. *Annalen der Naturphilosophie*, ed. Wilhelm Ostwald, vol. 14, parts 3 and 4, pp. 184–262 (Leipzig: Verlag Unesma G. m. b. H., 1921).

Perhaps word of this did not reach Russell in China: at any rate after his return in the autumn of 1921 he evidently began to discuss publication in England with C. K. Odgen and applied to Miss Wrinch from whom he heard as follows:[69]

Dear Bertie,
About Wittgenstein's Mss.—some months ago I got the Mss. accepted for publication in a certain German philosophical periodical. The Mss. is in the hands of the Editor and will appear shortly.
When I had arranged these matters I sent full details to you in Pekin. It was, I imagine, somewhere about last February. I have all the details at Cambridge but don't remember them off-hand.
Would you send on these details to Ogden if he wants to take further steps? The articles could be published as a book subsequently, but I imagine that nothing can be done until they appear.
Yours ever.
Dorothy

By 5 November 1921 Ogden had seen an off-print of the Ostwald publication[70] and readily agreed to have the work re-published in England. Indeed he expressed surprise that Russell, Nicod, and Miss Wrinch had made so little of it. Russell wrote to him on 8 November:

I dare say I could part with Wittgenstein's MS without consulting him, but I thought it better to tell him what was being done. I wrote some days ago, and if I hear nothing by the end of next week I shall assume he has no objection. He certainly won't make a fuss anyhow, but I have as yet nothing definite in writing giving me the rights.[71]

By "parting with Wittgenstein's MS" Russell probably meant 'permitting it to be published', because he himself seems at this time to have had no copy of Wittgenstein's manuscript. This is an inference from his letter of 5 December 1921 to Ogden enclosing Wittgenstein's permission to go ahead: Rus-

69. The letter (also in the Russell Archives) is dated simply "Winchelsea, Tuesday".

70. Cf. his letter of that date to Russell, printed in *The Autobiography of Bertrand Russell: 1914–1944*, pp. 121–122.

71. Ogden's letters to and from Russell (the latter in photo-copy) and Miss Wrinch's correspondence with Russell are in the Russell Archives. I am indebted to Mr. Kenneth Blackwell, the archivist, for locating this material and giving us access to it.

sell goes on to ask, "let me see proof or typescript of Ostwald's stuff if you have it". This seems to imply both that Russell had not received back the typescript that Miss Wrinch sent to Ostwald (which I have conjectured to be the only copy he had) and that it was envisaged that the printing would be from "Ostwald's stuff".

It seems, therefore, that in early November Russell had written to Wittgenstein telling him of the Ostwald publication and of definite plans for publication in England. As will be seen, he did not succeed in making clear to Wittgenstein (perhaps he himself did not know) that the Ostwald publication was already in print. Wittgenstein's reply is probably the permission to go ahead referred to above. It is dated Trattenbach, 28 November 1921, and in it Wittgenstein says:

> Dank Dir vielmals für Deinen lieben Brief. Ehrlich gestanden: es freut mich, daß mein Zeug gedruckt wird. . . . Liest Du die Korrekturen? Dann bitte sei so lieb und gib acht, daß er es genau so druckt, wie es bei mir steht. . . . Am liebsten ist es mir, daß die Sache in England erscheint. Möge sie der vielen Mühe die Du und andere mit ihr hatten würdig sein. . . . Von Ostwald habe ich keinen Brief erhalten.[72]

A student of the Ostwald edition of Wittgenstein's work is struck by a number of oddities in the use of logical symbols. For example, exclamation marks '!' are used for the Sheffer stroke, a slanted stroke '/' for the negation sign (occasionally also for the Sheffer stroke) and the capital letter C for material implication. The explanation of these eccentricities is as follows:

> The typewriter which was used for making the typescript of the book did not have the proper symbols. Rather than having

72. "Thank you very much for your kind letter. To be honest, I must confess that I am pleased that my stuff is being printed. . . . Are you going to read the proofs? If so, please be so good as to see that he prints it exactly the way I have it. . . . What pleases me most is that the thing is going to come out in England. I hope that it may be worth all the trouble that you and others have had with it. . . . I have received no letter from Ostwald."

them inserted by hand, Wittgenstein let them be typed with signs that were available. Russell made no changes—and so it was that the text became printed with the odd symbols.[73]

In the "Prototractatus" manuscript Wittgenstein uses, for example, '|' for the Sheffer stroke, '~' for negation, and the horseshoe for implication. But in the second part of the manuscript he uses '/' for negation (in 5.253). This gives strong support to the idea that the second part of the manuscript is a draft of additions to a typescript which had just been made (cf. above, p. 108). It should also be noted, that the words '6 Zeilen frei' in 6.241 on p. 118 of the manuscript sound like a directive from the author to a typist—to leave six lines free. The space reserved was for the proof of the proposition that 2 × 2 = 4.

It seems to me intrinsically unlikely, indeed impossible, that Wittgenstein would have left unchanged the symbolism of the typescript which Ostwald was printing, if he had checked the proofs. The printing of the eccentric symbolism and the occurrence of a very considerable number of uncorrected misprints constitute by themselves conclusive evidence that Wittgenstein had no hand at all in the production of the Ostwald edition. (It is also evident from the account given above that Russell never saw the proofs.) We have, moreover, evidence that the production greatly annoyed Wittgenstein. In a letter, dated 5 August 1922, he tells Engelmann that the book is shortly to appear in England, with a translation. Of the Ostwald edition he now says: "Diesen Druck betrachte ich aber als Raubdruck, er ist voller Fehler."[74] It is difficult to see why Wittgenstein calls the printing "pirated", considering that he had left the question of its publication in Russell's hands and had even expressed pleasure when he heard that the work was being printed. But he had reason to be annoyed at the errors and the barbarous typography which, we must assume, he would not himself have let pass uncorrected.

73. This is established by Wittgenstein's own comments on the symbols in a letter to C. K. Ogden dated 23 April 1922. Wittgenstein says he was "too lazy" to put the proper Russellian symbols in afterwards.

74. "However, I consider this a pirated edition. It is full of errors."

Ostwald also printed a German translation of Russell's Introduction ("Vorwort von Bertrand Russell").[75] He placed it *after* Wittgenstein's Preface ("Vorwort"). This translation is most probably *not* the one referred to in the Russell-Wittgenstein correspondence of 1920, but one which Ostwald had made or let be made for his printing. There is a letter from Ostwald to C.K. Ogden, dated 11 November 1921, which is a reply to a request from Ogden to return the English original of Russell's Introduction. Ostwald was not able to comply with the request, for, he says, he had destroyed the English copy after he got the German translation. Russell subsequently found a second copy, to which he made a certain number of additions for the forthcoming English printing of Wittgenstein's work. The printed English version of Russell's Introduction is dated "May 1922".

A comparison between the 1921 German version and the 1922 English version of the Introduction shows that the two for the most part correspond sentence by sentence though there are a number of errors of translation in the German. Only in the beginning are there some significant discrepancies consisting in substantial additions to or expansions of the earlier German text. The most expanded passage is the one dealing with Wittgenstein's concern with the conditions for a logically perfect or ideal language. This passage in the Introduction is well known and has, I am afraid, contributed to some current misunderstandings about Wittgenstein's concern with language in the *Tractatus*. In the 1922 version there are a few quotations from the book, in English translation, which are not in the German version.

6

It seems no longer possible to tell exactly when the English translation of the "Logisch-Philosophische Abhandlung" was made. Unless a new typescript copy had been taken for the purpose in England, work on the translation could not have gone on during the time when the work was being printed with Ostwald. We do not know how long Ostwald kept the

75. It is not listed in the Bibliography of the Writings of Bertrand Russell in the Schilpp volume on Russell's philosophy.

typescript. The only information relating to this matter which we have is a letter of a much later date, 5 November 1954, addressed to Professor Max Black and signed by Mr. Colin E. Franklin of the publishing house Routledge & Kegan Paul, but largely composed, it seems, by C. K. Ogden. In this letter it is said, "It seems that the German text, as corrected by Wittgenstein, reached us from Wilhelm Ostwald in January 1922 with instructions from the author to treat the translations in Russell's Introduction as having equal authority with the original." The "instructions from the author", however, can hardly have been given in January, since the exchange of letters between Ogden and Wittgenstein, as far as we know, did not begin until a few months later. It is therefore at least a possibility that the date "January 1922" is an error of memory.

We know, however (see above, p. 127), that Ogden already in the beginning of November the year before had in his hands an off-print of the work from Ostwald's *Annalen*. It is therefore a plausible conjecture that the off-print was used for the translation. Otherwise it would be surprising that the translation was finished already in March, since we know for certain that some time in March 1922 Wittgenstein got from C. K. Ogden the completed translation of his book into English. In a letter, dated 28 March, he acknowledges receipt. It is plain from the letter that Wittgenstein at that time had no copy of the German text with him. From Ostwald he had heard nothing—he even thinks that Ostwald is not going to print the work after all. He says he could obtain an uncorrected copy of it from Vienna and repeats that he had given the corrected copy to Russell. And he wonders where this typescript is now.

Very soon after this Wittgenstein must have received, probably from Ogden, the typescript which Ostwald had used for printing and (at least) one offprint of the paper in the *Annalen*. By 23 April he had finished work on checking the translation and revising the original. That he had taken great pains with this double task is clear both from his letter to Ogden of that date, from his 20 pages of attached comments on specific points in the translation, and from the physical marks on the German and English text which he returned.

The corrections to the German original were made by Wittgenstein both in the off-print from Ostwald and, in some cases, in the Engelmann-TS. The off-print he returned to Ogden. It is a plausible conjecture that he did *not* send the typescript, but kept it himself until he later (we do not know when) gave it to his friend Engelmann. If this conjecture is right, the German text of the Kegan Paul edition was printed, not from the Engelmann-TS, but from a heavily corrected off-print of the paper printed in Ostwald's *Annalen*.

The author must have found revising the corrupt Ostwald text an exasperating job. A detailed comparison of the German of the Ostwald and of the (first) Kegan Paul edition shows, beside the alterations of the symbolism and the correction of numerous misprints, also several changes of a more substantial nature. Sometimes a word or short phrase is added to the Ostwald text, sometimes another word is substituted for the one originally printed, sometimes a factual mistake in a logical formula has been corrected. The most important changes are in 4.003, the last paragraph of which does not occur in Ostwald, and in 6.2341, which in the *Annalen* has nearly the same formulation as 6.211 of the "Prototractatus". Finally, the following puzzling thing should be mentioned:

At 4.0141 in the Ostwald text stand only the words "(Siehe Ergänzung Nr. 72)". The remark itself is missing. Nor does it occur in the "Prototractatus" or in the second part of the manuscript.

In the typescript of the English translation which Ogden sent to Wittgenstein for revising, there are typed the words "4.0141 (See supplement No. 72)". In the off-print of the Ostwald edition which Wittgenstein returned to Ogden with his revisions, Wittgenstein has crossed out the printed words "Siehe Ergänzung Nr. 72" and written instead "Insert from MS attached". This evidently is a directive to the English printer. Attached to the same page is a slip of paper with the actual remark in Wittgenstein's handwriting. In the Engelmann-TS, finally, there are the words "4.0141 (Siehe Ergänzung Nr. 72)" in handwriting, and also the "Ergänzung" itself typed on two small slips of paper.

From this it must be concluded, I think, that the "Ergänzung Nr. 72" existed at the time when the Engelmann-TS was finally left with Russell. When was this? As we noted above (p. 116f.), the typescript which Wittgenstein had sent to Russell from the prison-camp, Russell returned to Vienna in the autumn of that same year (1919). After the two friends had met in the Hague in December, Russell wrote the Introduction. When writing it, he must again have had a typescript of the book. It is reasonable to think that this was the Engelmann-TS which Wittgenstein had given back to Russell, at or soon after, the meeting in Holland. We have no evidence that Russell returned the typescript, which he had in 1920 before going to China, when he gave it to Miss Wrinch. If this is right, the *terminus ante quem* of the "Ergänzungen" would be December 1919.

One is struck by the relatively high number of this particular supplement, 72. This is much greater than the number of remarks, or paragraphs in remarks, which appear in the *Tractatus* but which are neither in the "Prototractatus" nor in the rest of the manuscript-book. There is some reference to these supplements in a letter from Wittgenstein to Ogden of 5 May 1922. Ogden had evidently asked the author, whether he was not willing to let more "Ergänzungen" be printed. Wittgenstein firmly declined this proposal. He mentioned that there were about a hundred supplements, but we do not know what happened to the rest of them. Probably Wittgenstein destroyed them, not having found any use for them in the final text.

If the "Ergänzung Nr. 72" was attached to the typescript used by Ostwald's printer, it is surprising that the supplement was not printed. This must then have been due to carelessness—a hypothesis which does not seem to me too unlikely. It is also surprising that Ogden did not originally translate the supplement. This fact constitutes additional evidence for the hypothesis that the translation too, and not only the printing in England, was done from an off-print (or from proofs) of the Ostwald edition.

When Ogden had got the translation back from Wittgenstein

with the latter's comments and corrections, he still had a number of questions, on which he wanted to hear the author's opinion. In the beginning of May he therefore sent to Wittgenstein a questionnaire, which Wittgenstein returned with his annotations.

In a letter, dated 22 June 1922, Wittgenstein gave to the English publisher Kegan Paul all publication rights in his book. The agreement concerning the publication is between C. K. Ogden and Kegan Paul Ltd, and is dated 11 July 1922.

The printing in England took place in the summer. Proofs of both the German and the English texts were sent to Wittgenstein, who corrected and returned them to Ogden on 4 August. He dispatched the packet from Hallein near Salzburg, where his uncle, Paul Wittgenstein, had a house. Wittgenstein asked Ogden to check certain places in the German from the printer's 'manuscript'. This, however, does not prove that the Engelmann-TS, too, was at that time in England. It probably only means that Wittgenstein did not have the typescript with him in the place where he did the proofreading, and wished Ogden to consult the corrected Ostwald off-print which the printer was using as 'manuscript'.

Wittgenstein's letters and comments and the physical marks in the preserved proofs and typescripts conclusively establish the veracity of C. K. Ogden's words in the Editor's Note to the Kegan Paul edition: "The proofs of the translation and the version of the original which appeared in the final issue of Ostwald's *Annalen der Naturphilosophie* (1921) have been very carefully revised by the author himself." Later some people, among them the present writer, had expressed doubts about this. Although these doubts were based on statements by Wittgenstein himself later in his life, they appear to have been completely mistaken.

In the first half of August 1922 Russell and Wittgenstein met at Innsbruck. No letters between the two men relating to this meeting have been preserved. In a letter to Engelmann after the meeting (10 August 1922) Wittgenstein intimates that Russell had come to Innsbruck specially for the purpose of seeing him. We do not know exactly what were the topics of their conversation.[76] The revision of the text and translation of the book was by then completed and the proofs had been returned for the final printing.

When the *Tractatus* had been published, Wittgenstein received some author's copies of the book. In a letter of 15 November 1922 he thanks Ogden for the copies. He seems, however, to have given them all away to other people. One was a schoolmaster by the name Josef Putre, with whom Wittgenstein had made friends during his time in Trattenbach; another was Rudolf Koder, a schoolmaster at Puchberg; and a third was Arvid Sjögren: these last two remained life-long friends of his. Through Ogden Wittgenstein also arranged for a copy to be sent to David Pinsent's mother and to J. M. Keynes. When, in December 1924, Moritz Schlick in a letter asked the author for advice and help in obtaining copies of either the Ostwald or the Kegan Paul edition for Schlick's circle of students in Vienna, Wittgenstein replied (7 January 1925) that he himself had *no* copy of the book.

7

The Editor's Note to the 1922 edition ends with the words: "the Editor further desires to express his indebtedness to Mr. F. P. Ramsey, of Trinity College, Cambridge, for assistance both with the translation and in the preparation of the book for the press."

It is no longer possible to tell exactly how large Ramsey's share in the translation was. But there is evidence that it was considerable.

We have the beginning of a draft of a letter from Wittgenstein to Ramsey, in which the letter-writer excuses himself for switching from English to German with the words: "Now as you have so excellently translated the Tractatus into English I've no doubt you will be able to translate a letter too and therefore I'm going to write the rest of this in German." The letter has no date, but is probably from 1923.

In a letter from Schlick to Wittgenstein, dated 25 December

76. There is a brief mention of this meeting in Russell's *Autobiography: 1914–1944*, p. 100.

1924, we read: "(Nebenbei bemerkt hatte ich im Sommer die Freude, Herrn Ramsey, den Übersetzer Ihrer Arbeit, in Wien kennen zu lernen.)"[77] Since this was the letter in which Schlick introduced himself to Wittgenstein and there had been no communication between the two men before, Schlick's view of Ramsey as 'the translator' of the *Tractatus* can hardly have had Wittgenstein as its source.

We know that Ramsey had visited Austria in 1923 and again in 1924. On both visits he met Wittgenstein, who was at that time a schoolteacher at Puchberg, a village at the foot of the Schneeberg. When on his visit to Austria in 1924 Ramsey wrote from Vienna to Wittgenstein:

> . . . Ogden also asked me to get from you, if possible, while I was here any corrections in case there should be a second edition of your book. (This is not really likely.) I have got marked in my copy a lot of corrections we made to the translation, and 4 extra propositions you wrote in English. Obviously I think the corrections to the translation should be made in a new edition, and the only doubt is about the extra propositions; and also you might have had something else you would like altered. . . .

The letter tells of a previous occasion on which the two had met and made "a lot of corrections" to the translation. This evidently was in September 1923, when Ramsey had spent a couple of weeks with Wittgenstein discussing the *Tractatus*. Ramsey's copy of the book has been preserved and contains a number of corrections in Wittgenstein's hand.[78] Many, though not all of them, were incorporated into the second edition of the work which appeared in 1933. The four "extra propositions" were *not* incorporated. They appear, in the margin of Ramsey's copy, in English, in Wittgenstein's hand.[79] Their German version, if they had one, has not been preserved.

77. "Incidentally, I had the pleasure of meeting Mr. Ramsey, the translator of your work, in Vienna this summer."

78. A detailed study of this copy of the *Tractatus* has been made by Dr. Casimir Lewy and is published in *Mind* 76 (1967), 416–423 ("A Note on the Text of the *Tractatus*").

79. They are printed in Lewy's "Note", pp. 421–422.

8

Originally the proposed English title of the book was "Philosophical Logic." The proposal evidently was due to Ogden and Russell jointly.[80] Wittgenstein, however, disliked this title. In his letter of 23 April 1922 to C. K. Ogden he said:

> As to the title I think the Latin one is better than the present title. For although "Tractatus logico-philosophicus" isn't *ideal* still it has something like the right meaning whereas "Philosophic logic" is wrong. In fact I don't know what it means. There is no such thing as philosophic logic. (Unless one says that as the whole book is nonsense the title might as well be nonsense too.)

Who invented the Latin title, to which Ogden evidently had referred in a previous letter as being an alternative to the English? In my Biographical Sketch (1955) I said that the Latin title under which the work has become known was originally suggested by G. E. Moore. I cannot recall the source of my information. When I later had occasion to ascertain its truth, Moore was already dead.

In the letter of 5 November 1921 from Ogden to Russell, which is printed in Russell's *Autobiography* there is also mention of "Moore's Spinoza title"—and doubts are expressed whether Wittgenstein would like it. That phrase can hardly mean anything other than the title *Tractatus Logico-Philosophicus*. The letter thus seems to establish beyond reasonable doubt that the Latin title is Moore's invention. There is also direct evidence for this of a much later date. It is a letter of 3 March 1953 from Professor Gilbert Ryle to Professor Max Black. Ryle says in the letter: "Moore told me the other day that the title *Tractatus Logico-Philosophicus* was his own suggestion which Wittgenstein gladly adopted, partly because of its Spinozistic ring." (There are no further comments in the letter relating to this.)

80. See the letter of 5 November 1921 from C. K. Ogden to Bertrand Russell which is reproduced in *The Autobiography of Bertrand Russell: 1914–1944*, pp. 121–122.

5 The Origin and Composition of Wittgenstein's *Investigations*

GEORG HENRIK VON WRIGHT

A Summary

I think the reader will find it helpful if I begin this paper with what usually goes at the end, viz. a summary.

The *Philosophische Untersuchungen* was published posthumously two years after Wittgenstein's death. Wittgenstein did not regard it as a finished work. It consists, in its printed form, of two parts. If Wittgenstein had published his work himself, he would presumably have formed the two parts into a more unified whole.

In August 1936, Wittgenstein began to work on a revision, in German, of the *Brown Book* which he had dictated at Cambridge in the academic year 1934–1935. He had then withdrawn to solitude in Norway, where he remained, with interruptions, until towards the end of the following year. He called the revision *Philosophische Untersuchungen, Versuch einer Umarbeitung.*[1] Before finishing it he became dissatisfied with what he was doing and wrote at the end "Dieser ganze 'Versuch einer Umarbeitung'—ist *nichts wert*".[2] Thereupon he set himself to writing, in November and December of that same year, 1936, a new version which he also called *Philosophische Untersuchungen*. What he then wrote is, broadly speaking, the beginning of the book, as we have it. It answers, roughly, to

1. Published under the title *Eine philosophische Betrachtung*, ed. Rush Rhees, (Frankfurt am Main: Suhrkamp, 1970); (Ludwig Wittgenstein, *Schriften* 5).

2. MS 115, p. 292. I refer here to the manuscripts and typescripts of Wittgenstein using the catalogue numbers given in G. H. von Wright, "The Wittgenstein Papers," *Philosophical Review* 78 (1969). As a result of the research embodied in the present essay, some of the dates and figures given in the Catalogue stand in need of correction.

the first 188 numbered remarks of the printed text. (See below, p. 141). However, in the course of the years which followed, Wittgenstein made many additions and changes even in this first part of his work.

About one year later, from mid-September to mid-November 1937, Wittgenstein wrote the main part of a continuation to this manuscript. Again a year later, in August 1938 at Cambridge, he dated the Preface to a typescript essentially based on what he had written in Norway in the two periods mentioned. This typescript constitutes what I propose to call *the early version* of the *Investigations.* Some time later, presumably at the beginning of 1939, Wittgenstein added another sixteen pages to this typescript.

The early version of the *Investigations* thus consists of two parts written, mainly, in the autumn of 1936 and the autumn of 1937 respectively. The two parts form a consecutive whole. For this reason and because they are of almost equal length, they could also be described as the two halves of this early work. The first half, as mentioned, corresponds to the first 188 remarks of the printed final version. The second half, however, does not belong in the final version. A rearrangement, made by Wittgenstein himself, of its main content was published posthumously as Part I of the work called, by the Editors, *Bemerkungen über die Grundlagen der Mathematik.*

In the seven years from 1937 to 1944 Wittgenstein's chief preoccupation was with the philosophy of mathematics. It was only in the second half of 1944, it seems, that he resumed work on what was eventually to become the final version of the *Investigations.* In that same year he produced something which I propose to call an *intermediate* version of the work. For it he wrote the Preface, dated Cambridge, January 1945, which is printed with the final version.

The intermediate version of the *Investigations* consists, substantially, of a revision of the first half of the early version and of a continuation to it of remarks written in 1944. The continuation is about half as long as the part written earlier. Its content is in the final version dispersed over the remarks from 189 to 421.

In the summer of 1945 Wittgenstein prepared a typescript, called by him "Bemerkungen I".[3] A considerable proportion of the remarks in this collection had been written after the completion of the intermediate version. But the major part of them Wittgenstein had selected from earlier manuscripts, dating back as far as 1931. Presumably in the academic year 1945–1946 Wittgenstein expanded the intermediate version of the *Investigations* with no less than 386 remarks from "Bemerkungen I" into what is essentially the *final version of Part I* of the printed work.[4]

This means that of the 693 remarks which make up Part I of the *Investigations* more than half are new relative to the first and second versions of the work.

The manuscripts from which the remarks were selected which form Part II of the *Investigations* were written in the three-year period from May 1946 to May 1949.

The names "Teil I" and "Teil II" for the two parts composing the printed version of the *Philosophische Untersuchungen* were given to them by the Editors.

The Manuscript Sources

The primary task set for the research embodied in the present paper was to trace the remarks in the *Investigations* back to their sources in Wittgenstein's manuscripts. This task was performed, with great perseverance and skill, by Mr. André Maury. I take this opportunity to thank him and Mr. Heikki Nyman for their labours and for their helpful role in innumerable discussions from which gradually emerged the picture which is here set forth of the origin and composition of Wittgenstein's chef d'oeuvre.

It was possible to find manuscript sources for all but 109 of the remarks in Part I and for all but 27 remarks in Part II of the *Investigations*. As a 'remark' in Part II every paragraph, or group of paragraphs, separated from other paragraphs by a 'space', i.e. by an empty line, has been counted.

3. TS 228 of the Catalogue.
4. TS 227 of the Catalogue.

In some cases the sources are for a part of a remark only. In other cases different parts (paragraphs) of a remark have their sources in different manuscripts.

Sometimes a remark passed through several manuscript versions before it was dictated for a typescript. Frequently Wittgenstein made further changes in handwriting to the typescripts, but on the whole the assignment of a manuscript source to a printed remark is *univocal* and the changes *slight* from the formulation in manuscript to the final formulation.

One of the 109 remarks in Part I, for which no manuscript source is known, occurs in an early typescript (213) prepared by Wittgenstein. It is possible that some of the remarks for which no manuscript source has been found were dictated ex tempore by Wittgenstein to the typist. It is, of course, also possible that the sources of some remarks have simply escaped the searcher's notice. A further, more important, possibility is that the sources are in manuscripts which no longer exist. This last calls for a comment.

It is reported that when he was on his last visit to Vienna in the early months of 1950, Wittgenstein had ordered a great many papers, belonging to all periods of his work, to be burned.[5] It is also reported that when living in Ireland after his retirement from Cambridge, he destroyed old material which he considered useless.[6] It seems to me unlikely that there were several manuscripts containing unidentified source material for the *Investigations* among the material destroyed by him. Perhaps there were *no* such manuscripts at all.

One most important manuscript, however, is missing—and perhaps destroyed. This is a big manuscript book written in Norway late in 1936 and containing most of the content of remarks 1–188 of the printed text of the work.

This manuscript[7] Wittgenstein gave to his sister, Mrs. Margarethe Stonborough, as a Christmas present. To the dedication he had added "ein schlechtes Geschenk" ("a poor gift"). I

5. See Editor's Preface to *Notebooks 1914–1916* (Oxford: Basil Blackwell, 1961; New York: Harper & Row, 1969). The report is from Miss Anscombe.

6. Report from Mr. Rush Rhees to G.H. von Wright.

7. Listed in the Catalogue as MS 142.

saw and studied the manuscript when I visited Mrs. Stonborough at Gmunden in 1952. After her death in 1958, several manuscripts were with her son, Mr. Th. Stonborough, in Vienna. In 1965 I went there to check the material. Much to my surprise, I found none of the things I had seen at Gmunden thirteen years earlier— but also found some things, among them the "Prototractatus", which had until then been unknown to me. A subsequent search in the house at Gmunden brought to light some hitherto unknown typescripts—but not the 1936 manuscript of the *Philosophische Untersuchungen*. I cannot regard it as out of question that it has been destroyed.

It has been possible to identify manuscript sources for 98 of the first 188 remarks in the *Investigations*. Twenty-four of the "identified" remarks go back to the attempted revision in German of the Brown Book, 37 to earlier manuscripts from the years 1930–1934, 23 to a notebook from 1936, 13 to manuscript writings from 1937 and 1938, and one—added in pencil to the final typescript—to 1945. It is also possible to trace to manuscripts all but one of the "*Randbemerkungen*", which appear at the bottom of a page in the printed version of the work. It is a reasonable conjecture that of the 90 'unidentified' ones among the first 188 remarks the vast majority, perhaps all, have their source in the now lost manuscript (MS 142). Accepting this conjecture as true, we could say that the manuscript sources for only some 20 of the 693 remarks in Part I of the *Investigations* are completely unknown, or never existed.

The Early Version of *Philosophische Untersuchungen*

The Preface to the printed version of the *Investigations* is dated Cambridge, January 1945. But there existed an early version of the work with a Preface dated Cambridge, August 1938. (See above, p. 139.) Incidentally, the early Preface does not differ very substantially from the printed one.

This early version is based on material written in the years 1936–1939. Wittgenstein had it typed. The typescript comprises in all 272 pages. It falls into two parts. The first, of 137 pages and 161 numbered remarks, is that part which is, broadly speaking, identical with the first 188 remarks of the printed version. It is, for all we can tell, a typescript based directly on the lost manuscript (142) which had been written in Norway in November and December 1936. The master copy of the typescript, TS 220, contains changes and insertions in Wittgenstein's hand.

The second typescript, TS 221 of 135 pages, contains 281 remarks not, however, numbered by Wittgenstein himself. Two copies of the typescript exist; in them there are some, but rather few, marks in Wittgenstein's hand. A third copy Wittgenstein cut up in "Zettel" which he clipped together in a great number of bunches and on which he made further changes and annotations. This typescript of cuttings, TS 222, was printed posthumously as Part I of the work named by the Editors *Bemerkungen über die Grundlagen der Mathematik*.

Typescript 221 was evidently dictated at two different periods. There is a first, main part of it comprising pages 1–119 and a second part covering pages 120–135. The immediate reason for calling them two 'parts' is that they were typed on different typewriters. The first part is extracted from MSS 117, 118, and 119. The selections from 118 and 119, which take up fifty pages of the typed text, were written during the time from 10 September to 9 October 1937. The selections from 117, which compose the first sixty-nine pages of the whole thing (221), were written beginning on 11 September 1937. We cannot give them a definite *terminus ante quem*. But the writings in 117 which were dictated for TS 221 precede writings which Wittgenstein continued in a manuscript (MS 121) begun in April 1938. It is my conjecture that the part of MS 117 which was used for TS 221 was also written in Norway in the autumn of 1937.

It is of some interest to note that the greatest part of what I have called the early version of the *Investigations* was the result of two relatively short periods of concentrated writing—one in November-December 1936 and another in September-November 1937, both periods in Norway.

The second part of TS 221 is extracted from three MS sources separated by several years. Pages 120–130 are based on sections in MS 115 which were probably written early in 1934.

The remaining pages, 131–135, are based on writings in MS 121 and MS 162a, written at the turn of the years 1938–1939.

It is an open question whether the two TSS 220 and 221 (up to page 120) were dictated at the same or at different times. But it is noteworthy that they seemed to have been typed on the same typewriter—with the exception of some twenty pages in TS 220 which were typed on a different typewriter, *not*, however, the same as the one used for typing pages 120–135 of TS 221. TS 221 cannot have been dictated until some time in 1938; but TS 220 Wittgenstein *may* have dictated on a visit to Cambridge from Norway the year before.

It is known that Wittgenstein had a typescript with him in Norway in the autumn of 1937, which most probably was a typescript of what he had written one year earlier. But there is some evidence which points to it *not* being the typescript (TS 220) which has been preserved of the first half of the early version. I would therefore conjecture that the entire 'early version', i.e. both the typescripts 220 and 221, were made at Cambridge in 1938—and that the concluding part of 221 was added some time after January 1939.

When did Wittgenstein cut up TS 221 in "Zettel", composing TS 222? This we cannot tell with certainty. It is noteworthy that pages 120–135 were not cut up. This might indicate that the cutting up happened before these pages were even dictated. Pages 120–130, based on the much earlier MS 115, were clipped together and added as a separate bunch to the collection of "Zettel".

In MS 124 we find, for 18 March 1944, two references "to the Typescript". They can easily be identified as referring to TS 221 (or 222), and have the character of additions. They were included, by the Editors, in their proper places in the printed text of Part I of the *Bemerkungen über die Grundlagen der Mathematik*. But Wittgenstein did not himself insert them in the typed text. It is interesting to notice that as late as in 1944 he was still making additions to the second half of the early version of his work.

I incline to think that the cutting up of TS 221 in "Zettel" took place in connection with a revision of the *entire* Early

Version. Wittgenstein then decided to continue the revised TS 220 in a new direction—leading eventually to what is now Part I of the *Investigations.* This decision he probably made in 1944. Having made it, Wittgenstein laid aside the cut-up version of TS 221, i.e. TS 222, and never again returned to further work on it.

In MS 117 there are several drafts of a Preface to a book. They are from the time June-August 1938. Their typed and final version is dated "Cambridge, August 1938". This Preface was typed on the same typewriter as the second part of TS 221. This is an indication, I think, that the first and main part of TS 221 was typed not later than June or July 1938.

Early Plans for Publication

Wittgenstein left Norway in mid-December 1937 and travelled to Vienna, where he seems to have stayed until the middle of January 1938, when he went to Cambridge. In the first half of February he moved to Dublin and late in March back to Cambridge. This was the time of the Nazi invasion of Austria, which for natural reasons much troubled Wittgenstein and made him decide to apply for British citizenship. It seems that it was not until late April that he was again able to do concentrated philosophical work.

In February 1938, evidently before going to Dublin, Wittgenstein deposited with Trinity College Library a number of manuscripts and typescripts and gave to the college the publication rights in the event of his death. It has not been possible for me to identify the papers then deposited in the Library. In 1944 Wittgenstein withdrew the entire deposit.

In 1938, but presumably later in the year, perhaps at the time of writing the Preface, Wittgenstein also approached the Cambridge University Press about publication.[8] According to their minutes, the Syndics of the Press on 30 September 1938 offered to publish the German original with a parallel English

8. For information relating to Wittgenstein's contacts with the Cambridge University Press I am greatly indebted to Mr. Jeremy Mynott. However, no correspondence with Wittgenstein has been preserved; there are only a few records in the Syndicate's minutes.

translation of a work referred to as Wittgenstein's "Philosophical Remarks". In spite of the somewhat puzzling reference to the title, there can be little doubt that the work meant was what I have here called the early version of the "Philosophische Untersuchungen".

Wittgenstein, however, hesitated. In the minutes of the Syndics for 21 October 1938 we read that "the Secretary reported that Wittgenstein was uncertain about the publication of his *Philosophical Remarks* but was making arrangements with a translator". The translator referred to was evidently Mr. Rush Rhees, who at that time produced a translation of a considerable part of the text.

It is a reasonable conjecture that Wittgenstein's hesitation about publication is connected with his continued work on the part of the book dealing with the philosophy of mathematics, i.e. with the work which resulted in the addition of pages 120–135 to TS 221 at the turn of the year 1938–1939 and eventually in the cutting up in "Zettel" and rearranging of the content of TS 221.

Wittgenstein's next contact with the Press was in September 1943. What prompted him to make it then is not quite clear to me. One circumstance of importance, however, seems to have been his conversations in 1943 with Nicholas Bachtin.[9] The two were together reading the *Tractatus*—and, as Wittgenstein says in the printed Preface to the *Investigations,* it then suddenly seemed to him that he "should publish those old thoughts and the new ones together". The work now offered to the Press is referred to in the minutes under the title "Philosophical Investigations" and the Syndics "agreed to the author's condition that a reprint of the *Tractatus* should be included in the volume". The acceptance was confirmed on 14 January 1944. Permission for the reprinting had then been obtained from the publishers of the *Tractatus,* Routledge and Kegan Paul. (This permission was later withdrawn.)

9. From the printed Preface one would conclude that the reading of the *Tractatus* with Bachtin happened in 1941. This, however, is an error. The correct year is 1943.

A question of some interest is how the work offered by Wittgenstein to the Press in 1943 was related to the work the publication of which was being discussed in 1938. As we shall soon see, there existed a version of the *Investigations* intermediate between the early (1938) version and the final printed version. *This* intermediate version, however, did not yet exist in 1943. (The additional writings for it date from the second half of 1944.) It does not follow, however, that the work of 1943—which was going to be printed together with the *Tractatus*—was identical with the early version. We can, in fact, be certain that it was not. It is known[10] that Wittgenstein made extensive revisions in the first half of the typescript of the early version at the end of 1942 or beginning of 1943. Twelve typed pages of the revised text have been preserved, corresponding to sixteen (consecutive) pages in the earlier typescript (TS 220). The revisions and rearrangements are considerable—in relation both to the early version and the existing later versions. It is evident from the revised pages that also the numbering of the remarks in this version of 1942–1943 differed from the existing versions.

It is possible that the work, as conceived by Wittgenstein in 1943, consisted of a corrected version of both halves of the early version. Some evidence for this can be found in TS 222. Another possibility—less likely, however, in my opinion—is that Wittgenstein had already then decided to separate the writings on the philosophy of mathematics from the *Investigations*. In any case it is a fact that the version of the *Investigations* which Wittgenstein in 1943 was offering to the Cambridge University Press *cannot be reconstructed.*

The Big Manuscript Book (MS 116)

A major difficulty confronting the dating of the manuscript sources for the *Investigations* is caused by MS 116. This is the biggest of all Wittgenstein's preserved manuscript books. The number of written pages in it is 347. There is only one date in the book. It occurs on page 316 and reads (in English) "May 1945". There is every reason to think that the part from page

10. I am indebted to Mr. Rush Rhees for this information.

316 to the end was written in May or in May and June 1945. Of the remarks in this part of the manuscript, twenty-seven occur in the *Investigations*. They are, in the order of their writing, the latest remarks in Part I of that work.

When had the rest of MS 116 been written? This remaining and major part of the manuscript can be divided into three sections. The first covers pages 1–135, the second pages 136–264, and the third pages 265–315.

As far as its content goes, the first section clearly stands apart from the rest. An examination reveals that pages 1–135 in fact consist of selections with revisions from the beginning (pages 1–197) of the typescript with the number 213. This "Big Typescript" of in all 768 pages was probably dictated in 1933. It in turn is based on a typescript (TS 211) which Wittgenstein cut up into "Zettel" and rearranged before dictating TS 213. The underlying manuscript writings are from the years 1929–1932.

In manuscripts from 1933 and 1934 Wittgenstein revised parts of the content of TS 213. His efforts were evidently aimed at the composition of a work representing his position in philosophy at that time. These efforts he abandoned—under the influence, it seems, of the new developments of his thoughts which first manifested themselves in the *Blue Book* and then were continued in the *Brown Book*. Pages 1–135 of MS 116 were perhaps a last effort to revise the earlier work. When was this revision undertaken?

The Big Manuscript Book had been purchased in Bergen (Norway). After the end of the academic year 1935–1936 Wittgenstein went to stay in his hut in Norway for the greater part of the time from August 1936 to December 1937. Here he started (August 1936) a translation into German, with important revisions and additions, of the *Brown Book* which he had dictated at Cambridge in the year 1934–1935. He was then writing in the manuscript book MS 115. Later in the autumn he abandoned the efforts at an "Umarbeitung" and proceeded to the writing of the now lost manuscript book (142) which was the first version of the beginning of the final *Investigations*. This he finished in December. Preliminary materials for it are found in the notebook MS 152. For the sections 151–188 (including the long passage on "Lesen") he used materials in the "Umarbeitung" which were new relative to the *Brown Book.*

Two pocket notebooks, MS 157a (second half) and MS 157b, are all that we possess of writings by Wittgenstein which can be dated with certainty to the first half of 1937. They relate to the beginning of the *Investigations* and some of the remarks were selected and revised for the typescript of the first half of the early version (TS 220) which Wittgenstein dictated in 1937 or 1938.

It may seem intrinsically unlikely that Wittgenstein had written the first section of MS 116 *after* having written the beginning of the *Investigations* in the autumn of 1936. Nor is there much reason to believe that he wrote it simultaneously with either the revision of the *Brown Book* or the beginning of the *Investigations.* These facts speak in favor of the view that Wittgenstein began writing in MS 116 *before* going to live in Norway in 1936. It would follow that he must have acquired the book in Norway on some previous visit. (It is improbable that he had ordered the book or that it was sent to him from Norway.) Since he called it "Band XII" and the manuscript book in which he was writing in the beginning of 1934 was "Band XI" (MS 115), it is reasonable to assume that the earliest date of the writings in MS 116 is 1934.

It is not known with certainty that Wittgenstein had visited Norway in the period between his return to Cambridge in 1929 and the year 1936. For this and other reasons one must, I think, keep open the possibility that Wittgenstein's revision, in MS 116, of the beginning of the "Big Typescript" (TS 213) was, after all, made in 1936 or 1937. If this is the truth, the writings in the first part of MS 116 would thus be *later* than the writings for the first part of the early version of the *Investigations.* It is a fact that Wittgenstein later selected forty-seven remarks (and a few "Randbemerkungen") from pages 1–135 of MS 116 to be included in the final version of Part I of his great work.

The second part of MS 116, pages 136–264, is a revision of MS 120, a manuscript written late in 1937 and in the first third of

1938. At the very end of this part there are, however, a couple of remarks which had originally been written in MS 121 in July 1938 and five remarks which are selected from MS 115.

The third part of MS 116, pages 265–315, cannot be directly related to any other writings by Wittgenstein. But it is noteworthy that it deals to a large extent with topics which are also dealt with in MS 128. This latter MS contains a sketch of a Preface for a new version of the *Investigations* (in fact for the preface to the work as printed). MS 128 was most probably written in 1944, and it seems that this was also the year when MS 116, pages 265–315, was written.

It would then follow that the second part of MS 116 was written during the time between 1938 and 1944, limits inclusive. I should hazard a conjecture that it was actually written late in that period, perhaps as late as 1944. There is internal evidence—closeness of the thoughts to those in MS 129 written in the autumn of 1944–to support this conjecture.

The Intermediate Version of Part I of the *Investigations*

Even with due regard to the uncertainties pertaining to the dating of MS 116, it seems safe to say that only a very minor part of the *Investigations* stems from the years 1937–1943 inclusive. During those seven years Wittgenstein's main concern was with the philosophy of mathematics. In 1937–1938 he wrote what was originally the second half of the early version of the *Investigations* printed as Part I of the *Bemerkungen über die Grundlagen der Mathematik.* (See above p. 143.) In the beginning of 1944 Wittgenstein was still writing about the philosophy of mathematics—but then he shifted to work on the philosophy of psychology, which was to become a source for a new version of the *Investigations.* After 1944 he did not write anything about mathematics.

An examination of the final typescript of Part I of the *Investigations* (TS 227) reveals that there must have existed an intermediate typescript between it and the typescript of the early version. This one can see from the fact that the page-numbers and the numbers of remarks on some pages have been crossed out and changed in handwriting.

Some time in 1949, or possibly 1950, Wittgenstein put in my hands some twenty typed pages and said that I could destroy them, since they were no longer of any use. This I did not do, but put them aside in an envelope. This was fortunate. For it turns out that the pages with a changed page-number in the final typescript *and* those discarded pages together, without gaps, make up pages 145–195 of one and the same typescript. The first 144 pages are pages 1–144 of the final typescript (TS 227). Page 195 has only four lines typed on it. It may very well be the last page of the entire typescript. The last remark has the number 300. It is identical with remark 421 in the printed work.

An examination of pages 144–195 of that earlier typescript shows that almost all of them contain remarks from the first half of manuscript MS 129. The exceptions are only four in number. One is from the beginning of MS 130, one from the end of MS 129, one cannot be traced to any manuscript at all, and finally there is one which begins with a paragraph from MS 124 while the rest of it cannot be identified in the manuscripts. MS 129 was begun on 17 August 1944 and MS 124 was probably finished by that time. The beginning of MS 130 is undated. The later parts of that manuscript are from the time May–August 1946. There is independent evidence (cf. below p. 153) for thinking that the beginning of MS 130 was written considerably earlier.

The remarks from MS 129 were not, however, sifted directly into the typescript pages 144–195. They made the passage by the route of another, preparatory typescript (TS 240). This typescript was not known to exist until 1976 when it was found. There are, moreover, two copies of it. In both copies there are (different) corrections and insertions in handwriting. The typescript has 33 pages and 114 numbered remarks. (The occurrence of the number "115" after the last remark *could* indicate that Wittgenstein had thought of continuing it—but I think this possibility unlikely.) All remarks on pages 144–195 with exception of the four mentioned above correspond to remarks in this typescript TS 240. Virtually, TS 240 is thus a first typescript version of the new stuff which, together with the revised TS 220 and a brief section (pages 135–143) of remarks taken from TS 221, make up what I propose to call an intermediate version of the *Investigations*.

It seems to me a very safe conjecture that there existed in January 1945, or soon after, a typescript consisting of 195 pages and containing 300 remarks. It was for this "intermediate version" that Wittgenstein wrote the Preface, dated Cambridge, January 1945, which remains, with this somewhat misleading dating, the preface of the final, printed version of the *Investigations*.

The fact that Wittgenstein had re-written the Preface to the early version and dated the new preface January 1945 would indicate that he was again thinking of publishing. I do not know of any records, however, which show that he had then been in contact with the Cambridge University Press or any other publisher. We can only conjecture the reasons which kept Wittgenstein from proceeding with the publication plans. Presumably they have something to do with the fact that, soon after Wittgenstein had dated the preface for the "intermediate version", we find him busy at work composing yet a further, final version of that which is now Part I of the printed *Investigations*.

"Bemerkungen I"

On 13 June 1945, Wittgenstein wrote to Rush Rhees: "—I've been working *fairly* well since Easter. I am now dictating some stuff, remarks, some of which I want to embody in my first volume (if there'll ever be one). This business of dictating will take roughly another month, or 6 weeks.—"

This interesting record gives rise to a number of questions. Which are the writings Wittgenstein was then in a process of dictating? Can we identify the typescript which the dictating resulted in? And what does he mean by the phrase "my first volume"?

Wittgenstein says that he has been working "fairly well since Easter". This would mean April through May. As we know, the last part of the big manuscript book MS 116 was written in May 1945. There are no other writings of Wittgenstein's which can be dated with *certainty* to this period, nor to the earlier months of 1945. The most reasonable candidates are the later part of MS 129, the undated beginning of MS 130, and possibly some other portions of MS 116.

The time allowed for the dictating would indicate that there was a considerable amount of stuff to be typed. The resulting typescript, however, was neither the final nor yet another typescript of Part I of the *Investigations*. For all we can judge, the dictation resulted in a collection of 698 remarks, called by Wittgenstein "Bemerkungen I". A comparative study of remarks which appear both in "Bemerkungen I" and in the final typescript of the *Investigations* establishes beyond doubt that "Bemerkungen I" must be the earlier of the two typescripts.

The first 231 remarks of "Bemerkungen I", i.e. roughly the first third of the whole thing, are selected—in order of entry—from the first three parts of MS 116. Among them is included one single remark from MS 115. Then follow some 130 remarks from MS 129 (and one from MS 124), i.e. from the time 1944–1945. Then there is a jump back in time: after some 25 remarks in mixed order from TS 213, MS 114, and MS 119, more than 100 consecutive selections from MS 115 and more than 60 from MS 114 follow. All these latter sources are pre-war. But from remark number 563 to the end the selections are again mainly, though not exclusively, from later manuscript sources: chiefly from the beginning of MS 130 and from the concluding part, dated May 1945, of MS 116. Unless "Bemerkungen I" was dictated at different periods—for which there is *no* evidence—it was dictated in toto after May 1945 but, as mentioned, before the final typescript of Part I of the *Investigations*.

The Final Version of Part I of the *Investigations*

Wittgenstein selected 386 of the 698 remarks in "Bemerkungen I" to be included, occasionally with some changes, in the final typescript of Part I of the *Investigations*. Thirteen additional remarks from "Bemerkungen I" are included as "Randbemerkungen". It should be noted that these inclusions amount to more than half of the total number (693) of remarks in the printed Part I. (Of the remaining 299 remarks in "Bemerkungen I", 211 are printed in the "Zettel", occasionally with some "cuts".)

There is a list, made by Wittgenstein himself, of the selections from "Bemerkungen I" for the final typescript. This list also makes reference to pages where the selected remarks were to be inserted. A comparison with the intermediate typescript of the *Investigations* shows that the page references are to it. After the last page reference (to page 194) a long list of remarks from "Bemerkungen I" follows. They correspond, in their order, fairly well with the remarks from number 421 to the end of Part I of the printed text of the *Investigations.*

The final typescript of Part I was evidently composed on the basis of the intermediate typescript and the "Bemerkungen I" with the aid of the list. There is no indication that the final typescript contains remarks from manuscript sources of a later date than the composition of "Bemerkungen I", i.e. approximately June 1945. The version that was there in January 1945 had 195 pages, as against the 324 pages of the final typescript.

When was the final typescript of Part I made? It *could* have been made immediately after the production of "Bemerkungen I". *For* this speaks the time allowed for the dictations and perhaps the words in the letter to Rhees that Wittgenstein was dictating stuff (evidently "Bemerkungen I") *some of which* he wanted to embody in his "first volume". On existing evidence I find it likely that the typescript was made either immediately after "Bemerkungen I" or in the academic year 1945–1946. But Wittgenstein must have continued to work on the typescript after that and as late as in 1949 or 1950. The fact that he then gave me the loose typescript pages mentioned above (p. 151) can hardly mean anything else but that he was then still revising from the "intermediate" to the "final" typescript of Part I of the *Investigations.*

The table below shows how the remarks are distributed over the manuscript sources:

MS	Year of writing	Number of selected remarks (or parts of a remark)	"Randbemerkungen" (or parts of them)
108	1930	2	
109	1930–1931	1	
110	1931	7	
112	1931	6	
153 a	1931	1	
114	1933–1934	39	3
115 (1)	1933–1934	79	2
140	1933–1934	1	
116 (1)	1934? (1937?)	49	5
115 (2)	1936	26	
152	1936	34	
157 a	1937	8	
157 b	1937	10	
117	1937	14	
119	1937	10	
121	1937–1938	1	
162 b	1939–1940	4	
163	1941	3	
116 (2)	1938–1944	46	
116 (3)	1944?	27	1
124	1944	16	
128	1944	3	
180 a	Circa 1945		1
129	1944–1945	199	3
130	1945?	14	
116 (4)	1945	29	
Sum total		629	15

Comments on the table:

1. When one and the same remark in the *Investigations* has several manuscript sources, we have in the "statistics" of the table taken notice only of the source which has the *latest* date and which therefore, in time, is closest to the printed remark. Then it should be remembered, however, that a majority of the identified MS sources for the first 188 remarks in the book were presumably sources, *immediately* for the now lost MS 142, and only *remotely* for the typescripts TS 220 of the early version and TS 227 of the final version. It must be left to future research to try to trace all MS sources back to their *earliest* appearance in the manuscripts.

2. The total number of remarks in Part I of the *Investigations* for which a manuscript source has been found is 584. The sum of figures given in the third column in the table is considerably higher, 629. This is due to the fact that many remarks have partial sources in several manuscripts. (Cf. above p. 141).

3. The remarks in MS 114 (from the part which is paginated 1–228), those from the beginning part of MS 115, and those from the first of the four distinguishable parts of MS 116 (cf. above p. 148) are revisions, sometimes containing considerable additions and changes, of the writings in TS 213 ("Big Typescript"). This typescript was probably dictated in 1933 and had a predecessor in a typescript probably dictated the year before. The chief manuscript sources (MSS 109–114) for these typescripts are writings from the years 1930–1932. As a consequence, the remarks in the *Investigations* which were selected from MS 114 and from the first parts of MS 115 and MS 116 respectively have remoter manuscript sources in writings from 1930–1932—in some few cases even in writings from 1929.

4. The second half of MS 115 was written in Norway in 1936 and is (see above p. 148) a revision, with additions, in German of a substantial part of the *Brown Book.* Wittgenstein broke off the work before finishing it and then started to write the now lost MS 142 which became the beginning of the present *Investigations.* As seen from the table, there are twenty-six remarks in the *Investigations* for which we have indicated a manuscript source in the 1936 part of MS 115. They were presumably "lifted" from MS 115, with many revisions, into MS 142. (See above p. 148). In addition, the beginning of the printed text (*roughly* remarks 1–21) is close in content and sometimes also in formulation to the beginning of the 1936 part of MS 115. It would not, however, be correct to regard *these* passages in MS 115 as "manuscript sources" for remarks in the beginning of the final *Investigations.* They are therefore not included in the statistics of the above table.

"Bemerkungen II"

What do the words "my first volume" in the letter to Rhees refer to?

In a letter to Moore (M 40) from February 1939 Wittgenstein also refers to something with the words "my first volume".[11] There can be little doubt but that he then means the first half (TS 220) of the early version of the *Investigations.* It seems to me obvious that in the letter to Rhees six years later he uses the phrase for referring to the revision and enlargement of this "first volume", i.e. to what I have here termed the intermediate version of the *Investigations.*

But which is the other volume or volumes referred to by implication? Was Wittgenstein in 1945 contemplating a second

11. Ludwig Wittgenstein, *Letters to Russell, Keynes, and Moore,* ed. by G. H. von Wright (Oxford: Basil Blackwell; Ithaca, N.Y.: Cornell University Press, 1974), p. 176.

volume dealing with the philosophy of logic and mathematics? This volume would presumably have embodied a new version of the second half of the early version of the *Investigations*, with additions from his many writings on those topics during the time 1937–1944. This is *one* possibility—and the one I consider most likely. But it must remain a conjecture. The conjecture would get considerable support if it could be shown that Wittgenstein had done the cutting up of the second half of the early version roughly at this time (1944–1945). We have no direct evidence for this. (See above p. 144.) But the fact is that Wittgenstein made additions to the cut-up version from writings from the year 1944 (above p. 144) and this at least shows that he was still working on it then.

Another possibility is that Wittgenstein had then already planned the continuation to Part I of the *Investigations* which eventually resulted in what is now Part II of the printed work. Against this, however, speaks the fact that Wittgenstein did not begin the writings which are the manuscript sources for Part II of the *Investigations* until about one year after the letter to Rhees, or in May 1946. (See below.)

Some time after the completion of "Bemerkungen I", but *before* the commencement of the writings for Part II of the *Investigations*, Wittgenstein composed a typescript (TS 230), called by him "Bemerkungen II". It contains 542 remarks, practically all of which are also in "Bemerkungen I". Furthermore, practically all remarks from "Bemerkungen I" which were selected for Part I of the *Investigations* also occur in "Bemerkungen II". Therefore it seems out of question that "Bemerkungen II" was a projected "second volume"—assuming that Part I was the "first volume".

Why did Wittgenstein compose "Bemerkungen II" at all? The remarks in "Bemerkungen I" had been selected from manuscript sources mainly in chronological order of writing, though with some 'jumps' back and forth in time among the manuscripts. "Bemerkungen II" is definitely an arrangement with a view to subject matter. With a certain justification "Bemerkungen II" may be regarded as an independent and final work by Wittgenstein.

Wittgenstein must have worked hard on the composition of "Bemerkungen II". Three typescripts of it are preserved. All three contain further corrections and additions in Wittgenstein's hand—not always the same in the three copies. Wittgenstein also made a list of correspondences between the remarks in "Bemerkungen I" and "Bemerkungen II".

Part II of the *Investigations*

The undated beginning of MS 130 was evidently written mainly in the first half of 1945 and several remarks from it were selected for the "Bemerkungen I". About half way through the book there appears the date "26 May 1946". After this the rest of the book, 293 pages in all, is dated. Continuous with this manuscript are the manuscripts 131–138. These consecutive writings end in MS 138 with the date 22 March 1949. There is an additional entry dated 20 May of that year.

It is from these manuscripts, covering a period of almost exactly three years, that practically all the remarks in Part II of the *Investigations* are selected. There are also some remarks selected from the pocket notebook 169. They probably date from the spring of 1949. Wittgenstein then visited Vienna from Dublin in April and returned to Dublin in May. It is possible that he wrote the pocket notebook in Vienna and that this piece of writing thus bridges the gap between the penultimate and the ultimate insertion in MS 138.

On the basis of selections from manuscripts 130–135 Wittgenstein dictated a typescript, TS 229. Its pagination continues that in "Bemerkungen I". The numbers of the remarks also continue those in "Bemerkungen I"—with the exception of an intermediate 'zone', where the numbers start with 699 but then drop back to 670. The 'zone' is somewhat longer than the overlap of numbers of remarks; it ends with remark 701. Of the 33 remarks constituting the 'zone' all but the first 5 can be traced to the undated part of MS 130. They were thus probably written in 1945. I find the existence of the 'zone' somewhat puzzling.

The last remark in TS 229 has the number 1804. The typescript is a collection of in all 1,137 remarks. Only some 70 of them were selected for Part II of the *Investigations*. 142 are (sometimes with cuts) printed in *Zettel*.

On the basis of the concluding part of MS 135, from 9 November 1947, and up to the entry of 23 August 1948 in MS 137, Wittgenstein made selections for another chronologically arranged typescript, TS 232. It has 736 numbered remarks. The page numbers are from 600 to 773—a fact for which I can offer no explanation. Of the 736 remarks, 36 were selected for Part II of the *Investigations*; 227 are (in toto or with cuts) printed in *Zettel*.

Some time in 1949, probably before he went to visit Norman Malcolm and his wife in the United States in July, Wittgenstein composed a handwritten selection of remarks from all his writings from the three-year period 1946–1949 (beginning with the latter part of MS 130). This manuscript, MS 144, is, save for minor discrepancies, identical with Part II of the *Investigations*. There was also a typescript, based on this manuscript. The printing of the book took place from the typescript which is now, unfortunately, lost.

The Unity of the *Philosophische Untersuchungen*

How did Wittgenstein himself view the relation between the two parts, which now jointly make up the *Investigations*? Did he regard them as being essentially *one* work—and was it his intention, if possible, to knit the two parts together so as to form a more complete whole? The Editors of the *Investigations* indicate in their Preface that they think this was so. Perhaps they are right—and perhaps this was one reason why Wittgenstein could not bring himself to publish the book in his lifetime. One would then be justified in calling the *Investigations* an unfinished work.

I am not sure, however, that this is the only right view to take. I lean, myself, towards the opinion that Part I of the *Philosophische Untersuchungen* is a complete work and that Wittgenstein's writings from 1946 onwards in certain ways represent departures in *new* directions. But this fact, which seems to me interesting and noteworthy for a full understanding of Wittgenstein's achievement, need not exclude the possibility that he himself had wanted the two parts of the work to form a more integrated whole than they as a matter of fact do.

In this connection it is also worthwhile to contemplate the position of the work of Wittgenstein's which was published under the title *Zettel.* It is not known with what end in view Wittgenstein kept this collection of cuttings from various typescripts. Well more than half of the remarks which occur in *Zettel* were written in the period May 1946–August 1948. Of the remaining number the overwhelming majority belong to the typescript "Bemerkungen I" (TS 228), which seems to have been composed in 1945 and from which Wittgenstein selected 386 remarks to be included in Part I of the *Investigations.* (See above p. 153) It is not an unplausible hypothesis that Wittgenstein's plan was to use the fragments (the "Zettel" as he called them) for "bridging the gap" between the present Part I and Part II of the *Investigations.* In any case it seems safe to say that *Zettel* belongs between the two disconnected members of the chef d'oeuvre of Wittgenstein's "later" philosophy and thus constitutes the middle part of what could also be thought of as a trilogy.

Addendum (October 1978)

In 1977 a hitherto unknown typescript version of the first half of the early version of the *Investigations* came to light. It is now with the other Wittgenstein papers in the Wren Library, Cambridge. This typescript is evidently the revision of TS 220 which Wittgenstein made at the end of 1942 or beginning of 1943. (See above, p. 147.) The relevance of its discovery to the history which is told in this essay cannot be assessed until a detailed examination of the typescript has taken place.

6 Wittgenstein, Ficker, and *Der Brenner*

ALLAN JANIK

The publication of Wittgenstein's correspondence has greatly altered our understanding of his *Tractatus.* In this essay I should like to indicate the significance of his letters to Ludwig von Ficker for comprehending his aims in writing that mysterious little book. I should like to begin with a brief survey of what I take to be the significance of other recently published Wittgenstein correspondence for interpreting the *Tractatus* so that one may see why I assign such a special position to the Ficker letters.

In general, the publication of Wittgenstein's correspondence with his Cambridge friends and colleagues[1] has tended to bear out the fact that the Russellian interpretation of the work as fundamentally concerned with "the conditions for accurate symbolism" was off the mark. The letters to Russell in particular indicate this. Wittgenstein described the *Tractatus* to Russell as his life's work.[2] He expressed anxiety to him over the fact that publishing the book, which he had completed in the prisoner of war camp at Cassino, would be slow and involved. He yearned to see the book in print, yet he recognized that it was bound to be misunderstood. Even Russell himself would probably misunderstand it: "Don't think that everything that you won't understand is a piece of

1. Ludwig Wittgenstein, *Letters to Russell, Keynes, and Moore,* ed. G. H. von Wright, assisted by B. F. McGuinness (Oxford: Basil Blackwell; Ithaca, N.Y.: Cornell University Press, 1974). Hereafter cited as *R* with the appropriate letter number.

2. *R* 36.

stupidity,"[3] he wrote in December of 1919. Six months later he described Russell's Introduction to his Austrian friend Paul Engelmann as "impossible."[4]

Indeed, the publication of Wittgenstein's letters to Engelmann with Engelmann's *Memoir* provided the first clear-cut evidence that Wittgenstein's lifelong refusal to discuss the *Tractatus* was rooted in a profound disappointment at the universal misunderstanding to which it was subject. Paul Engelmann's friend and associate was clearly not a positivist nor a British empiricist. He was an Austrian, passionately concerned with all of the moral and cultural issues of his countrymen, not the least of which was the tendency to distort the beautiful and trivialize the profound. In Wittgenstein's view this problem was the result of confusing those occasions on which one ought to speak from those upon which one should best remain silent.

Engelmann's *Memoir* was an effort to provide us with a deeper understanding of this silence. He related it to the aesthetics of Tolstoi and the activities of the contemporary Viennese social critics Adolf Loos and Karl Kraus as well as to certain classical German authors and poets such as Keller, Mörike, and Uhland. This was indeed a breakthrough, for it confirmed what such literary critics as George Steiner,[5] Werner Kraft,[6] and Erich Heller,[7] who were thoroughly familiar with the Austrian cultural milieu in the early part of this century, had suspected for some time. However, as informative as this might be, it was still secondhand.

It was only with the publication of Wittgenstein's correspondence with Ludwig Ficker[8] that we came to possess evi-

3. *R* 36.

4. Paul Engelmann, *Letters from Ludwig Wittgenstein with a Memoir,* trans. L. Furtmüller, ed. B. F. McGuinness (Oxford: Basil Blackwell, 1967), #31. Hereafter cited as E with the appropriate letter number.

5. George Steiner, *Language and Silence* (New York: Athenum, 1967), pp. 51 passim.

6. Werner Kraft, "Ludwig Wittgenstein and Karl Kraus," *Neue Rundschau* 72 (1961), 812–844.

7. Erich Heller, "Ludwig Wittgenstein: Unphilosophical Notes," *Encounter* 13 (1959), 40–48.

8. Ludwig Wittgenstein, *Briefe an Ludwig von Ficker,* ed. G. H. von Wright

dence from the hand of Wittgenstein himself that there was a good deal more to the book than his Anglo-Saxon expositors had hitherto suspected. The twenty-nine brief letters and cards which Wittgenstein wrote to Ficker between July 1914 and January 1920 provide us with a context for reading the *Tractatus* and are, consequently, of the highest significance for comprehending the work. But that is not their whole significance. They also afford us glimpses of Wittgenstein in two other roles: that of patron of the arts and that of soldier. I should like to examine these in chronological order and analyze their import for our knowledge of his life and work.

Out of the blue during the third week of July 1914, Ludwig Ficker received a letter from Ludwig Wittgenstein requesting Ficker's assistance in disseminating 100,000 crowns[9] among worthy young artists. Ficker was nonplussed and replied so. Wittgenstein wrote to assure him that the offer was genuine and that he would prove it by giving the money to Ficker in two weeks' time. He explained that he had chosen Ficker to assist him in donating a part of his inheritance from his father to a worthy cause "because of what Kraus wrote about you and your journal in the *Fackel,* and because of what you wrote about Kraus."[10] At this point I should like to explain how Ficker and Wittgenstein would have appeared to one another after this second letter.

Ludwig Wittgenstein was the twenty-five-year-old youngest son of Karl Wittgenstein, the Dual Monarchy's premiere steel baron until his retirement in 1913, not long before his death. Karl Wittgenstein's home was perhaps the foremost musical

assisted by Walter Methlagl (Brenner Studien, I: Salzburg: Otto Müller, 1969). Translated as Ludwig Wittgenstein, "Letters to Ludwig von Ficker," this volume, Chapter 3. Hereafter cited as *F* with the appropriate letter number. Ficker was required by law to drop the noble 'von' after World War I, when the Austrian Republic abolished titles.

9. At the time the equivalent of $20,500. While estimates of relative buying power are subject to question, a conservative estimate would place the value of that amount at ten times the face value.

10. *F* 2.

salon in Vienna, frequented by Brahms and Joachim, Mahler and Casals.[11] He had financed the construction of the Secession building where the Viennese avant-garde painters exhibited, and contributed lavishly to needy musicians and musical institutions such as the Gesellschaft für Musikfreunde. His contributions to Vienna's cultural life warranted a full-page obituary in the art section of the *Neue Freie Presse* (as well as two other full pages elsewhere). Karl's brother Louis was among the most prominent Lutherans in Austria. In short, Ludwig was from one of the wealthiest and most distinguished families in Austria. He had studied abroad and had just returned from nearly a year's stay in Norway. He was impressed by Karl Kraus and his *Fackel*.

Kraus had written of Ficker's *Brenner*, "That Austria's only honest review is published in Innsbruck should be known, if not in Austria, at least in Germany, whose only honest review is published in Innsbruck also."[12] Ficker returned Kraus's esteem. Indeed, the periodical which he founded in 1910 as a journal of art and culture had been named *Der Brenner* (The Burner) because it was conceived as a kind of extension of what Kraus was doing in *Die Fackel* (The Torch).[13] From 1899 Kraus had wielded the weapon of satire deftly against the hypocrisy and corruption in the Habsburg Monarchy.[14] The press was a main target of his attacks. The Austrian press reciprocated by having recourse to what is known as *totschweigentaktik* against Kraus. It was the same weapon that the medical profession wielded against Freud and psychoanalysis (which Kraus also detested), the conspiracy of silence: Kraus was not mentioned in any newspaper with the exception of the Social Democratic *Arbeiterzeitung*. Thus, for example, Vien-

11. Allan Janik and Stephen Toulmin, *Wittgenstein's Vienna* (New York: Simon and Schuster, 1973), p. 169.

12. Cited in the notes to *F* 2.

13. Walter Methlagl, "Ludwig Ficker," *Neue Österreichische Biographie* (Vienna: Amalthea Verlag, 1968), p. 22. I am deeply indebted to Dr. Methlagl for my understanding of Ficker and *Der Brenner*.

14. On Kraus see Frank Field, *The Last Days of Mankind: Karl Kraus and His Vienna* (London: Macmillan; New York: St. Martin's Press, 1967). Also Janik and Toulmin, *Wittgenstein's Vienna*, ch. 3.

na's *Neue Freie Presse* refused to print anything about the death or funeral of writer Peter Altenberg because Kraus gave the funeral oration. Ficker not only mentioned Kraus in the *Brenner*—he championed him from the very outset. This, however, is not sufficient to identify Ficker and his journal.

Born in 1880, Ludwig von Ficker was the son of a distinguished historian. After pursuing studies in law and art history, Ficker turned to the stage and was for a time an actor and playwright. He soon decided, however, that none of these careers was for him, that his efforts in these directions were, at the very best, second-rate. Knowledge of his personal limitations was one of Ficker's primary qualities. In 1905 he met Carl Dallago, a poet and, in his own words, an "nonwriter." Dallago, whose ideas I shall discuss subsequently, made a deep impression on Ficker and they became fast friends. Dallago, surprisingly, could express himself in writing only with difficulty, so Ficker assisted him by editing what he wrote. Beginning in 1910 with the founding of the *Brenner* by Ficker and Dallago and extending beyond the last *Brenner* of 1954, Ficker was ever the editor, the mediator, the transmitter of thought and culture for the journal. In short, he found himself in a kind of Socratic role of midwife to poets, writers, and even philosophers.

By July 1914, the *Brenner* had come a long way from its provincial origins as an outlet for the poetry and thought of Dallago as well as other Tyroleans, to the position of one of the leading literary journals of the German avant-garde.[15] In December of 1910, Hugo Neugebauer published an enthusiastic essay on Theodor Däubler's *Das Nordlicht* which started a chain of events that would lead the *Brenner* to gain a reputation as one of the leading organs of innovative writing in the German-speaking world and lead to the association of Ficker and the *Brenner* with some of the leading lights of German Expressionism. In particular, Ficker was the first to publish the work of a sensitive, anxiety-ridden Salzburg pharmacist,

15. Walter Methlagl's dissertation "*Der Brenner:* Wissenschaftliche Wandlungen vor dem Erstem Weltkrieg" (Leopold Francens Universität, Innsbruck, 1966) is an admirable study of the early *Brenner*.

Georg Trakl, perhaps the foremost Expressionist poet and certainly one of the finest writers of German lyrics in modern times. It was thus to one of the most prominent new figures on the Austrian scene that Wittgenstein turned when he wished to become a benefactor of deserving talented people, for by mid-1914 Ficker had published Däubler, F. T. Csokor, Else Lasker-Schüler, and Hermann Broch, to cite the most prominent. He had achieved notoriety as a champion of the Krausian cause with his volume of *Studien über Karl Kraus* (the fourth volume to be published by Ficker's Brenner Verlag) as well as with his *Rundfrage* (questionnaire) on the importance of Kraus, which appeared in the *Brenner* in June and July 1913 and was later also printed separately. The questionnaire contained tributes to Kraus from such notables as Frank Wedekind, Thomas Mann, Adolf Loos (who occasionally contributed to the *Brenner*), Arnold Schoenberg, Albert Ehrenstein, Stefan Zweig, Lanz von Liebenfels, Franz Werfel, and Oskar Kokoschka. The man who produced this questionnaire would surely know how to place the 100,000 crowns in the right hands.

In the very last issue of the *Brenner*, which appeared in 1954, after the death of Wittgenstein, Ficker, who had been sworn to secrecy by Wittgenstein in this affair, recounted the story of Wittgenstein's benefaction in the essay "Rilke und der Unbekannte Freund."[16] After receiving Wittgenstein's second letter which assured him that the offer was genuine, Ficker proceeded to Vienna as Wittgenstein suggested to receive the money. He spent 26 and 27 July in Vienna with Wittgenstein, whom he found to be most impressive. Wittgenstein's knowledge and learning seemed astonishingly wide to him. He recalled Wittgenstein's appearance as "a picture of stirring loneliness at the first glance,"[17] and he compared it to what one associates with such Dostoevskian characters as Aloysha in *The Brothers Karamozov* or Prince Myshkin in *The Idiot*.

16. Ludwig Ficker, "Rilke und der Unbekannte Freund," *Der Brenner* 18 (1954), 234–248. Reprinted in Ludwig Ficker, *Denkzettel und Danksagungen* (Munich: Kösel, 1967).

17. Ficker, "Rilke," p. 236.

Wittgenstein considered Ficker's introducing him to Adolf Loos, the architect, at the Café Imperial to be a highlight of the trip. So much did the iconoclastic architect and the young Wittgenstein prove to have in common that Loos would remark, "You are me."[18] Wittgenstein wrote to Ficker of Loos, "It makes me *very* happy to have been able to meet him."[19] Ficker returned to Innsbruck on the night train 31 July to discover on his arrival home that the world was at war.

By 14 August, Wittgenstein had volunteered for military service and was already stationed in Kraków. He wrote Ficker often during the first year-and-a-half of the war, on several occasions to inform Ficker of a change of address, and once even to send a card which was "Just a line so that you do not forget me!"[20] (In his 1954 essay Ficker remarked that it simply would not have been possible to forget Wittgenstein.[21]) Meanwhile, Ficker was beginning the disbursement of the 100,000 crowns which would continue into 1915. Georg Trakl, always in need of money, was to receive 20,000; R. M. Rilke also 20,000; Dallago, 20,000; Oskar Kokoschka, 5,000; Adolf Loos, 2,000; Karl Borromäus Heinrich, 1,000; Hermann Wagner, 1,000; L. E. Tesar, 2,000; Richard Weiss, 2,000; Franz Kranewitter, 2,000; Hugo Neugebauer, 1,000; Josef Georg Oberkofler, 1,000; Theodor Haecker, 2,000; Theodore Däubler, 2,000; the *Brenner* was to receive 10,000 for editorial expenses at Wittgenstein's request; Else Lasker-Schüler (probably) also received 4,000 crowns.[22]

Wittgenstein had been assigned to serve on the steamer *Goplana* on the river Vistula after his arrival in Kraków. While assigned to the *Goplana* his time was divided between service on the river and in port at Kraków.[23] Sometime in October he

18. Engelmann, *Memoir,* p. 127. It is not clear just when Loos made this remark; it may have been at a later meeting. On Loos see Ludwig Münz and Gustav Künstler, *Adolf Loos: Pioneer of Modern Architecture* (New York: Praeger, 1966); also Janik and Toulmin, *Wittgenstein's Vienna,* pp. 93–101.

19. *F* 3.

20. *F* 5.

21. Ficker, "Rilke," p. 241.

22. Walter Methlagl, "Erläuterung zur Beziehung zwischen Ludwig Wittgenstein und Ludwig von Ficker," appended to *F.*

23. See the note appended to *F* 5.

received the message from Ficker that Georg Trakl was also stationed on the Eastern Front. He replied that he should like to meet Trakl if it were possible. Meanwhile, he informed Ficker that he had received a letter, presumably of thanks, from Rilke. He also hinted to Ficker that he had found fulfillment in his war work, which was hitherto lacking in his life. "Just imagine," he wrote, "*I* have been working in the last six weeks as seldom before! May it be with many as it has been with me!"[24] Ficker reports that (from 24 to 26 October) he visited Kraków, where he met an officer who described an exciting philosophical conversation with Wittgenstein which took place on the deck of the *Goplana* while Wittgenstein peeled potatoes.[25] Surely this was one of the occasions when Wittgenstein was able to fulfill his aspiration to live a Tolstoian, simple life which contributed positively to his community. Just as he was leaving port for river duty he got word that Trakl would meet him in Kraków. He returned from river duty on 5 November. On the sixth he proceeded to the garrison hospital where he discovered that Trakl had died three days prior. "This hit me *very* hard,"[26] he recorded in his diary.

Trakl had suffered much before the war and had sought solace in alcohol, which he is reputed to have consumed in enormous quantities, and in drugs, which were easily obtainable for a pharmacist. The torments of people in war were simply too much for him to bear. Intentionally or unintentionally, he took his own life by an overdose of alcohol and drugs. His last poems bear witness to the pathos which the war had evoked in him. "Grodek," his last poem, was named for the scene of a battle in which Trakl, the medic, could not soothe the pain of the serious casualties. It epitomizes his experience of the war:

At eventide the autumnal woods
With weapons of death resound, across golden fields
And lakes of blue, solemn the sun
Rolls on; the night embraces

24. *F* 8.
25. Note to *F* 5.
26. Ibid.

Soldiers dying, the wild lament
of their shattered mouths.
Still soundlessly from the meadowland
The scarlet clouds of an angry god
Gather the spilled blood up, moonly cool;
Every road leads to black decay.
Under golden boughs of night and the stars
Through the quiet glade moves the sister's shadow
Greeting the spirits of the heroes, the bleeding heads;
And soft the dark flutes of autumn sound in the reeds.
O prouder grief! O altars of brass,
The searing flame of the spirit is fed by a mighty sorrow today,
The grandchildren not to be born.[27]

The task was left to Wittgenstein to inform Ficker of the cause of Trakl's death and, later, the location of his grave. Ficker in the meantime had sent Wittgenstein some of Trakl's poetry. Wittgenstein replied with thanks, saying that he did not understand his works but that their tone made him happy. "It is the tone of the true genius,"[28] he wrote.

Wittgenstein wrote Ficker twice around the middle of February 1915, once to acknowledge Ficker's gift of a volume of Trakl's verse and again to acknowledge letters of thanks from some of the people to whom he had anonymously donated money. The first letter of the ninth laments the fact that Wittgenstein is unable to appreciate Trakl's work because he was going into a fallow period (as he frequently did) when he could do nothing, when, as he put it, he was "completely burnt out."[29] In the letter of the thirteenth he writes to thank Ficker for forwarding to him a letter that the poet had sent to Ficker and a gift (possibly a poem) from Rilke to his unknown benefactor. In the same letter he criticizes the letters sent him via Ficker as thanks to an unknown benefactor. He deplores them and their "degrading, *almost* swindling tone."[30] He was returning these banalities that so contrasted with Rilke's letter, which he called "a support in the unsteady balance of my

27. Georg Trakl, "Grodek," trans. Kate Flores in *An Anthology of German Poetry from Hölderlin to Rilke in English Translation*, ed. Angel Flores (Magnolia, Mass: Peter Smith, Publisher, 1960), pp. 368–369.
28. *F* 12.
29. *F* 16.
30. *F* 17.

life."[31] Thus Wittgenstein's initial exhilaration at being in the army was definitely on the wane.

By this time Ficker, too, was in the war. He had begun his active duty with the 2nd Kaiserjager Regiment in Brixen on 15 February 1915. Wittgenstein's letter, postmarked 24 July 1915, implies that Ficker, as might be expected, found the war absurd. However, Wittgenstein had made a breakthrough in understanding and, uncharacteristically and with reluctance, offered Ficker some advice. He dared to suggest that Ficker read Tolstoi's *Gospel in Brief*, since "you are living, as it were, in the dark and have not found the saving word."[32] Tolstoi's *Gospels* somehow had come into his hands at just the right moment and made an emormous impact upon him (as is corroborated also in Russell's *Autobiography*)[33] and had in some sense or other wrought "salvation" for him. Perhaps it might help Ficker as well. Those who knew Wittgenstein best, his family, insist that the war changed him radically. I should like to suggest that Tolstoi's "saving word" was an integral part of the man who emerged from the war with his life's work in seventy-five pages of aphorisms which could be epitomized in the statement, "What can be said at all can be said clearly, and what we cannot talk about we must pass over in silence." This, however, belongs to another part of the essay. What remains without doubt is Wittgenstein's experience of the horror of war and the saving character of the *Gospels*, which he always carried with him. Indeed, he was known by his comrades at the front as "the man with the Gospels."[34]

Wittgenstein's letter of advice was followed by a series of very brief communications informing Ficker of a change of address and expressing the hope that he could write. These cover the period up to the beginning of November 1915. Then the correspondence ceases until the end of the war and Witt-

31. Ibid.
32. *F* 18.
33. Bertrand Russell, *The Autobiography of Bertrand Russell: 1914–1944* (London: George Allen & Unwin; Boston: Little, Brown, 1958), p. 134.
34. Hermine Wittgenstein, "Family Recollections," in Bernhard Leitner, *The Architecture of Ludwig Wittgenstein: A Documentation* (Halifax, N.S.: The Press of Nova Scotia College of Art and Design, 1973), p. 19.

genstein's release from the prisoner of war camp at Cassino in 1919. It resumes again in 1919 with Wittgenstein's uncharacteristic request for assistance. He had written a book and hoped that Ficker, once again publishing *Der Brenner* after a four-year pause, would publish it. These letters constitute the correspondence central to any assessment of the *Tractatus Logico-Philosophicus,* for they, more than any other document discovered to date, reveal what Wittgenstein was hoping to do in writing the book. The book, Wittgenstein explained, was "strictly philosophical and, at the same time, literary,"[35] it was his "life's work"[36] which had occupied his efforts since 1911. It treated of the presentation of a system, "and this presentation is *extremely* compressed since I have only retained in it that which really occurred to me—and how it occurred to me."[37] It is clear that the form of the book, which incorporated the manner in which the ideas had come to him, was of paramount importance to him. Thrice before he had endeavored to interest publishers in the book.[38] The third effort was through a German professor (presumably Frege), who had connections with a journal but who would only agree to assist Wittgenstein if the latter would, in Wittgenstein's words, "mutilate it from beginning to end and, in a word, make another work out of it."[39] For Wittgenstein this was out of the question—it must appear exactly as written.

Before proceeding to a discussion of just what Wittgenstein revealed to Ficker about the book, I should like to point out the significance of his first choices of publishers, who are mentioned by name in the correspondence. He first submitted the book to Jahoda and Siegel. This firm was also the publisher of Karl Kraus's satirical *Die Fackel.* We know from his

35. *F* 33.
36. Ibid.
37. Ibid. Cf. Ramsey's letter to his mother appended to Ludwig Wittgenstein, *Letters to C. K. Ogden with Comments on the English Translation of the Tractatus Logico-Philosophicus,* ed. G. H. von Wright (Oxford: Basil Blackwell; London and Boston: Routledge & Kegan Paul, 1973), p. 78.
38. For a full account of the publication history of the *Tractatus* see G. H. von Wright's essay appended to the correspondence with Ficker and Chapter 4, above.
39. *F* 22.

correspondence with Engelmann that Wittgenstein wanted to know Kraus's opinion of the work.[40] There are, therefore, good reasons for suspecting that he saw himself doing something which was essentially related to the efforts of the satirical moralist, Kraus, who sought to exhibit the hypocrisy that pervaded Viennese public life simply by quoting what people said without comment. Kraus had used this technique with devastating success in his monumental satire of World War I, *Die letzten Tage der Menschheit.* In any case, it is certainly possible to read Wittgenstein's central thesis in the *Tractatus* in a Krausian manner. Kraus wished to point out the ubiquitousness of the double standard in the Dual Monarchy by using people's very words to show the immorality of their actions. Wittgenstein's *Tractatus* could be viewed as an attempt to separate what could be said (reason) from that concerning which we must be silent (ethical and aesthetic values) but which nonetheless shows itself to those who know how to look.[41] In any case, Jahoda and Siegel was a literary publishing house and did not deal in philosophical books. Wittgenstein's choice would therefore be difficult to explain unless he considered that his work was somehow appropriate for that particular house, since he was a person for whom appropriateness was almost obsessional.

His second choice is also revealing because it, too, shows that he was attempting to relate his work to that of another Austrian moralist whom he admired. Braumüller, his second choice, had published Otto Weininger,[42] a figure Wittgenstein is known to have admired to the end of his life. "I thought of him [Braumüller]," Wittgenstein wrote to Ficker, "because he published Weininger."[43] In 1903, Weininger had published a book entitled *Sex and Character,* which became enormously successful and enormously controversial. Weininger's thesis

40. E 18.

41. Stephen Toulmin and I endeavored to make a case for this view in Chapter 5 of *Wittgenstein's Vienna.*

42. Very little of any value has been written about Weininger to date. David Abrahamsen's *The Mind and Death of a Genius* (New York: Columbia University Press, 1946) is the best work on Weininger presently available.

43. *F* 22.

was that humans are essentially bisexual and all that is evil and destructive arises from the feminine principle which is in all of us. He identified the feminine and the Jewish as one and the same. The human situation is essentially tragic because we are called to live up to a rational ideal of conduct (Kant's categorical imperative) which our feminine side, as purely sexual and egocentric, prevents us from realizing. All sexual intercourse is rooted in egoism, involves using human nature as a means only rather than as an end, and so is wholly immoral. Weininger's Eternal-Feminine was thoroughly demonic, a far cry from Goethe, but then this was also the time when Ibsen, Wedekind, and Strindberg were shocking and fascinating Europe with just such a literary portrait of woman. In short, Weininger's account was close enough to social reality to have a profound impact upon nearly all of the young Austrian writers.

It was less a matter of agreeing with Weininger than of admiring him for his daring and, in the eyes of many, his consistency. He had dared to say what many believed and had brought out the question of whether genuinely moral relations between the sexes were possible. His suicide, a mere six months after the publication of the book, confirmed what many believed regarding his profundity. The poets Trakl[44] and Hofmannsthal[45] read him with avid interest. Kraus defended him posthumously from Freud's attack that he had plagiarized the bisexuality theory from him. The questions he posed were never far from the minds of the contributors to *Der Brenner*, and in 1912 Carl Dallago published *Otto Weininger und sein Werk* in Ficker's Brenner Verlag after it had appeared in installments in *Der Brenner*. It is most unfortunate that despite all of this interest in Weininger we still do not have a critical analysis of his work. This, however, is indicative of the type of response which Weininger's work elicited, i.e., either deep admiration or equally deep revulsion, neither of which was

44. See Alfred Doppler, "Georg Trakl und Otto Weininger," *Peripherie und Zentrum* (Salzburg, 1971), pp. 43–54.
45. See Michael Hamburger, "Hofmannsthals Bibliothek: Ein Bericht," *Euphorion* 55 (1961), 27.

especially critical. While it is speculation to assert just what it was that so deeply impressed Wittgenstein about Weininger's work, I should like to suggest that one should look less to the sensational sexual part of the book and turn rather to those sections which deal with 'character' in endeavoring to answer this question, for there can be no doubt that Wittgenstein, like Weininger, viewed everything a man did *sub specie moralitatis.* There is insufficient space here to elaborate, but I should like to suggest that Wittgenstein's personal views of morality and character, as well as certain of his philosophical views—of, say, understanding—can be illuminated by comparing his views with what Weininger has to say about talent, genius, logic, ethics, and aesthetics. Not a little that strikes us as peculiar about the life and work of Wittgenstein might be illuminated through such a comparison.

Wittgenstein's abiding interest in Weininger is attested to by his friend Rudolf Koder, his student G. H. von Wright, and in a letter to his colleague G. E. Moore as well. Koder, who taught music in the elementary school at the Lower Austrian town of Puchberg, became acquainted with Wittgenstein as a result of their common interest in music. He reports that though they never discussed philosophy because he neither knew nor cared for the subject, Wittgenstein asked him if he had read Weininger and expressed interest in Weininger to him.[46] G. H. von Wright recalls Wittgenstein's discussing Weininger's posthumous *Über die letzten Dinge* with him and that Wittgenstein was particularly impressed with Weininger's discussion of animal psychology in which he attempted to relate different human character types to various animal species.[47] Apparently, he went farther than this with Moore and actually convinced him to read Weininger, from whom Moore could glean nothing at all, it seems. Wittgenstein wrote him in 1931:

I can quite imagine that you don't admire Weininger very much, what with that beastly translation and the fact that W. must feel very

46. In conversation, March 1974.
47. In conversation, February 1966.

foreign to you. It is true that he is fantastic but he is *great* and fantastic. It isn't necessary or rather not possible to agree with him but the greatness lies in that with which we disagree. It is his enormous mistake which is great, i.e. roughly speaking if you just add a "~" to the whole book it says an important truth.[48]

Hence, in submitting his work to Weininger's publisher, Wittgenstein was associating himself and his work with a thinker who was far removed indeed from the context in which that work would finally come into a position of preeminence.

Unfortunately, Braumüller would only publish the *Tractatus* if Wittgenstein paid for the printing and paper costs, which was the same to Wittgenstein as publishing the book with a vanity press, and consequently out of the question for him. It was then that he turned, rather in desperation, to the publisher of the "only honest periodical in Austria," Ficker. His failures to get the work published made him more convinced than ever that his book would not be understood by anybody. Yet he was determined that there was a profound dimension to the form and content of the book, something which someone who had had the thoughts it expressed would recognize. Nevertheless, he attempted to convey something of what he took to be the sense of the book to Ficker with the hope that he could convince him that his aims in writing the *Tractatus* were consonant with Ficker's program for the *Brenner*:

It will probably be helpful for you if I write a few words about my book: For you won't—I really believe—get too much out of reading it. Because you won't understand it; the content will seem quite strange to you. In reality, it isn't strange to you, for the point of the book is ethical. I once wanted to give a few words in the foreword which now actually are not in it, which, however, I'll write to you now because they might be a key for you: I wanted to write that my work consists of two parts: of the one which is here, and of everything which I have *not* written. And precisely this second part is the important one. For the Ethical is delimited from within, as it were, by my book; and I'm convinced that, *strictly* speaking, it can ONLY be delimited in this way. In brief, I think: All of that which *many* are *babbling* today, I

48. Wittgenstein, *R,* letter to Moore #17. Among the faults of the English translation is the omission of 135 pages of notes to the German edition.

have defined in my book by remaining silent about it. Therefore the book will, unless I'm quite wrong, have much to say which you want to say yourself, but perhaps you won't notice that it is said in it. For the time being, I'd recommend that you read the *foreword* and the *conclusion* since these express the point most directly.[49]

It is noteworthy that Russell already possessed the corrected copy of the *Tractatus* at this time because this indicates that Wittgenstein did not originally contemplate Russell's having any part in the publishing of the book (though he would have been naturally interested in Russell's reaction to it).

The *Tractatus* which he had endeavored to publish in Austria was a most curious ethical treatise, which was connected with what Ficker was attempting to do in *Der Brenner*. The authentic subject of the book, in its author's mind, was easily confounded by its appearance, but the author would only elucidate its true message in a private letter. What was Ficker to do with such a book?

Common sense dictated that a philosophical book be evaluated by a philosopher, and Ficker appears to have proposed to do just that. Wittgenstein's reply is characteristic of the attitude which he always maintained toward academic philosophers, but is perhaps more sharply phrased than other of his statements about philosophers: "As far as I am concerned you can show the manuscript to the philosophy professor (although showing a philosophical work to a professor of philosophy is like casting pearls . . .). At any rate he won't understand a word of it."[50] Ficker appears to have suggested that the book was not really suitable for publication in the *Brenner* and that Wittgenstein should look to some more suitable publisher, although he did not know which one to suggest. However, he immediately began to relent, and telegrammed that he would print the work as a favor to Wittgenstein. (The main problem was the financial solvency of the *Brenner* and the press in the face of the postwar economic crises.) This was precisely what Wittgenstein wished to avoid above all. He dreaded the thought of forcing something upon the world for

49. *F* 23.
50. *F* 24.

which the world had no desire. The *Tractatus* had to be published on its own merits alone.

Wittgenstein insisted that it was a book whose main lines of thought corresponded with those of *Der Brenner*:

> How can I recommend my own work to you?—I think in all such cases it is so: A book, even when it is written completely honestly, is always worthless from *one* standpoint: for no one would really need to write a book because there are quite different things to do in this world. On the other hand, I think I can say that if you print Dallago, Haecker, etc., *then* you can also print *my* book.[51]

Ficker doubtlessly was a bit annoyed at the deprecating tone in which his two chief contributors were mentioned. Wittgenstein seemed to be telling him how much better a job he had done in saying what they wished to say. Ficker turned to Karl Röck, another member of the *Brenner Kreis* who had become interested in logic and syntax through his interest in the poetry of Trakl. Röck rejected the work flatly as completely different from the *Brenner* in its conception of language. Because we possess far more information about Wittgenstein than Ficker and Röck did, especially his letters and the memoirs of Engelmann and von Wright, we are able to see something in Wittgenstein's final sentence that seems to have eluded Ficker, i.e., the sense in which Ficker should have seen the *Tractatus* as an effort to do what his contributors Dallago and Haecker were attempting. In short, we have all the benefits of hindsight which Ficker lacked and are consequently capable of using this reference to Dallago and Haecker to deepen our understanding of the *Tractatus*. A glance at the contributions of Dallago and Haecker to the *Brenner* up to the time when Wittgenstein was writing this to Ficker, I think, is helpful in illustrating Wittgenstein's point in insisting that his work was to be compared with theirs and the implication of his tone, namely, that they would come off much the worse in the comparison.

Carl Dallago (1869–1949) was one of the original dropouts from bourgeois society.[52] He viewed modern life as rooted in

51. *F* 25.

52. On Dallago see Methlagl, "*Der Brenner,*" pp. 14–86, 98–118 passim; also Hans Haller, *Der südtirolische Denker Carl Dallago: Die Mystik seines Schrifttums* (Innsbruck: Josef Winkler, 1938).

cynical utilitarianism and conformism and thus as something to be rejected. He believed that the march of reason and progress had stunted and perverted everything spontaneous in men. Urban existence reduced the individual to an object, a mere thing. He drew inspiration from the poetry of Walt Whitman and the painting of Millet and from the remarkable Giovanni Segantini, as well as a mystical reverence for landscape as the source of everything of abiding value, which he claimed to derive from Nietzsche. This led him to champion the solitary individual before the masses, the natural in the face of the conventional, the eternally beautiful before the transitory and profitable, in short, feeling above reason. Reason, he thought, only produces categories which by their very nature are employed in a manipulative manner. One must, in his view, turn one's back upon 'civilization', and return to the 'basics', the simple life close to nature, far from science, progress, and mass society. Nowadays this line of thought is 'old hat'. We can quickly associate the more extreme among organic food freaks, environmentalists, and Heideggerians (among whom Dallago would be quite at home) with such thinking. It is difficult to conceive that such ideas were then the very epitome of radicalism.

Dallago impressed Ficker and others because he actually lived according to these principles. He removed himself from the bourgeois city, sold his business, and withdrew to the countryside, where he could be close to the soil.[53] Security was to be rejected, for modern man was obsessed with it and had sacrificed something of his essential humanity by this obsession. Dallago's defiance of convention did not end there. He lived openly with a woman outside of wedlock while he inveighed against 'civilized' society's hypocritical concept of marriage in the pages of the *Brenner*. Bourgeois marriage, in Dallago's view, as indeed in the view of Kraus and many of his contemporaries, was the symptom of a spiritual malaise which afflicted modern man. Bourgeois marriages had more the character of business mergers than unions between lovers.

53. Dr. Adolf Klarmann, professor of German at the University of Pennsylvania, remembers Dallago's reputation among his fellow gymnasium students as that of a sort of hero. Conversation, October 1974.

Prostitution, which was the object of constant attack on the part of politicians and clergymen, was the inevitable consequence of the degeneration of marriage to the level of merger. Thus sexual mores were the focal point of his polemic but represented only the tip of the iceberg. Sexual hypocrisy, above all, indicted civilized society and reason, upon which it was constructed, as well. Dallago contrasted this rational and thoroughly unnatural institution, marriage-prostitution, with natural *Lust,* punning upon all of the various connotations that word implied: pleasure, delight, joy, even lust. *Lust* was spontaneous, not rational, unfathomable, rather than scientifically explicable.

We may find these notions quaint, but there is no doubt from his writing that Dallago was passionately devoted to them and lived by them rigorously until his death. Yet, quaintness apart, he expressed these thoughts in essays which were not without a certain charm. They were inevitably written in the form of meditations or soliloquies that always began with some reference to the way in which his experience of the landscape occasioned his reflections. They were thus thoroughly natural. They ended invariably with his return to the experience of the forest, animals, or streams whence they arose. The soliloquy was a particularly appropriate form for such an avowed individualist as Dallago. His was a mystical and pantheistic individualism. Paradox imbued what is most properly referred to as his *Weltanschauung.* He was endeavoring to express something inexpressible. "All science, all knowing in general," said Dallago, "produces its higher value through the discovery of new darkness. . . . As long as it comes forward to dominate nature and considers everything as explicable it is crude and unknowing."[54] Only feeling can grasp reality without distortion, from which it would follow that his insight was fundamentally incommunicable in arguments. He was consistent therefore in refraining from employing arguments in his writings except in the course of an exposition of the views of one of his heroes or in polemics.

The very titles of his works reflect the constituents of his *Weltanschauung*: the seasons, in which he found analogies for

54. Dallago, *Brenner* 1, p. 154.

discussing various types of human character, and the landscape, in *Peals of the Landscape, One Summer, Winter Days, New Spring*; his polemical side in "Philistines," "Decay"; his heroes in *Kierkegaard's Conception of the Christian,* "Lao Tsu and I"; his admiration for values which were antithetical to bourgeois society in *The Great Unknowing One, The Book of Insecurities.* These were some of the titles of his voluminous output of books, essays, and collections of poetry. During the whole of his life he eschewed the appellation 'writer', let alone 'philosopher', preferring to be known as a "nonwriter" (*Nicht-Schriftsteller*).

His prose works divided into polemics against the idols of civilized man and essays which are exhortations to embrace his concept of wisdom. The chief objects of his wrath were Ernst Haeckel and his Monist followers.[55] Theirs was a blind faith in the power of science to solve and to unify knowledge into a system which would be the realization of Descartes's dream. This ultimate solution would come in the form of the discovery of some basic substance which might even make the alchemists' wildest dreams of transmuting base metals into gold possible. In any case, it would leave the universe an open book, denuded of everything enigmatic. Science would supplant religion in a Comtean fashion. In short, they believed exactly those things which Dallago took to be the height of folly. The Monist attitude was at bottom precisely what caused modern society to be soulless and dehumanized.

Dallago believed that the fundamental truth of things was outside time. 'In the beginning was the completion' came to be his slogan, which emphasized the ahistorical nature of truth. Progress was illusory, only phenomenal; the human situation never altered. The great religious leaders, who all taught the same fundamental truth, realized this. Dallago grouped Jesus, Socrates, Lao Tsu, St. Augustine, Pascal, and Kierkegaard together under this rubric as the "Pure Men of Yore" (*Die reine Menschen der Vorzeit*). He thus identified truth with religious, rather than scientific, thought. These great religious thinkers all emphasized the paradoxical character of

55. On Haeckel and Monism see Daniel Gasman's *Scientific Origins of National Socialism* (London: MacDonald; New York: Elsevier, 1971).

man's condition. They knew that man is human only when he ceases to make demands, when he ceases to endeavor to master nature but begins to listen to her. By ceasing to speak (masculine) reason will be spoken to by (feminine) nature and a transformation will occur: reason will cease to be merely manipulative and become creative. The "Pure Men of Yore" were aware that discursive reason was incapable of conveying such a message. They consequently chose to transmit it through their lives, through their deeds rather than words. Everything about these "Pure Men of Yore" remains incomprehensible to calculating thought because their solution to the riddle of the universe is through a radical affirmation of it. The problem of the nature of reality is thus solved by recognizing that it is essentially an insoluble riddle. It is the unperturbed oriental, who has the *Tao*, and the Christian, who has made the leap into the absurd, who have solved the problem of the meaning of life by recognizing and embracing the unfathomableness of it all. Such was the message of one of the thinkers to whom Wittgenstein had related his work in 1919. Before attempting to answer the very difficult question as to what Wittgenstein affirmed and what he rejected in Dallago, let us briefly examine the output of the other figure with whom he compared himself, Theodor Haecker.

The Theodor Haecker (1879–1945) whom Wittgenstein compared, however unfavorably, to himself was not yet the figure whose theologically oriented literary criticism was deemed noteworthy by T. S. Eliot, nor was he yet the figure who was capable of inspiring the only overt civilian resistance that the Nazis would receive during World War II.[56] These dimensions of Haecker were present embryonically, but would develop only during the twenties and thirties. The Haecker whom Wittgenstein would have recognized was an admirer and imitator of Karl Kraus and had devoted much of his time to the

56. On Haecker see Eugen Blessing, *Theodor Haecker: Gestalt und Werk* (Nuremberg: Glock and Lutz, 1959); also Alexander Dru's Introduction to Theodor Haecker, *Journal in the Night*, trans. Alexander Dru (London: Pantheon Books, 1950). Eliot mentions Haecker in "Religion and Literature," *Selected Essays* (London: Faber and Faber, 1951), p. 388.

translation of the Danish religious thinker Søren Kierkegaard. He shared Dallago's views on the decadence of contemporary society. He was thus led to direct vitriolic, pseudo-Krausian satires against the Berlin Establishment (as a Swabian German he saw himself extending Kraus's social critique into his society). He believed that reason, in the form of science and technology, had gone wild and was responsible for the corrupt conditions which he found ubiquitous. Like Dallago, progress-oriented bourgeois capitalism appeared to him the enemy, the incarnation of reason gone wild.

Unlike Dallago, however, he identified the individuals responsible for this with the 'Jewish' element in society (a move which Dallago had explicitly rejected). The Jews seemed responsible for the spiritual malaise of modern life because there was an observable conjunction between their preeminence and the decline of traditional values of mutual trust and social cohesion into a competitive society, where one could turn a cold eye upon his neighbor's plight. Above all, Jews dominated the press, which was held to be the very essence of corruption because it sought to expose the evils of society while it drew its livelihood from the very scandals it claimed to expose. It was not unusual to find the same paper carrying on campaigns against moral 'permissiveness', especially prostitution, while its very pages contained advertisements for what was then the equivalent of 'massage parlors' and 'artists' models'. The *Berliner Tagblatt* was the archetypical representative of corrupt 'Jewish' journalism, of a value system in which objective good and evil are replaced by the whims of an easily manipulated public opinion.[57] Morality seemed to be dictated by the external standard of the preferences of the advertisers. News that was embarrassing to the editors, civic and ecclesiastical authorities, and the advertisers failed to appear in these papers.

57. Since 1945 we have become accustomed to condemning all forms of enmity toward Jews as fanatical, unwarranted, and irrational. Eva Reichmann argues that there were objective grounds for such beliefs in pre-1914 central Europe in her penetrating study *Hostages of Civilization* (New Haven: Greenwood Press, 1970). She identifies this enmity toward Jews with their role in the development of capitalism in the German-speaking world.

The full force of Haecker's ire was reserved for those writers, academics, and scholars who added 'a touch of class' to all this by being regular contributors to such papers. In the end, he lay the responsibility for World War I at the feet of a group which included such figures as Wilhelm Wundt, Rudolf Eucken, Hermann Bahr (one of Kraus's favorite targets), Emil Ludwig, Karl Lamprecht, Hermann Cohen, and Fritz Mauthner, among others, who sold their integrity to Mosse and Ullstein and other such unscrupulous publishers. Haecker assailed contemporary intellectuals for divorcing speculative thought from moral concerns and thereby opening the Pandora's Box, which ultimately proved to be the source of everything despicable and dishonorable in modern life. He lashed out at them in his satires, of which "Der Krieg und die Führer des Geistes"[58] was the best known, with a vitriol which is unusual even for a satirist.

Haecker differed from Dallago in that his satires and polemics were far more bitter in degree, but he differed from him more fundamentally in that he never ceased to believe in the value of intelligence and reason. Haecker saw the decay of modern life as resulting from the detachment of reason from concrete experience and, therefore, from moral values. Scientific and technological advances had put modern man 'out of touch', with the result that reason had run riot. Reason was abstracted from its human matrix and had become dehumanizing. It must be put back into its proper place. This major difference from Dallago is perhaps due to the fact that Haecker had an academic background. He knew and admired the writings of Bergson and had attended Dilthey's lectures. He had even become friendly with his philosophy professor at Munich, Max Scheler. He learned from these thinkers that it was not human reason, but Cartesian rationalism that must be opposed at all costs. A new Socrates was required, who would take up the cause of reason against rationalism. Haecker found just such a thinker in Kierkegaard, who had explicitly modeled himself on Socrates.

58. Theodor Haecker, "Der Krieg and die Führer des Geistes," *Brenner Jahrbuch*, 1915, pp. 130–187.

His enthusiasm for Kierkegaard led him to learn Danish so that he would have firsthand knowledge of his texts. He was to spend the period from 1910 to 1945, when he died, producing translations and expositions of the Dane's works, and thus he played a major role in the revival of interest in Kierkegaard in this century. In the period we are concerned with here, he published translations with commentary of Kierkegaard's "Prefaces," "Discourse on Death," and the influential *Present Age*. His "Afterword" to the latter drew favorable comment from none other than Edmund Husserl.[59] His *Søren Kierkegaard und die Philosophie der Innerlichkeit,* published in 1913, identified Kierkegaard with Dostoevski (another new figure in the German-speaking world at that time), Pascal, and Bergson, as well as with Karl Kraus, and did much to fix Kierkegaard's popular image. His works made their mark upon central European thinking inasmuch as they provided Christian philosophers and social critics with a believing counterpart to Nietzsche. The Christian, too, could oppose his values to those of the bourgeoisie and thereby claim a role in the existentialist revolt. Subsequent scholarship has not always borne out Haecker's interpretations and, indeed, they may be in part responsible for a distortion of certain elements in Kierkegaard's thinking; yet Haecker's work, even then, could not be entirely ignored.

After the war Haecker's translations continued with two volumes of selections from Kierkegaard's *Journals,* two volumes of religious discourses, *On Authority and Revelation,* and several short pieces. He wrote two more expository works, including one on the all-important Kierkegaardian notion of truth as subjectivity. He saw that the notion of truth as "an objective uncertainty held fast in an appropriation-process of the most passionate inwardness"[60] implied a logic of individual experi-

59. Hans Jaeger, Letter to Ludwig Ficker, 16 December 1923, Brenner Archive, Innsbruck. The Brenner Archive is preparing a multivolume edition of a large portion of Ficker's correspondence, in which this letter will be included.

60. Søren Kierkegaard, *Concluding Unscientific Postscript,* trans. David F. Swenson and Walter Lowrie (Princeton, N.J.: Princeton University Press, 1941), p. 182.

ence, to be constrasted with mechanistic formal logic. He endeavored to bring Kierkegaard and Cardinal Newman, whose *Grammar of Assent* he also translated, together into a synthesis which would articulate what Pascal termed the "reasons of the heart" in such a manner as to develop a logic of the concrete in which inference and action were intimately bound together. It will be recalled that this is a central theme in Kierkegaard's critique of the alleged mystic Adler.[61] But as this belongs to a different story, we must now return to the question of what Wittgenstein would have thought himself to be doing that was similar to and yet so much better than Dallago and Haecker.

Here, to be sure, we are on less than firm ground but, nevertheless, I believe that our perspective, some fifty-five years later, does enable us to draw some conclusions, especially in the light of the biographical data we have from such other sources as Engelmann. Wittgenstein insisted that he was defining the area of human experience about which we cannot speak, the ethical sphere, by being silent about it. He was criticizing Dallago and Haecker for saying that which can only be shown. They said too much. One need not read very much of the writings of either to realize that Wittgenstein's point is well taken. 'Excessive' best describes both Dallago and Haecker.

While Wittgenstein could concur with Dallago's emphasis upon the rootedness of all morality in the conduct of the solitary individual, there was much that he could take exception to in Dallago's writings. Dallago was a man with very few ideas, which he subscribed to rigorously but overstated through repetition. He never ceased to proclaim the ineffability of reality. He was trying to make a point about the futility of all efforts to explain the way things are in discourse which was itself expository. There was, however, an essential inconsistency in a man who *wrote* so much about *acting* spontaneously, who continually extolled the simple life, unencumbered

61. Søren Kierkegaard, *On Authority and Revelation,* trans. Walter Lowrie (New York: Harper & Row, 1966), passim. This is the book which Haecker translated as *Der Begriff der Auserwählten* (Hellerau: Jakob Hegner, 1917). It was reissued through Ficker's Brenner Verlag in 1926.

by conventions, close to nature, by writing in a semimonthly avant-garde journal. Wittgenstein, on the other hand, endeavored to do this but with the crucial difference that his book was trying to get at the limits of discourse from within; to show that the essential characteristic of our thinking apparatus indicated that the whole realm of value lay beyond those limits. It was not a matter of rejecting science and reason in favor of morality and value, for that was, in the end, fruitless. The scientist need merely assert that science, on Dallago's own view, was incapable of grasping the message about the Eternal-Unfathomable nature of reality, that this notion had no consequences for him, and consequently need not be considered by him. It was a scientific critique of science and in that respect wholly opposed to Dallago's irrationalism.[62] For Wittgenstein it was neither a matter of the solution of the riddle of the universe nor of its eternal affirmation, but of seeing that this was the wrong question from the start. What can be said can be said clearly; when we cannot speak we ought to remain silent. Dallago's attempt to say what shows itself only in action is as much a trespassing against the limits as Haeckel's view that there are no limits at all. Dallago should have devoted more time to living the simple life, which Wittgenstein always advocated, rather than "babbling" about it. The ethical *Weltanschauung* of the author of the *Tractatus* was to be found in his actions (where Dallago had insisted that it should be), and not in his words (which both men considered impossible anyway). The only way in which this could be rigorously expressed was to show what science and reason are by saying just what they are not, i.e., in a remarkably indirect manner.

Wittgenstein disparaged Haecker because he, too, spoke when he ought to have remained silent. Haecker's polemics were uncontrolled, little more that diatribes, at the very best a pale imitation of what Karl Kraus did so subtly and brilliantly. Wittgenstein could agree with Haecker's intention. Indeed, at this time he was a great admirer of Kraus, but *for that reason*

62. See Janik and Toulmin, *Wittgenstein's Vienna,* ch. 6, pp. 167–201.

he could not admire Haecker's feeble efforts at satire. Wittgenstein certainly shared Haecker's moral absolutism as well as his dislike for academics, but the essential point of his *Tractatus* was that one could only put such beliefs into action. Words failed (and had to fail) to express them. Haecker above all, as the translator of Kierkegaard's *Present Age,* should have known that well. Had not Kierkegaard written

> What is talkativeness? It is the result of doing away with the vital distinction between talking and keeping silent. Only someone who knows how to remain essentially silent can really talk—and act essentially. Silence is the essence of inwardness, of the inner life.[63]

Haecker berated Fritz Mauthner for saying too much, whereas he was himself guilty of the same offense. Haecker simply was not Kierkegaardian enough for Wittgenstein, despite the fact that Haecker was the most enthusiastic of Kierkegaardians, because the essence of keeping silent was such that no one should be aware that one is keeping silent. Unfortunately, since there was no way that Ficker would have grasped all of this, he had no choice, given the grave financial difficulties of the postwar era, but to decline publishing the *Tractatus.*

The final letters deal with Wittgenstein's efforts, through Ficker, to get Rilke's publisher Insel Verlag to publish the *Tractatus.* Rilke seems to have made inquiries and discovered that Insel did not handle such subject matter. Wittgenstein would face yet another rejection from Reclam before the work was printed. It was clearly a difficult time for him. The postscript of his last letter to Ficker read, "I too am struggling against great adversities now."[64] The correspondence thus ended with Wittgenstein's request for the return of his manuscript so that he could send it on to Reclam. Wittgenstein seems to have been upset by Ficker's abysmal failure to understand him and came to consider him a "dubious" person.

Ficker simply could not understand anything in the book

63. Søren Kierkegaard, *The Present Age,* trans. Alexander Dru (London: Oxford University Press, 1940; New York: Harper & Row, 1962), p. 69.
64. *F* 29.

and in this respect was not unlike the publishers who preceded him in reading the text. He did not know how to take Wittgenstein's strange book seriously. As far as he could tell this book stood for quite the opposite of what he was coming to believe about the spiritual nature of "The Word." It seemed too scientific for him. Ficker probably was "dubious," in Wittgenstein's sense, since he did believe that all of the things Wittgenstein wished to remain silent about, not only can, but *must* be said; he had come to believe that language is the gateway to spiritual reality.[65] Ficker had recently encountered this notion in the writings of a Lower Austrian schoolteacher, self-taught in philosophy, Ferdinand Ebner.[66] It was Ebner, rather than Wittgenstein, whom he felt he must publish. There did not seem to be room in the *Brenner* for both. In later life he came to regret the rejection of the *Tractatus* more than any other editorial decision he had ever made, but it is difficult to conceive any other course of action on his part. How could he grasp a book that even the great Frege had failed to understand?[67] The high regard that such philosophers as Martin Heidegger and T. W. Adorno came to have for Ficker would attest to the fact that he was anything but dubious, but this, too, is another story.[68]

The Ficker episode indicates the degree to which Wittgenstein both was and was not a part of the Austrian cultural

65. On Ficker's conception of language see the dissertation of Sr. Margit Riml, "Das philosophische Verhältnis zur Sprache im Brenner" (Leopold Franzens Universität, Innsbruck, 1973), pp. 15–36.

66. On Ebner see Theodor Steinbüchel, *Der Umbruch des Denkens: Die Frage nach der christlichen Existenz erläutert an Ferdinand Ebners Menschdeutung* (Regensburg: Verlag Friedrich Pustet, 1936); also William M. Johnston, *The Austrian Mind: An Intellectual and Social History* (Berkeley: University of California Press, 1972), pp. 217–220, and Sr. Margit Riml, "Sprache im Brenner," pp. 37–53.

67. Hermine Wittgenstein, "Family Recollections," p. 20.

68. See Martin Heidegger's remarks on the occasion of Ficker's reception of an honorary degree from the Free University of Berlin, 13 April 1969 (in *Ludwig von Ficker zum Gedächtnis seines achtzigsten Geburstags* [Nuremberg: private, 1960], pp. 19–20). For Adorno's estimate of Ficker see *Kösel Nachrichten,* no. 26 (1967), pp. 6–7. Ficker's forthcoming correspondence contains many letters from the former and one from the latter, whom Ficker came to know personally only within a year of his death in 1967.

scene. Wittgenstein saw his *Tractatus* first and foremost as something Austrian, but there is much doubt whether any Austrian publisher would have accepted his work (indeed, without Russell's "impossible" Introduction it is unlikely that it ever would have seen the light of day). In retrospect, one can well understand why Ficker rejected it and why Wittgenstein was so remarkably reticent to discuss it for the rest of his life. For its author the *Tractatus* was a symbol of *failure,* a thorn in his flesh.[69]

69. I gratefully acknowledge the support of La Salle College during the academic year 1973–1974, when I was researching materials relating to Ludwig Ficker and *Der Brenner* at the Brenner Archive in Innsbruck.

7 The Relation between Wittgenstein's Picture Theory of Propositions and Russell's Theories of Judgment

DAVID PEARS

"Form is the possibility of structure" (*Tractatus* 2.033). My aim in this paper is to show how far this idea, which is part of the picture theory, is a reaction against Russell's unpublished 1913 theory of propositions.[1] There is more to the picture theory than this, and more could be said about Russell's theories of propositions and judgment than is necessary for the presentation of his 1913 theory. But I shall confine myself to fixing the two points and drawing the line that connects them.

There is a letter from Russell to Lady Ottoline Morrell, dated 28 May 1913, in which he reports the fact that Wittgenstein had criticized the book that he was writing, but does not give the details of the criticism:

> We were both cross from the heat. I showed him a crucial part of what I had been writing. He said it was all wrong, not realizing the difficulties—that he had tried my view and knew it wouldn't work. I couldn't understand his objection—in fact he was very inarticulate—but I feel in my bones that he must be right, and that he has seen something that I have missed. If I could see it too I shouldn't mind, but as it is, it is worrying, and has rather destroyed the pleasure in

This essay appeared in slightly different form in the *Philosophical Review* 86 (April 1977), 177–196.

1. Contained in a MS entitled "Theory of Knowledge" in the Bertrand Russell Archive, McMaster University. Russell published the first six chapters of this book as articles in the *Monist* from January 1914 to April 1915. He never published the remaining chapters.

my writing—I can only go on with what I see, and yet I feel it is probably all wrong, and that Wittgenstein will think me a dishonest scoundrel for going on with it. Well, well—it is the younger generation knocking at the door—I must make room for him when I can, or I shall become an incubus. But at the moment I was rather cross.[2]

In "Theory of Knowledge" Russell recognized that the primary relation between a person and a proposition is understanding, and he investigated it more fully than belief and other secondary relations. The theory of judgment that he had published in 1910 had combined the two topics, to the detriment of the first one. The fact that in 1913 he gave a separate and more detailed account of understanding propositions was probably the effect of earlier discussions with Wittgenstein.

Russell's 1910 theory of judgment was very sketchy. When a subject *S* judges that *aRb,* the theory presupposed that *S* is acquainted with each of the constituents of this proposition.[3] Otherwise he would not understand it. *S*'s acquaintance with *a* and *R* and *b* are three separate instances of a relation that takes only two terms. But judging is a relation that takes at least three terms, viz. the subject and the two constituents that are the minimum requirement for a proposition. When the proposition is *aRb,* judging takes four terms, viz. the subject and the three constituents of this proposition. The advantage of this theory, according to Russell, is that it allows for the possibility that *S* may judge that *aRb* when the proposition is in fact false because the three constituents are not arranged as it says that they are. If the theory had treated judging as a relation taking only two terms, *S* and the complex *a-in-the-relation-R-to-b,* it would have excluded this possibility.[4]

But the theory had several connected faults. It did not do justice to the fact that the subordinate relation *R* is judged to

2. Quoted by Ronald W. Clark, *The Life of Bertrand Russell* (London: Weidenfeld and Nicolson; New York: Alfred A. Knopf, 1976), pp. 204–205.

3. *The Problems of Philosophy* (Oxford: Oxford University Press, 1912), p. 58.

4. "On the Nature of Truth and Falsehood," in *Philosophical Essays* (London: Longmans, Green, 1910), pp. 177–178.

relate *a* and *b*,[5] or to the consequence that *R* must be the kind of relation that can relate things like *a* and *b*. There is also a difficulty about asymmetrical relations: when *R* is asymmetrical, it "must not be abstractly before the mind, but must be before it as proceeding from *a* to *b* rather than from *b* to *a*."[6] But this leaves the difference between these two ways of being before the mind unexplained.

These deficiencies in Russell's 1910 theory of judgment all result from neglect of the primary relation between *S* and the proposition *aRb*, viz. understanding. In order that *S* should understand this proposition, it may be necessary that he should be acquainted with its three constituents, but it certainly is not sufficient. Russell's 1913 theory is an attempt to specify what more is needed, drawing only on resources supplied by acquaintance.

He suggests that the extra thing that is needed is acquaintance with the pure form of the proposition, which he calls "the utmost generalization" of it: e.g. the pure form of *aRb* is x χ y, in which each of the three names has been replaced by a variable. The suggestion that anyone who understands *aRb* must be acquainted not only with *a*, *R*, and *b*, but also with this form, seems to imply that it is a fourth constituent of the proposition. But though he calls it an object, he insists that it is a logical object and not a constituent of the proposition. For if it were a constituent, "there would have to be a new way in which it and the . . . other constituents are put together, and if we take this way as again a constituent, we find ourselves embarked on an endless regress". He also denies that logical objects are "entities" or "things".[7]

The difference between an object and an entity (or thing) is not a clear one. We need to be told more about logical objects. But though Russell tells us something about the membership of the class, he never explains the qualifications for membership. "Besides the forms of atomic complexes, there are many other logical objects which are involved in the formation of

5. Russell himself makes this criticism in "The Philosophy of Logical Atomism" (1917) in *Essays in Logic and Knowledge*, ed. R. C. Marsh (London: George Allen & Unwin, 1956), p. 226.

6. "On the Nature of Truth and Falsehood," pp. 183–184.

7. "Theory of Knowledge," pp. 182–185.

non-atomic complexes. Such words as *or, not, all, some,* plainly involve logical notions; and since we can use such words intelligently, we must be acquainted with the logical objects involved."[8] In general, "there certainly is such a thing as 'logical experience', by which I mean that kind of immediate knowledge other than judgement, which is what enables us to understand logical terms. Many such terms have occurred in the last two chapters, for instance, particulars, universals, relations, dual complexes, predicates. Such words are, no doubt, somewhat difficult, and are only understood by people who have reached a certain level of mental development. Still, they are understood, and this shows that those who understand them possess something which seems fitly described as 'acquaintance with logical objects'."[9]

Another approach to this elusive theory would be to ask whether acquaintance takes on a special character when it is directed onto logical objects. On this point Russell is more informative. He warns us at the start that "acquaintance has, perhaps, a somewhat different meaning, where logical objects are concerned, from that which it has when particulars are concerned."[10] Later, he explains that acquaintance with the form $x \chi y$ is "understanding what is meant by something having some relation to something." But he also equates this form with the fact that "something has some relation to something."[11] Here he is not using the word 'fact' loosely to mean 'possibility'. For in his detailed account of acquaintance with pure forms he says,

> I do not think there is any difference between understanding and acquaintance in the case of 'something has some relation to something'. I base this view simply on the fact that I am unable introspectively to discover any difference. In regard to most propositions—*i.e.* to all such as contain any constants—it is easy to *prove* that understanding is different from acquaintance with the corresponding fact (if any): understanding is neutral as regards truth and falsehood, whereas acquaintance with the fact is only possible when there is

8. Ibid., p. 186.
9. Ibid., p. 181.
10. Ibid.
11. Ibid., p. 212.

such a fact, that is, in the case of truth; and understanding of any proposition other than a pure form cannot be, like acquaintance, a two-term relation. But both these proofs fail in the case of a pure form, and we are therefore compelled to rely on direct inspection, which, so far as I can discover, reveals no distinction, in this case, between understanding and acquaintance.[12]

In this passage acquaintance with the pure form has become acquaintance with the fact that something has some dual relation to something. Later Russell makes it quite clear that he regards this as a logical truth: "The importance of the understanding of pure form lies in its relation to the self-evidence of logical truth. For since understanding is here a direct relation of the subject to a single object, the possibility of untruth does not arise, as it does when understanding is a multiple relation."[13] On the other hand "something is similar to something" is not a pure form, and, if true, is only contingently true, because in this case the subject is related to two terms, the form and similarity.[14] Pure forms are simple,[15] but when a constituent is added to a pure form the result is something that is not simple.

It is surprising to find Russell treating the proposition that something has some relation to something as a logical truth. But it does explain why he says not only that logical words, such as 'or' and 'not' involve logical objects but also that pure atomic forms are logical objects. The reason is that " 'logical constants', which might seem to be entities occurring in logical propositions, are really concerned with pure *form,* and are not actually constituents of the propositions in the verbal expression of which their names occur," and some of these propositions evidently are logical truths.[16] So he associated the dubious logical truths that he called "pure atomic forms" with those molecular propositions that evidently are logical truths and owe this status to their pure forms and the logical words that occur in their construction. In both kinds of case he took logical truth to be self-evident.

12. Ibid., p. 246.
13. Ibid., p. 250.
14. Ibid., pp. 252–253.
15. Ibid., p. 243.
16. Ibid. p. 183.

The ascription of logical truth to the proposition that something has some dual relation to something is not the only surprising feature of Russell's 1913 theory of propositions. It is also a remarkably Platonic theory, because the apprehension of logical truths does not develop in any way out of the understanding of ordinary propositions. On the contrary, an ordinary proposition, such as *aRb*, could not be understood unless the appropriate logical truth had already been understood and accepted.

This makes it all the more necessary for Russell to put logical truth on a firm, independent foundation. But he does not attempt that task. Instead, he offers an account of the way in which people come to know logical truths. His idea is that pure forms are completely general complexes, which are either atomic or molecular, and that, when someone achieves acquaintance with a complex of either of these two kinds, he also achieves acquaintance with a fact. Error is out of the question, because the proposition that expresses the fact cannot be false.

This should be seen as a transference to the Platonic world of an idea which Russell first applied to judgments of immediate perception. When a subject, *S*, makes a judgment of immediate perception, he is acquainted with a particular complex, and, as long as he confines himself to analyzing it into its constituents, his judgment cannot be false.[17] But even if this were a correct account of judgments of immediate perception, it is not easy to see how it could be transferred to knowledge of logical truths. A perceived complex could have been arranged differently, and so *S*'s judgment is only contingent, even, if, given certain conditions, it could not be mistaken. But when it is a logical truth that has to be explained, it is not enough to establish that *S* could not make a mistake; if *S*'s knowledge of the logical truth is based on acquaintance with a completely general complex, it has to be established that this complex is necessarily as it is.

17. See *Principia Mathematica*, 1st ed. (Cambridge: Cambridge University Press, 1910), I, p. 43, and *Problems of Philosophy*, pp. 178ff.

But Russell makes no attempt to establish this. Instead, he argues that completely general complexes are really simple, because they have no constituents,[18] and that, therefore "understanding is a dual relation, the object-term being a pure form,"[19] and that "the dualism of true and false . . . presupposes propositions, and does not arise so long as we confine ourselves to acquaintance, except, possibly, in the case of abstract logical forms; and even here there is no proper dualism, since falsehood is logically impossible in these cases."[20] But this is unconvincing. Completely general complexes cannot be regarded as simple merely because they have no constituents. Indeed, the point of introducing such complexes was that they should be isomorphic with particular perceived complexes, which are not simple. In any case, if completely general complexes were simple, the possibility of truth would be eliminated together with the possibility of falsehood, and so logical truth would remain unexplained.

Russell's 1913 theory of language and logic is an attempt to exploit the resources of two worlds. We understand propositions in part by achieving acquaintance with the things, qualities, and relations signified by the non-logical words that occur in their expression. But these resources, which are supplied by the world that we perceive, are not enough in themselves to yield understanding of propositions. We also need acquaintance with abstract objects in another world, because, without such acquaintance we would be unable to understand the forms of propositions or the logical words that occur in their expression. Any theory of this kind has to face the question, where the boundary between the two worlds should be drawn, and Russell's demarcation can be challenged because he ascribes logical truth to generalizations which are only capable of achieving contingent truth. It is also necessary for any such theory to face the question, why elements taken from the two worlds can be fitted together.

18. "Theory of Knowledge," p. 243.
19. Ibid., p. 347.
20. Ibid., p. 271.

But Russell never faces this question, and, for all that he says, the harmony might be pure coincidence. Finally, a two-world theory, like any other theory of language and logic, has to explain what logical truth is. It is on this point that Russell's theory is weakest. For instead of offering an explanation of the nature of logical truth, he merely tells us how it is known. Here, as elsewhere, he relies on acquaintance, and he tries to explain the necessity of a logical truth by making the abstract object simple, so that acquaintance in this kind of case will be a dyadic relation between subject and object without the dualism of truth and falsehood in the object and simultaneously he tries to explain the truth of a logical truth by representing the abstract object as 'a complex'.

Wittgenstein's picture theory of propositions may be classified as a one-world theory of language and logic, not because it is an empiricist theory (it is not), but because it explains logical truth as a natural development out of contingent sense, without the need for any resources drawn from elsewhere.

> It is clear that whatever we can say *in advance* about the form of all propositions, we must be able to say *all at once*.
>
> In fact elementary propositions themselves contain all logical operations. For '*Fa*' says the same thing as
>
> $$'(\exists x).\ Fx\ .\ x = a'.$$
>
> Wherever there is compositeness, argument and function are already present, and where these are present we already have all the logical constants.[21]

The general opposition between Wittgenstein's picture theory and Russell's 1913 theory is clear enough. Instead of trying to remedy the deficiencies in Russell's theory, Wittgenstein offered something radically different. But what is needed is a detailed demonstration that he was reacting against particular things Russell had said. However, that would require a commentary on much of the *Tractatus* and much of *Notebooks 1914–1916*, and even on some of "Notes on Logic," since

21. *Tractatus Logico–Philosophicus* (London: Routledge & Kegan Paul, 1922; New York: Humanities Press, 1961), 5.47 i–iii.

Wittgenstein must have been familiar with the direction that Russell's thoughts were taking before he wrote "Theory of Knowledge." I have space only to make a few salient points.

Wittgenstein's rejection of logical objects is his best-known criticism of Russell's theory. "There are no 'logical objects' or 'logical constants' (in Frege's and Russell's sense)."[22] "My fundamental idea is that the 'logical constants' are not representatives; that there can be no representatives of the *logic* of facts."[23] This is more than a denial that logical words stand for constituents of propositions. The point is that they do not even stand for objects in a Platonic world.

Before Russell showed him the "crucial part" of his 1913 manuscript, Wittgenstein was aware that his theory of logical objects was part of a general theory of pure forms, both atomic and molecular. In "Notes on Logic" there is an ironic comment on his claim that pure forms are complexes, in order to allow for logical truth, but simple ones, in order to exclude the possibility of falsehood: "Russell's 'complexes' were to have the useful property of being compounded; and were to combine with this the agreeable property that they could be treated like 'simples'. But this alone makes them unserviceable as logical types (forms), since there would then have been significance in asserting of a simple that it was complex. But a *property* cannot be a logical type."[24] Here Wittgenstein does not mention Russell's idea that knowledge of a logical truth comes from acquaintance with an abstract complex, construed as a fact, but he does mention it and rejects it in an early entry in *Notebooks 1914–1916:* "If the existence of the subject-predicate sentence does not show everything needful, then it could surely only be shown by the existence of some particular fact of that form. And acquaintance with such a fact cannot be essential for logic."[25] In the *Tractatus* he criticizes the next step in the development of Russell's theory. Russell believed that,

22. Ibid., 5.4; cf. 4.441 i.
23. Ibid., 4.0312 ii.
24. *Notebooks 1914–1916* (Oxford: Basil Blackwell, 1961; New York: Harper & Row, 1969), p. 99.
25. Ibid., 4.9.14, p. 3.

when someone achieves acquaintance with an abstract complex, the associated logical truth becomes self-evident to him. This receives the following comment:

> Self-evidence, which Russell talked about so much, can become dispensable in logic, only because language itself prevents every logical mistake.—What makes logic *a priori* is the *impossibility* of illogical thought.[26]

The *Tractatus* also contains a long and detailed criticism of Russell's whole theory of pure forms.[27] Wittgenstein's central contention is that he was mistaken in supposing that there is any such thing as 'logical experience'. For experiences issue in truths, but logic and the elementary propositions out of which it develops do not depend on any truths. The idea that they depend on truths about a Platonic world comes from a failure to understand the nature of propositions.

> The 'experience' that we need in order to understand logic is not that something or other is the state of things, but that something *is:* that, however, is *not* an experience.
>
> Logic is *prior* to every experience—that something *is so.*
>
> It is prior to the question 'How?', not prior to the question 'What?'[28]

This passage introduces an important doctrine: sense never presupposes truth. Russell, of course, did not accept this doctrine, but what he says on the subject contains another controversial feature. According to him, the presupposed truths are logical truths learned by acquaintance with a Platonic world, and some of them are atomic, but the examples of atomic logical truths that he gives, such as "Something has some dual relation to something", are evidently contingent. Wittgenstein criticizes this feature of Russell's theory in another part of the *Tractatus,* because it is part of his general tendency to include

26. *TLP* 5.4731; cf. 5.1363 and 6.1271.
27. Ibid., 5.55–5.5561.
28. Ibid., 5.552.

propositions that are really contingent among the axioms of logic.

> The mark of a logical proposition is *not* general validity.
>
> To be general means no more than to be accidentally valid for all things. . . .[29]
>
> The general validity of logic might be called essential, in contrast with the accidental general validity of such propositions as "All men are mortal'. . . ."[30]

The application of this criticism to Russell's theory of pure forms is given in *Tractatus* 5.553–5.5542:

> Russell said that there were simple relations between different numbers of things (individuals). But between what numbers? And how is this supposed to be decided?—By experience?
>
> It is supposed to be possible to answer *a priori* the question whether I can get into a position in which I need the sign for a 27-termed relation in order to signify something.
>
> But is it really legitimate even to ask such a question? Can we set up a form of sign without knowing whether anything can correspond to it?

Here Wittgenstein touches on one of the questions that Russell failed to ask: If the understanding of propositions requires the resources of another world, what guarantees that elements taken from the two worlds will fit together?[31]

Wittgenstein's picture theory of propositions is, in part, a reaction against Russell's theory of language and logic. Before he formulated it, he had explored the possibility of a theory like Russell's. He told Russell in May 1913 that he had tried his view and knew that it would not work.[32] There is a clear reference to this false start in an entry in the *Notebooks* dated 21 October 1914: "I thought that the possibility of the truth of the proposition 'ϕa' was tied up with the fact $(\exists x, \phi) \,.\, \phi x$. But

29. Ibid., 6.1231.
30. Ibid., 6.1232.
31. Cf. *TLP*, 5.5521.
32. See Russell's letter to Lady Ottoline Morrell, quoted on pp. 190–191.

it is impossible to see why 'ϕa' should be possible only if there is another proposition of the same form." He means "only if there is another true proposition of the same form." For he continues, "ϕa surely does not need any precedent. (For suppose that there existed only the two elementary propositions 'ϕa' and 'ψa' and that 'ϕa' were false: Why should this proposition only make sense if 'ψa' is true?)"[33]

Here Wittgenstein makes it clear that, unlike Russell, he assumed that, if $(\exists x, \phi)\phi x$ is true, it is only contingently true. So in his version of the theory the sense of one elementary proposition depended on the truth of another one of the same form, rather than on a logical truth about an abstract complex in another world. This is a step forward, but it led very quickly to the collapse of the theory.

The picture theory emerges in the early entries of the *Notebooks,* and it is developed rapidly against the background of the discarded theory. The problem that it was designed to solve is put concisely in an entry dated 29 October 1914: "This is the difficulty: How can there be such a thing as the form of p when there is no state of affairs of this form? And in that case, what does this form really consist in?"[34] Russell poses the problem in a similar way in "Theory of Knowledge,"[35] and his solution is that the form is an abstract complex with which anyone who understands the proposition, p, must be acquainted. Wittgenstein explains in a later entry why he cannot accept any such solution: "The reality that corresponds to the sense of a proposition can surely be nothing but its constituents, since we are surely *ignorant* of everything else. If the reality consists in anything further, this can at any rate neither be denoted nor expressed; for in the first case it would be a further constituent, and in the second case the expression would be a proposition, for which the same problem that arose for the original proposition would arise again."[36] The second argument is directed against Russell's theory that the

33. *NB,* p. 17.
34. Ibid., p. 21.
35. "Theory of Knowledge," p. 185.
36. *NB,* 20.11.14, p. 31.

form is a completely general fact. The conclusion is important, because it severely restricts the resources available to any theory of propositions. "The knowledge of the representing relation *must* be founded only on the knowledge of the constituents of the state of affairs."[37]

Given this restriction, the inevitable solution is that forms are possibilities inherent in the constituents of states of affairs.

> If I know an object I also know all its possible occurrences in states of affairs.
> (Every one of these possibilities must be part of the nature of the object).[38]

This solution is Aristotelian in spirit. The forms that Russell had placed in a Platonic world were treated by Wittgenstein as essential features of objects. But it is a strange version of Aristotelianism. For the union of an object and a form is not a genuine kind of complexity, and so it cannot be reported in a proposition. Consequently, though the metaphysic is much more empirical than Russell's, it cannot be expressed in language.

Wittgenstein's objects cannot be decomposed into further constituents, and are, to that extent, simple. If their possession of forms does not make them complex, they are perfectly simple. The theoretical advantage of an object's simplicity is that it either exists or does not exist and there is not the third possibility that its components might be combined in a different way. If it exists it can be the meaning of a name, which would have lacked a meaning had it not existed.[39] But neither its existence nor its non-existence can be expressed in a proposition,[40] because a proposition requires some compositeness in "the reality that corresponds to (its) sense."[41] Here we might echo Wittgenstein's ironic comment on Russell's theory: Wittgenstein's 'simples' were to have the useful property of being non-composite, and were to combine with this the agreeable property that they could be treated as if they had a certain kind of complexity.

37. Ibid., 3.11.14, p. 24.
38. *TLP*, 2.0123.
39. Ibid., 3.2–3.203.
40. Ibid., 4.1211–2, 4.1272, 5.535.
41. *NB*, 20.11.14, p. 31; cf. *TLP*, 4.023, 4.0311.

But he could reply that even if the possession of a form is a kind of complexity it certainly is not compositeness, and so a proposition containing the object's name cannot be said to need further analysis, on the ground that, without further analysis, its sense would depend on the truth of a further proposition which decomposed the object into its constituents.[42] However, he felt doubts about this point in the period preceding the compilation of the *Tractatus*. For example, in the *Prototractatus* he says: "If '*A*' is used to signify a person, the proposition, '*A* is sitting', is admissible, but not if 'A' signifies this book.—But once a proposition is completely analysed, everything that depends on the understanding of its form must be unaffected by the meanings of its parts."[43]

In the *Tractatus* he seems to have overcome these doubts,[44] perhaps rightly, but it must be observed that he substituted an ineffable Aristotelian metaphysic for Russell's Platonic metaphysic.

If the form of a state of affairs is the possibility of its structure,[45] and if this possibility is an extract from the possibilities of combination inherent in its constituents, the next question is how this form is absorbed by a proposition. Here we must speak of 'absorption' partly because, for reasons already given, a proposition does not stand in any semantic relation to its form. It does not denote it or express it,[46] but rather, makes it its own. When this idea first occurs in the *Notebooks*, Wittgenstein says that a proposition acquires its sense through a formal match between it and the reality with which it is concerned. But when two structures match each other formally, they have the same form. Now there could not be identity of form unless both structures contained the same number of

42. *TLP*, 2.0211–2; cf. "Notes Dictated to G. E. Moore in Norway," in *NB*, p. 116, lines 18–23.

43. *Prototractatus* (London: Routledge & Kegan Paul, 1971; Ithaca, N.Y.: Cornell University Press, 1971), 3.201412 ii; cf. *NB*, 22.6.15 viii–xi, p. 70.

44. See *TLP*, 2.013 and 2.0131.

45. Ibid., 2.033.

46. *NB*, 20.11.14, p. 31, quoted on p. 201.

constituents and a relation capable of relating them. But Wittgenstein adds the further requirement that the constituents of the proposition must not be combinable in ways that are not matched by the combinability of the constituents of the state of affairs. This is an important addition to the theory if, as has just been suggested, the forms of objects are choosy, and it gives us another reason for using the phrase 'absorption of form'.

The picture theory is a theory about the absorption of form. The points that have just been ascribed to Wittgenstein first appear as stages in the development of the theory in the *Notebooks*.

> The proposition must enable us to see the logical structure of the state of affairs that makes it true or false. (As a picture must show the spatial relation in which the things represented in it must stand if the picture is correct (true).)
>
> The form of a picture might be said to be the respect in which it MUST agree with reality (in order to be capable of picturing it at all). . . .
>
> The theory of logical picturing by means of language says quite generally: In order for it to be possible that a proposition should be true or false—agree with reality or not—for this to be possible, something in the proposition must be *identical* with reality.[47]
>
> There is, after all, no need for the state of affairs itself actually to be the case.
>
> One name stands for one thing, another for another thing, and it is they that are combined with one another; in this way the whole group—like a *tableau vivant*—presents the state of affairs.
>
> The logical combination must, of course, be one that is possible as between the things that the names stand for, and this will always be the case if the names really do stand for the things. . . .[48]
>
> In this way the proposition represents the state of affairs as it were off its own bat.

47. Ibid., 20.10.14, p. 15; cf. *TLP*, 2.18.
48. *NB*, 4.11.14, iii–v, p. 26; cf. *TLP*, 4.0311 and 2.15.

But when I say that the combination of the constituents of the proposition must be possible for the things that are represented, does this not contain the whole problem? How can a combination of objects be possible when it does not exist?

'The combination must be possible' means that the proposition and the constituents of the state of affairs must stand in a determinate relation.

Then, in order for a proposition to present a state of affairs, it is only necessary for its constituents to represent those of the state of affairs, and for the former to be combined in a way that is possible for the latter.[49]

The salient feature of the picture theory is that a proposition achieves sense independently, or, as Wittgenstein puts it, "off its own bat [auf eigene Faust]." "The precedent to which we are constantly inclined to appeal must reside in the symbol itself."[50] A proposition achieves its sense without the help of any apparatus of truths, either about the referents of its names or about its form. An elementary proposition must be true or false, with no third possibility, because the referents of its names are simple objects. So "when I say '*p* is possible', does that . . . not . . . try to say what '*p* v ≃ *p*' shows?"[51] And in a letter to Russell, he explains, "I can now express my objection to your theory of judgment exactly: I believe it is obvious that from the proposition 'A judges that (say) *a* is in a relation R to *b*', if correctly analyzed, the proposition '*a*R*b*. v. *a*R*b*' must follow directly *without the use of any other premiss.* This condition is not fulfilled by your theory."[52] This letter antedates the formulation of the picture theory, but it is a clear statement of the requirement that it had to meet: the sense of a proposition must not be dependent on any truth.

49. *NB*, 5.11.14, i–iv, pp. 26–27; cf. 3.4.15, iii, p. 41.
50. *TLP* 5.525.
51. *NB*, 10.11.14, i, p. 28.
52. Letter to Russell dated June 1913 in *NB*, p. 121. The immediate referent of "your theory" is Russell's 1913 theory, but the criticism also applies to his 1910 theory. A similar criticism of "Russell's theory" is made in "Notes on Logic" before Wittgenstein had seen the "crucial part" of "Theory of Knowledge." Cf. *TLP*, 5.5422.

The development of logic out of elementary propositions is equally independent. "Logic must take care of itself,"[53] and the theory that its propositions are tautologies explains how it manages to do so. "The propositions of logic demonstrate the logical properties of propositions by combining them to form propositions that say nothing."[54] "It follows from this that we can actually do without logical propositions, for in a suitable notation we can in fact recognise the formal properties of propositions by mere inspection of the propositions themselves."[55] So though tautologies are genuine logical truths, unlike the propositions that express Russell's forms, they too are an unnecessary apparatus.

The whole theory rests on the idea that propositions absorb the forms of states of affairs. But Wittgenstein describes this fundamental process very rapidly, and it is not entirely clear what the exact analogy between propositions and pictures is. So it is worth taking a closer look at the mechanism of absorption, and we may at the same time succeed in making out more of the details of the difference between Russell's and Wittgenstein's metaphysics.

The main lines of the picture theory are drawn in the second part of the second of the seven sections of the *Tractatus*.[56] The presentation is abstract, and it will help to have some concrete examples to illustrate it, and some sense of the direction in which it moves. So I shall first state what I take to be the point of the analogy between propositions and pictures, and then I shall give three examples, and finally, using the examples, argue that the analogy is introduced to make that point.

The point of the analogy is that, when we choose a method of symbolization, we really make a number of choices, many of which are independent of one another, but there are some things that we do not choose, because they are forced on us by the nature of reality. Now we tend to call a method of symbolization pictorial when it exploits material likeness, especially

53. *NB*, 22.8.14, i, p. 2; cf. *TLP*, 5.473.
54. *TLP*, 6.121, i.
55. Ibid., 6.122.
56. Ibid., 2.1–2.225.

visual likeness, and in such cases we feel that the rules of symbolization are forced on us, because we take a natural package deal. But we were not really forced to symbolize by material likeness because we could have used words instead. When we do use words, many of the rules of symbolization are chosen not as a package deal, but independently, since that is how vocabularies are set up. But underneath these options there is something that is not optional, and that is the necessity of constructing our sentences in such a way that they reflect the possibilities of combination inherent in things. This is not a choice, because the only alternative is silence. In fact, reflection of form by form, or formal likeness, is essential even to pictures that exploit material likeness. It is, therefore, more illuminating to treat material likeness as inessential, and to treat this very abstract type of reflection as the essence of all pictures. Thus the concept of a picture is generalized to include propositions.

Naturally, this does not exhaust the picture theory. But it does give the point of the analogy. The question with which I am concerned is whether the analogy throws any light on the way in which a proposition absorbs the form of a state of affairs.

If it is necessary to chart the position of the icebergs in a certain part of the North Atlantic at a particular moment, there are various ways in which it might be done.

I. An aerial photograph could be used.
II. It would be possible to pin flags to a map.
III. Each iceberg could be named, as hurricanes are, and its bearing and distance from a reference point could be given.

Method I is the extreme case of the package deal. Of course, another method could have been used instead, but, given that this one is used, there are few possible variations of it. The height at which the photograph is taken could be varied, or the curvature of the lens, but not much else. Method II allows more independent choices. The map-projection could be varied,[57] and the choice of one flag to stand for a particular iceberg is not only arbitrary, but also independent of other similar choices. The same is true of the assignment of names, if Method III is used. But this method introduces another range of choices that are both arbitrary and independent of one another, the choices of methods of symbolizing directions and distances.

The introduction of pictures in *Tractatus* 2.1–2.225 can be divided into two sections. The first, which runs down to 2.174, is primarily about material likenesses, and the concept of a picture has not yet been explicitly generalized. The second section, which starts at 2.18, argues for a generalization of the concept. The essence of a picture, in the generalized sense, is, of course, shared by material likenesses, and many of the remarks in the first section, which are primarily about material likenesses, apply to pictures in general. The result is that we are led to generalize the concept of a picture by stealth without quite knowing at what point we took the decisive step. But it is clear that 2.18 gives the argument for it: "What any picture, of whatever form, must have in common with reality, in order to be able to depict it—correctly or incorrectly—in any way at all, is logical form, i.e., the form of reality."

The generalization varies everything that can be varied in order to arrive at the invariable essence of all pictures. It is designed to give us an intellectual jolt. Those features of material likenesses that strike us as natural and inevitable are really optional, and those that really are inevitable and forced on us by the nature of things[58] are too abstract to be noticed at first. Only the features of Methods I and II that are shared by Method III are essential to pictures.

Before the point of generalization is reached, Wittgenstein says, "What a picture must have in common with reality, in order to be able to depict it—correctly or incorrectly—in the

57. See Wittgenstein, "Some Remarks on Logical Form," *Proceedings of the Aristotelian Society*, Supplementary Vol. 9 (1929); reprinted in *Essays on Wittgenstein's Tractatus*, ed. I. M. Copi and R. W. Beard (London: Routledge & Kegan Paul, 1966; New York: Hafner Press, 1973).

58. See *TLP*, 6.124, quoted on p. 212.

way it does, is its pictorial form."[59] Here the words "in the way it does" are to be contrasted with the words "in any way at all" in 2.18. The point is that there are options between different ways of depicting the same state of affairs, and this is illustrated by the next remark:

> A picture can depict any reality whose form it has.
>
> A spatial picture can depict anything spatial, a coloured one anything coloured, etc.[60]

These are only examples of methods of symbolizing something spatial or something coloured, and there is no suggestion that Method I or even Method II must be used. But they are carefully chosen examples, because we all start with the idea that a picture is a material likeness, and Wittgenstein's strategy is first to get us to see that this kind of picture must have the same form as the reality that it depicts, and then to generalize the requirement.

There is a risk attached to this strategy. Some of the points made in the first section may be expressed in a way that applies only to material likenesses, and so imply that all pictures must use Methods I or II:

> The fact that the elements of a picture are related to one another in a determinate way represents that things are related to one another in the same way.
>
> Let us call this connection of its elements the structure of the picture and let us call the possibility of this structure the pictorial form of the picture.
>
> Pictorial form is the possibility that things are related to one another in the same way as the elements of the picture.[61]

But can he really mean in the *same* way? The apparent insistence on material likeness is all the more surprising because it occurs in the definition of the concept of pictorial form, and we know that the point of his theory is that Method III is also

59. Ibid., 2.17.
60. Ibid., 2.171.
61. Ibid., 2.15 and 2.151.

pictorial. So we might suppose that the criterion of the sameness of way could be sufficiently relaxed to fit propositions. However, that would be a strained use of the phrase "same way," and in the sequel he does not apply the remark to propositions,[62] but always uses some more complicated form of words instead.[63] It is, therefore, probably best to take the phrase to imply material likeness, and to assume that, when the concept of a picture is generalized, the definition of "pictorial form" is tacitly adjusted.

After the generalization in 2.18 he says:

> A picture whose pictorial form is logical form is called a logical picture.
>
> Every picture is *at the same time* a logical one. (On the other hand, not every picture is, for example, a spatial one).[64]

The distinction between being a logical picture and being called a logical picture is not immediately clear. All pictures, including material likenesses, are logical pictures, because they present logically possible combinations of objects. But Wittgenstein implies that the pictorial form of a picture is not always logical form. This is presumably because when we characterize the pictorial form of a picture, we use the most specific characterization that is applicable. For example, the pictorial forms of the pictures produced by Methods I and II are spatial,[65] and the pictorial form of the picture produced by Method III is logical. So the point is that, though we call a picture "logical" only when this is the most specific characterization that applies to its pictorial form, nevertheless all pictures are *au fond* logical. Not surprisingly, the next step is to maintain that what any picture must have in common with the reality that it depicts is logical pictorial form.[66]

62. E.g., not at *TLP*, 3.14, where it might have been expected. However, in *Notebooks 1914–1916*, he does make this strained use of the phrase "in a way that," and so he may be allowing himself the same license here.

63. See *TLP*, 4.023, v, or 4.031.

64. Ibid., 2.181 and 2.182.

65. As it is in the first example suggested in *TLP*, 2.171. This provides some support for the suggestion made above, that 2.15 and 2.151 define "pictorial form" for material likenesses.

66. Ibid., 2.2.

I have dwelt on the details of Wittgenstein's introduction of the analogy between propositions and pictures because its obscurity is the key to understanding it. The concept of a picture is generalized by stealth, so that we will feel it as something inevitable. But though this gradualism may help to convince us that a proposition is like a picture, it may also leave us in some doubt about the precise content of our conviction. So Wittgenstein's remarks need to be focused onto the main point of the analogy.

The picture theory is a general theory of language and logic. The specific point of the analogy between propositions and pictures is that both must have the same form as the reality with which they are concerned. Wittgenstein makes this point by reducing the shared form to the indispensable minimum, so that the scope of the requirement that form must be shared is enlarged to the maximum and includes propositions expressed in words. It is in this way that the concept of a picture is extended to cover propositions. This theory of language inevitably yields, as a metaphysical by-product, a theory of forms. The metaphysic, unlike Russell's, is Aristotelian. There is also another respect in which it is unlike Russell's: it contains no more than the necessary features of reality. It is not necessary that reality should consist of specific types of objects with specific forms. All that is necessary is that it should contain some objects with some forms. This extremely general theory is matched by, and deduced from, an equally general theory about the necessary features of propositions.

The propositions of logic describe the scaffolding of the world, or rather they represent it. They have no 'subject-matter'. They presuppose that names have meaning and elementary propositions sense; and that is their connection with the world. It is clear that something must be indicated about the world by the fact that certain combinations of symbols—whose essence involves the possession of a determinate character—are tautologies. This contains the decisive point. We have said that some things are arbitrary in the symbols that we use and that some things are not.[67] In logic it is only the latter that express: but that means that logic is not a field in which *we* express what we wish with the help of signs, but rather one in which the

67. A reference to *TLP*, 3.342.

nature of the natural and inevitable signs speaks for itself. If we know the logical syntax of any sign-language, then we have already been given all the propositions of logic.[68]

The theory of logic rests on the picture theory of propositions, which also yields a metaphysic. The foundation of the whole edifice is the requirement of sameness of form. Even when the picture is a material likeness, this identity of form depends on the semantics of its elements.

> The pictorial relationship consists of the correlations of the picture's elements with things.
>
> These correlations are, as it were, the feelers with which the picture touches reality.[69]

When the picture is not a material likeness, these correlations are not arranged in a package deal. So it is easier to violate the syntax which is imposed on the picture's elements by their semantics. A string of words is less foolproof than a material likeness, and the form that it is supposed to have absorbed is more likely to be violated.[70] But this is not a profound difference. For there are impossible 'likenesses', and, in any case, language and logic take care of themselves in another way: violations simply lack sense.

68. Ibid., 6.124.
69. Ibid., 2.1514 and 2.1515.
70. I.e., a string of words may fail to meet the condition laid down in *NB*, 4.11.14 iii–v, p. 26, and 5.11.14 i–iii, pp. 26–27, quoted on pp. 204–205.

8 Semantic Holism: Frege and Wittgenstein

P. M. S. HACKER

Introduction

The dictum 'A word has a meaning only in the context of a sentence' was propounded by Frege in the *Foundations of Arithmetic.*[1] It is emphatically stated, in four separate places, as a fundamental semantic principle. Of this dictum, or holistic principle, as I shall call it, Michael Dummett has written, "[it] is probably the most important philosophical statement Frege ever made."[2] Yet what the dictum means, and what role it plays in Frege's philosophy of language, is both obscure and debatable.

The dictum is quoted by Wittgenstein, with evident approval, in both his masterpieces, in the *Tractatus* 3.3 and in the *Investigations* §49. Was Wittgenstein's understanding of the principle similar to Frege's? Did his conception of it remain constant between the *Tractatus* and the *Investigations* or was it transformed? Did he add anything to the philosophical significance of the principle?

Irrespective of the historical-exegetical issues raised by examination of the sources of the principle, philosophical issues

I am deeply indebted to my colleague Dr. G. P. Baker for his aid, advice, and criticisms of the earlier drafts of this paper.

1. In the sequel the following editions of Frege's works are cited: *Foundations of Arithmetic,* trans. J. L. Austin (Oxford: Basil Blackwell, 1953); *The Basic Laws of Arithmetic,* trans. and ed. M. Furth (Berkeley and Los Angeles: University of California, 1964); *On the Foundations of Geometry and Formal Theories of Arithmetic,* trans. Eike Henner W. Kluge (New Haven: Yale University Press, 1971); *Translations from the Philosophical Writings of Gottlob Frege,* ed. P. Geach and M. Black (Oxford: Basil Blackwell, 1960).

2. Michael Dummett, "Nominalism," *Philosophical Review* 65 (1956), 491.

surround it too. After all, it is prima facie disproved by the extensive use of words *outside* the context of a sentence: e.g. the use of numerals to paginate or number licences, or the use of personal names to call or greet, or the use of concept-words to label. Moreover, on one reading, the dictum would immediately render unintelligible our capacity to understand sentences we have never heard before. For if the sentence is the minimal unit of meaning rather than the word, how can we understand words in novel combinations? Again, on another reading, if the meaning of a word consists in its contribution to the meaning of any sentence in which it occurs, it seems to follow that to know its meaning would require one to know (or be capable of understanding) the sense of all possible sentences in which it can occur. But what delimits the 'possible sentences in which it can occur'? These problems will be examined in the sequel, and, it is to be hoped, some light will be shed upon them by way of a historico-exegetical investigation.

Frege: The Origin of the Dictum

The dictum is prominent in the *Foundations of Arithmetic*, but much to the bafflement of commentators, it apparently sinks from sight in Frege's later works. Our initial problem is to explain what Frege meant by this enigmatic slogan, and what justification he had for asserting it. We must also examine the purposes which the principle serves in the *Foundations.* The second central task is to discover whether Frege did indeed abandon the principle. In particular it will be necessary to see whether, as Dummett suggests, assimilation of sentences to proper names in the 1890s, and repudiation of piecemeal definition, forced Frege to relinquish the holistic principle which was, it is alleged, one of his greatest insights.

A fundamental programme, a fundamental principle, and a fundamental analogy dominate Frege's philosophy of language. The fundamental programme, only fragmentarily executed, is to display language as a kind of calculus. The fundamental principle is that to know the meaning of a sentence is to know its truth-conditions. The fundamental analogy is between concepts and mathematical functions. The principle and analogy interlock: a function is fully defined only if it has a determinate value for every possible argument (within its range). *Pari-passu* a concept-word has a determinate meaning only if it is defined for every possible argument (Frege misguidedly took concepts as functions ranging over the totality of objects). Concepts are functions whose values are truth-values, and unless they are completely defined it will be possible to generate well-formed sentences lacking a truth-value. Such sentences would violate the Law of Excluded Middle. So a logically adequate language must have rules ensuring determinacy of sense thus interpreted.

When Frege wrote "Begriffsschrift" he worked with an undifferentiated notion of content (*Inhalt*). However, the fundamental principle and analogy were already formulated. The mathematical analogy introduced new principles of parsing sentences which freed logical analysis from the trammels of conventional grammatical parsing, made possible Frege's sophisticated analysis of generality, and led to his theory of types. The holistic principle first appears in the following passage from "Begriffsschrift":

> Comparing the two propositions 'the number 20 can be represented as the sum of four squares' and 'every positive integer can be represented as the sum of four squares', it seems possible to regard 'being representable as the sum of four squares' as a function whose argument is 'the number 20' one time and 'every positive integer' the other time. We may see that this view is mistaken if we observe that 'the number 20' and 'every positive integer' are not concepts of the same rank.[3] What is asserted of the number 20 cannot be asserted in the same sense of [the concept] 'every positive integer'; of course it may in certain circumstances be assertable of every positive integer. The expression 'every positive integer' just by itself, unlike 'the number 20', gives no complete idea; *it gets a sense only through the context of the sentence.*[4]

3. To be sure, Frege was, by his own lights, confused here. 'The number 20' is not a concept (nor a concept-word) but a proper-name that stands for an object. The expression 'every positive integer' is not a concept either, but a complex consisting of a second-level concept-word 'every' and only *part* of its argument-expression. Hence it does not express 'a complete idea'. Nevertheless, the type-theoretical point made here is clear enough.

4. My italics.

> We attach no importance to the various ways that the same conceptual content may be regarded as a function of this or that argument, so long as function and argument are completely determinate. But if the argument becomes *indeterminate*, . . . then the distinction between function and argument becomes significant as regards the *content*. Conversely, the argument may be determinate and the function indeterminate. In both cases, in view of the contrast *determinate—indeterminate* or more or less *determinate*, the whole proposition splits up into *function* and argument as regards its own content, not just as regards our way of looking at it.[5]

In this passage many strands of Frege's thought are closely interwoven. The mathematical analogy is applied to language in order to illuminate its logical structure. The parsing of an atomic sentence into function and argument is arbitrary (concerns only our way of looking at it). But the parsing of a sentence containing an expression of generality is not. If a proper name in an atomic sentence is replaced by a quantifier, the quantifier cannot be considered the argument-expression of the concept-word. The universal quantifier takes the concept-word as *its* argument-expression, and its meaning is explained by its determining the truth-conditions of the resultant sentence, i.e. that the concept applies to everything. The conception of step by step construction of a sentence, as opposed to assemblage of independently significant units,[6] involves a theory of types which precludes treating different types of expression as arguments of the same type of function. It is, of course, striking that the slogan, as it appears here, seems to be restricted to expressions which do not give a 'complete idea'. The logico-mathematical principles of parsing a sentence force us to realize that the meanings of some types of expression are to be explained only by reference to their effect in determining the truth-conditions of a sentence which results from their being combined with other types of expression. Equally, Frege stresses, the meaning of certain symbols

5. "Begriffsschrift," pp. 13–14, in *Translations from the Philosophical Writings of Gottlob Frege*.

6. M. Dummett, *Frege: Philosophy of Language* (London: Duckworth, 1973), ch. 2.

may vary according to their position in a sentence.[7] Finally, we must realize that some word sequences have a sense at all only in virtue of their position in a sentence. 'Every positive integer' would, in Aristotelian logic, be classified as a subject term. Now it is denied that it may be so treated. Unlike 'the number 20', it does not 'express a complete idea' (any more than 'the cup drank' in the sentence 'the girl who held the cup drank her tea'), for it is not a logical unit of significance. Unlike 'the number 20', which is a proper name (singular referring expression) and can fulfil the role of argument expression for the relevant function-name, 'every positive integer' is an expression of different level or rather a complex consisting of a second-level concept-word and *part* of its argument-expression, and cannot do so. These type-theoretical considerations intimate the concept/object distinction which is later to play a major role in Frege's thought—what can intelligibly be said of an object (e.g. the number 20) cannot be said of a concept (e.g. positive integer). It is evident that the principle that an expression, or at least some types of expressions of logically fundamental importance, gets a sense only through the context of a sentence is wholly dependent upon the novel conception of logical syntax, and the truth-conditional principle. A sentence is the fundamental unit of truth or bearer of truth-value, whose significance is given by its truth-conditions. A subsentential expression that does not express a 'complete idea' has a sense only qua contributor to determining the truth-conditions of the sentence in which it occurs.

Frege: The Emergence of the Dictum

In the *Foundations of Arithmetic* the holistic principle is invoked no less than four times. On page x of the Introduction Frege lays forth his famous principles of semantic inquiry:

> always to separate sharply the psychological from the logical, the subjective from the objective;
> never to ask for the meaning [*Bedeutung*] of a word in isolation but only in the context of a proposition [*Satzzusammenhange*];
> never to lose sight of the distinction between concept and object.

7. "Begriffsschrift," p. 17.

What do these principles amount to, and what rationale is offered for them? The Introduction opens with a Kantian cry that it is a scandal to mathematics that there is no satisfactory answer to the question what a number is. In the brief polemical Introduction Frege adamantly rejects psychologism in semantics in general and in the philosophy of mathematics in particular (i.e. numerals are not names of ideas or mental pictures). The second principle, as it occurs in the Introduction, is invoked against psychologism, for, Frege insists, "if the second principle is not observed, one is almost forced to take as the meanings of words mental pictures, or acts of the individual mind." Compliance with the holistic principle is a condition of compliance with the first principle; semantic atomism leads to psychologism. Frege does not explicitly explain why this is so—why the view that words, in some sense, have a meaning outside the context of a sentence should lead to identifying their meaning with mental representations. Frege's reasons for this claim turn on the peculiarities of his own semantic theory. In his view, every significant expression (barring, e.g., the assertion sign and variable letters) stands for something, but only in the context of a sentence. What type of entity an expression stands for depends on its logical form: a proper name stands for an object, a first-level concept-word stands for a concept, etc. But the logical form of an expression is determined by logical syntax, itself a quasi-mathematical structure of argument and function. 'Vienna' in 'Vienna is the capital of Austria' stands for Vienna, but in 'Budapest is no Vienna' it is part of an expression that stands for a concept. 'Horse' in 'Black Beauty was a horse' stands for a concept, but in 'The concept horse . . . ' it is part of the name of an object. So what entity an expression stands for depends on its logical form, which is determined by its mode of occurrence in a sentence. Outside a sentential context it has no logical form, and does not stand for anything. Hence grasping its meaning (which Frege will later identify as its *sense*, i.e. the 'route' to its reference) presupposes knowledge of its logico-syntactical role. It is not obvious, indeed it is false, that semantic idealism is the only alternative to Frege's bizarre semantics and ontology. We manifestly do explain the meanings of words irrespective of their sentential occurrence, but we are not thereby committed to identifying their meanings with ideas. Semantic atomism, as embraced by idealist theories of meaning, is not the only alternative to Frege's brand of holism.

The third principle is closely related to the second, which, in view of the source of the holistic principle in "Begriffsschrift," is not surprising. The connection is via the type-theoretical implications. "As to the third point", Frege explains, "it is a mere illusion to suppose that a concept can be made an object without altering it." The point, unhappily phrased, is that the meaning or content[8] of an expression is different according as to whether it occurs predicatively (or as part of a predicate) or substantivally (or as part of a proper name). In the one case it (or the complex expression of which it is a part) stands for a concept, in the other for an object. What can intelligibly be asserted of the one cannot be asserted of the other. It is, however, another aspect of the distinction which is emphasized by Frege here. The principle entails, he says, that a certain formalist theory of fractional, negative, etc. numbers is untenable. He clarifies this in §97: the error of the formalists is to suppose that by postulating properties objects can be ensured existence. We *can* introduce concept-words, e.g. 'square root of −1', even though nothing falls under them. All that matters is that they be sharply defined. But we may not, without further ado, add the definite article to the concept-word (i.e. purport to 'transform the concept into an object'). For we would have no guarantee that the resulting proper name has any meaning—it may well not stand for anything (or for more than one thing). But we must ensure that every well-formed expression has a meaning *(Bedeutung)*, otherwise we will generate well-formed sentences without a truth-value. Keeping in mind the distinction between concept and object will prevent us from introducing complex proper names, on the basis of 'postulating' a concept without first proving the unique existence of a bearer.

8. Note that meaning (*Bedeutung*) in the *Foundations* is equivalent to content *(Inhalt)* in "Begriffsschrift."

The holistic principle occurs again in §60 in another anti-psychologistic polemic. If we consider words in isolation, then

> any word for which we can find no corresponding mental picture appears to have no content [*Inhalt*]. But we ought always to keep before our eyes a complete proposition [*Satz*]. Only in a proposition have the words really a meaning. It may be that mental pictures float before us all the while, but these need not correspond to the logical elements in the judgment. It is enough if the proposition taken as a whole has a sense [*Sinn*]; it is this that confers on its parts also their content.[9]

The argumentative context needs clarifying. Frege has argued that numbers are not physical objects or collections, mental objects or operations, nor are they properties of things. A statement of number (a statement as to *how many* of something there are) is an assertion about a concept. Accordingly he offers contextual definitions of numerals as they occur in the context of a statement of number, e.g. "The number 0 belongs to a concept, if the proposition that *a* does not fall under that concept is true universally, whatever *a* may be." Though this is a move in the right direction, it is immediately repudiated on the grounds that it defines (contextually) 'the number ξ belongs to' i.e. a predicative phrase in which a numeral occurs, but it does not define 0, 1, etc. Just because '0' is only an element in the predicative expression, it follows that a number is a self-subsistent object, for numerals are proper names (and so 'stand for' objects), they flank the identity sign (as in '1 + 1 =2'), and although they commonly appear in attributive constructions (e.g. 'Jupiter has 4 moons' or 'The number 4 belongs to the concept Moon of Jupiter') these are, in Frege's view, always eliminable in favour of substantival occurrences. Thus 'Jupiter has 4 moons' = 'The number of Jupiter's moons is four'. The expression on the right of the equivalence is to be taken to be an identity statement and '4' occurs in it substantivally. This too shows numbers to be objects. The initial definition of number as second-order property was further defective in failing to give us criteria of identity to pick out 0 and 1 as 'self-subsistent objects' that can be recognized as the same

9. The last clause reads "*dadurch erhalten auch seine Theile ihren Inhalt.*"

again—a requirement that must be met before any expression can be admitted as a name of an object.

It is in this context that the quoted passage occurs. It is designed to meet the objection that we can form no representation or idea of a number. All this shows, Frege insists, is that numbers are non-sensible, not that they are not objects. In general, we must distinguish meaning or content (which is public and communicable) from ideas (which are private, fleeting, variable). Ideas are irrelevant to meaning. Semantic atomism, he argues in §60, treats all expressions as if (1) they were of the same level, (2) their contribution to the meaning of a sentence were independent of their position within a given logical element of the sentence. But if we advert to the holistic principle it is evident that we must know what the whole proposition is before we can identify the logical elements (the function and argument) and thence identify the role of the problematic word in the logical element of which it is a part. If the sentence as a whole has a meaning, we can determine from this the content of its parts qua contributors to that meaning. That no associated ideas occur is irrelevant.

It is striking that Frege finds himself forced to the position of asserting, "It is enough if the proposition as a whole has a sense; it is this that confers on its parts also their content," a claim he would certainly not have made later. For this accords *priority* to the significance of a sentence which prima facie renders it unintelligible that we can understand new sentences composed of known expressions. Once the sense/reference distinction is drawn the position becomes much clearer. The sense of a sentence is composed of the sense of its parts, and is given by its truth-conditions. The sense of the parts of a sentence consists in their contribution to the sense of the sentence. The spurious priority is replaced by interdependency, as is appropriate for a holistic principle.

The sequel to the passage is also of interest. Frege continues thus:

> The self-subsistence which I am claiming for number is not to be taken to mean that a number word signifies something when removed from the context of a proposition, but only to preclude the use

of such words as predicates or attributes, which appreciably alters their meaning.[10]

There is a worry and a puzzle associated with this passage. The worry is that numerals clearly have an extra-sentential use—to number houses, pages, licences, to mark out distances, to label weights, lengths, prices, to pinpoint target areas on a butt, etc. Did Frege overlook this, or deny that such uses were, in some sense, significant? The issue will be examined in the sequel. The puzzle lies in the last words: does Frege mean that the word 'one' in an attributive position has a different meaning from that which it has in a substantival position? The answer is surely—yes. In Frege's view, implausible though it may be, a numeral in an attributive position contributes to the meaning of a second-level concept-word 'The number ξ belongs to', while in a substantival position it is a proper name.

Having rejected the initial contextual definition of number as a property of concepts, Frege now attempts a contextual definition of number qua object. The problem is stated in terms of the holistic principle at §62:

> How then are numbers to be given to us, if we cannot have any ideas or intuitions of them? Since it is only in the context of a proposition that words have any meaning, our problem becomes this: to define the sense of a proposition in which a number word occurs.

(I.e. occurs substantivally). This leaves a wide choice, but since Frege takes himself to have established that numbers are objects, there can be no doubt in his view that numerical identity statements have a sense. So Frege's task is to define contextually 'the number which belongs to the concept F is the same as that which belongs to the concept G' without using the expression 'the number which belongs to F'. This third invocation of the principle is obviously meant to justify contextual definition. This is confirmed by its final occurrence in

10. This is J. L. Austin's translation. The German runs thus: "*wodurch seine Bedeutung etwas verändert wert,*" which should perhaps be rendered: "by which means their significance is somewhat altered."

the summary §§106–108. It is noteworthy that Frege examines three objections to contextual definitions, and *sustains* the third objection that the definition will not decide for us the truth of identity statements in which one side is filled by the numerical operator 'The number which belongs to the concept F' and the other by a simple name (e.g. 'Julius Caesar'). Frege therefore moves on to an explicit definition in terms of extensions.

What can be concluded from this survey of the *Foundations*? It is disturbing that the principle is never supported by explicit justification, nor is Frege's skimpy elaboration in §60 such as to inspire confidence. It is evident that the application of the principle is wholly consonant with its origin in the mathematical analogy and truth-conditional semantic principle of "Begriffsschrift". The developments are both critical and constructive. Critically the principle is repeatedly invoked to combat psychologism, which is alleged (without explanation) to be a direct consequence of semantic atomism. Constructively the principle is used for three purposes: (1) to give prima facie justification of contextual definition; (2) to give explanatory support to Frege's type-theoretical distinctions between different levels of expressions. The way in which a word contributes to determining the truth-conditions of a sentence will vary according to its mode of occurrence (e.g. substantivally or attributively). Its meaning or content varies accordingly, and it has a meaning only in a sentential context, for outside a sentence it plays no role in fixing truth-conditions of anything; (3) to ensure, together with the third principle, that ambiguous names or vacuous names (i.e. names without meaning) are not introduced by 'transforming a concept into an object' and by disregarding the mode of occurrence of an expression within a sentence. The second constructive purpose is crucial to Frege's general programme of displaying language as a calculus, or *improving* it by reconstructing it as a *perfected* calculus. The sense of every sentence is argued to be derived from the senses of its constituents and their mode of combination as laid down by the type-theoretical combinatorial rules of the calculus of language.

Frege: The Transformation of the Dictum

After the *Foundations of Arithmetic* the holistic principle *seems* to disappear from sight. Dummett argues that the principle

> never reiterated though never repudiated, has no place in Frege's later philosophy, since it accords a distinctive position to sentences which he was no longer prepared to recognize.[11]

Elsewhere Dummett writes:

> It was Frege's adoption of this new doctrine [that sentences are complex names of truth-values] which, presumably, was responsible for the failure of thesis . . . to make a single reappearance in his subsequent writings.[12]

It is, of course, true that Frege's famous essays of the early 1890s involve not only the introduction of the sense/reference distinction, but also the misguided assimilation of sentences to singular referring expressions. However, closer examination reveals that the principle was transformed rather than repudiated, that it does actually occur in subsequent minor writings in very special and highly significant contexts, and that it is quite unaffected both by the assimilation of sentences to proper names and by the later repudiation of 'piecemeal' definition.

The most important advance Frege made after the *Foundations* was the replacement of the undifferentiated notion of content or meaning by the sharper notions of sense and reference. Sense is objective, public, communicable—it is what we grasp when we understand an expression. The sense of an expression determines its reference (together with the facts), but not vice-versa. If two expressions have identical sense, they also have identical reference, but not vice-versa. So they are substitutable *salva significatione* in contexts of identical degree of obliqueness. Sense must be determinate, and definitions complete, i.e. the sense of an expression (that has a *complete* sense) must unambiguously determine a reference. A thought (the sense of a sentence) must be either true or false,

11. Article in *The Encyclopedia of Philosophy*, ed. P. Edwards, entitled "Frege, Gottlob," by M. Dummett, III, 223.
12. Dummett, *Frege: Philosophy of Language*, p. 7.

a proper-name must uniquely identify an object, a concept-word must unambiguously determine, of any object, whether it falls under the concept or not. Otherwise the laws of logic will not apply universally to well-formed sentences. Most important for present concerns is the principle succinctly expressed in the *Basic Laws of Arithmetic* (Vol. I) §32:

> The names, whether simple or themselves composite of which the name of a truth-value consists, contribute to the expression of the thought, and this contribution of the individual [component] is its *sense*. If a name is part of the name of a truth-value, then the sense of the former name is part of the thought expressed by the latter name.

The sense of an expression therefore (taking 'expression' to indicate a logical unit of significance) consists of its contribution to the sense of a sentence (the latter being conceived as the *name* of a truth-value) and thereby of its contribution to determination of its reference (truth-value)—together with the facts. The sense of a sentence is made up, or composed, of the senses of its constituent expressions and is given by its truth-conditions. This principle effectively replaces the dictum 'A word has a meaning only in the context of a sentence' for all expressions that have a sense and a reference. How so?

The sense/reference distinction made it possible to sharpen the holistic insight embodied in the dictum while also avoiding some obvious difficulties. It made it possible to specify the interdependence of the notions of the sense of a sub-sentential expression and the sense of a sentence without wrongly allocating absolute priority to either. We understand sentences by understanding the senses of their constituent logical elements, yet what we know when we know the sense of a sentence are the conditions under which it is true and the conditions under which it is false. We grasp the sense of a sub-sentential element when we know the means whereby it determines a reference—but to know that is to know how the element contributes to determination of the truth-conditions of a sentence in which it occurs. To the extent that Frege's theory of sense implies a 'theory of understanding', then his holism and the calculus model of language imply that every well-formed sentence will be understood by anyone who understands its constituents and its structure.

The new notion of sense is explicitly invoked, like the holistic principle of the *Foundations,* to combat psychologism. Sense, unlike subjective representations, is public, communicable, and fixed. Colouring, sense, and reference are the business of a theory of meaning, ideas are not. The holistic principle gave hazy and tentative backing to Frege's distinctions between different logical types of expression—the holistic conception of sense fulfils this task more satisfactorily. The sense of a proper name determines its reference, to know its sense is to know the criterion for identifying an object as its referent. The sense of a concept-word fixes a concept as its referent and to know its sense is to know the criterion for deciding whether it applies to an arbitrary object. The distinction between object and concept is considerably sharpened. But it can no longer be invoked to warn against introducing 'meaningless' proper names. For now 'transforming a concept into an object' by affixing a definite article to a concept-word under which nothing falls will not be said to yield a name which lacks meaning or content, but rather a name which has sense but no reference. An ideal calculus of language will make this impossible. The holistic dictum was rooted in the functional analogy and truth-conditional principle that dominate Frege's philosophy of language. Neither analogy nor principle are in any way relinquished. Nor does the introduction of the notion of sense in any way weaken them. On the contrary it renders them more intelligible.

For the mathematical analogy which lies at the foundation of Frege's logical notation and philosophy of language determines an extensional semantics. Given an 'interpretation', an assignment of reference to all the primitive non-logical expressions, together with formation rules, the truth-conditions of all well-formed sentences will be determined. But this type of formal semantics is in no sense an account of meaning. The meaning of an expression, as Wittgenstein laboured to show with exhaustive detail, is not the object or entity for which a word stands (if, indeed, it stands for anything). Knowing the meaning of an expression is not a matter of simply associating a word with an object, and understanding an expression or sentence is not a matter of knowing a mysterious relation between an expression or sentence and an object. It is the introduction of the distinction between sense and reference, and the elaboration of the notion of sense as determinant of reference, that renders Frege's account a theory of meaning at all. Transformation of the holistic principle into a holistic conception of sense, and grafting the latter upon the type-theoretical account of the logical syntax of language immensely strengthens Frege's philosophy of language. To be sure, the dictum was employed in the *Foundations* to justify contextual definition, and Frege, in his later work, insists upon explicit definition. But since even in the *Foundations* contextual definition of numbers was ultimately rejected (on *fairly general* grounds) this is not to the point. Whatever inadequacies contextual definition may suffer from, this will not affect the validity of the dictum, nor of its transformation into the principle that the sense of an expression consists in its contribution to determining the truth-conditions of a sentence.

Dummett repeatedly insists that assimilation of sentences to proper names forces Frege to abandon the principle, since sentences are no longer accorded a unique position in Frege's semantics. Had Frege originally based the holistic principle upon considerations of speech and communication, then assimilating sentences to names would force abandonment of the principle since names have no unique position in acts of speech and communication. Had Frege argued, as Wittgenstein subsequently did, that the sentence is the minimal unit of communication, the elementary unit of language with which something is *said*, then assimilation of sentences to names (which cannot be used to *say* anything) would render it wholly obscure why the meaning of a word consists in its contribution to the meaning of just these kinds of complex names of truth-values rather than other complex names. But Frege's holistic principle was based upon the insight that the sentence is the sole bearer of truth-value (which is the value to be preserved through inference by the laws of logic, principles of valid inference), that the meaning of a sentence is given by its truth-conditions, and that the structure of a sentence splits up into function-name and argument expression. To be sure, the sentence is also what is *asserted* or judged, the thought is the content of judgement. But this is so because the sentence is the vehicle of truth, and we happen to go in for judging what is (or is taken to be) true. What is important and relevant about judgement, for Frege, is the extent to which contents of judgment affect possible inferences. Even in "Begriffsschrift" the nexus between judgment and content is external, assertability does not affect meaning. The failure to draw an adequate connection between judgment and content is a worrying lacuna in "Begriffsschrift," which *might* have been filled in by later developments. But this was not to be.

Conceiving of a sentence as a complex proper name is a retrograde step. But it does not affect the principle that the sense of an expression consists in its contribution to the sense of a sentence, which principle is the direct descendant of the holistic principle of the *Foundations*. What becomes completely obscure is the already weak connection between the bearers of, i.e. the complex names of, truth-values—and assertion. The connection between sentence and speech, in particular assertion, becomes *unintelligible*. By assimilating sentences to names it becomes *impossible* to fill in the lacuna in the skimpy account in "Begriffsschrift." Why we *assert* just these kinds of names and not others, why we cannot assert other kinds of complex names of truth-values (e.g. 'What Pontius Pilate wanted to have defined') let alone other names, why assertion has a peculiar connection with truth (and not falsehood—or indeed any other 'object' such as beauty, or the Koh-i-Noor), and indeed what it is to assert something, it is these issues which are rendered insoluble by the misguided assimilation of sentences to names of truth-values. But *just because* the holistic principle was *not derived* from consideration of the role of sentences in speech (but rather in inference) it was unaffected *at this level*—by the assimilation. The difficulties are deeper, and the assimilation places intolerable pressure at even more fundamental levels than that of the holistic principle.

This interpretation is supported by the fact that, contrary to Dummett's contention, the principle does reappear in Frege's writings after 1884. It occurs in the polemical debate with Hilbert in the first decade of the century. Two of the four relevant passages are worth quoting.[13]

(1) It is absolutely essential for the rigour of mathematical investigations that the difference between definitions and all other propositions be maintained throughout in all its sharpness. The other propositions (axioms, principles, theorems) must contain no word (sign) whose *sense and reference or* (in the case of form words, letters in formulae) *whose contribution to the expression of the thought is not already completely settled,* so that there is no doubt about the sense of the proposition [*Satz*]—about the thought expressed in it.[14]

(2) These letters [in algebraic formulae] are of a nature completely different from that of the number signs '2', '3', etc., or the relation signs '=', '>'. They are not at all intended to designate numbers, concepts, relations, or some function or other; rather, they are intended only to indicate so as to lend generality of content to the propositions in which they occur. Thus *it is only in the context of a proposition that they have a certain task to fulfil, that they contribute to the expression of the thought. But outside of this context they say nothing.*[15]

The italicized disjunction in (1) is noteworthy. If the sense of a sentence is to be determinate then either the sense and reference, or the general contribution to the sense of the sentence, must be fixed. Since the sense of a word *is* its contribution to the sense of a sentence, the disjunction may appear pleonastic. But it is not—for what Frege is emphasizing is that variable letters in algebraic notation do not have a sense or reference. The significance of 'a' in '(a + b) × c = a × c + b × c' can be seen only in the context of the general proposition in which it occurs. The sense of an expression is what determines its reference, contributes to the sense of any sentence in which it occurs by determining its truth-conditions which in turn determine its reference. Where the sense/reference distinction

13. The other two are on pages 23, footnote 2, and 53 of Kluge's edition of Frege's *On the Foundations of Geometry*.

14. Ibid., p. 8 (letter to Hilbert, date missing), my italics.

15. Ibid., p. 67 (written in 1906) my italics.

cannot get a grip, to ask for the meaning of an expression is not to ask for the means whereby it determines a reference, thereby partly determining the reference of any sentence in which it occurs. It is to ask for its role in determining the sense of the sentence in which it occurs, other than by way of determining its own reference, for it has no reference. But its role in fixing the truth-conditions of a formula can be specified.

These passages confirm the conjecture that Frege's holistic principle was transformed and sharpened, not relinquished, and that it was unaffected by the disastrous assimilation of sentences to names.

Wittgenstein: The *Tractatus*

Frege's dictum occurs in various formulations in the *Tractatus*. At 3.3 Wittgenstein writes, "Only propositions have sense; only in the context of a proposition does a name have a meaning (*Bedeutung*)." At 3.314 he adds, "An expression has meaning only in a proposition," and at 4.23, "It is only in the context of an elementary proposition that a name occurs in a proposition." The notebooks from which these remarks are taken no longer exist.[16] Nevertheless it is evident that the dictum is derived from Frege. For all that, it is put to use in novel ways. Wittgenstein accepted Frege's terminology of '*Sinn*' and '*Bedeutung*', but understood the notions differently and propounded quite different theses concerning sense and *Bedeutung*. Sentences have a sense, given by specification of their truth-conditions, but they do not have a reference. Nor are they a kind of name. Names, logically proper names, have a *Bedeutung* but no sense. Their having the *Bedeutung* they have is not a matter of their sense determining a reference, but a matter of a psychological correlation of name and metaphysical simple. But names do have a form—determined by the combinatorial rules of logical syntax, and only qua possessor of a given syntactical form can they stand for the type of object for which they do stand. Wittgenstein's commitment to Frege's

16. Although the principle occurs in the early writings, e.g. "Notes on Logic" (1913), App. I to *Notebooks 1914–1916* (Oxford: Basil Blackwell, 1961; New York: Harper & Row, 1969), pp. 98f.

calculus conception of language is whole-hearted, with one crucial difference. Where the fragmentary and skeletal calculus Frege constructed was conceived as an *improvement* over natural language with all its logical defects, Wittgenstein insisted that natural language *is* a calculus which is in *perfectly good order just as it is* (although that order is concealed by a confusing outward clothing).

The holistic principle is thoroughly integrated into the picture conception of language with its bizarre theory of isomorphism. The syntactical form of a name mirrors the logical form of an object. Just as names are significant, have a meaning, only in the context of a proposition, so too objects exist only concatenated in facts. There is no such thing as an object which is not an element of a fact, so too there are no meaningful names which are not elements of sentences with a sense. Parallel to sentences—the units of sense—are states of affairs—which are what can exist or fail to exist. A sentence itself is a fact—for *only* facts can express a sense. The sense of a sentence is given by its truth-conditions. If they are satisfied in the world then the state of affairs described by the sentence obtains.

The sole rationale for the principle that a name has a *Bedeutung* only in the context of a sentence occurs in a passage in the *Prototractatus*. It is, unfortunately, too obscure to offer much guidance. Wittgenstein is arguing for the principle that every possible combination of objects is necessarily possible. He moves abruptly from the metaphysical to the grammatical level:

> What this comes to is that if it were the case that names had meaning both when combined *in* propositions and outside them, it would, so to speak, be impossible to guarantee that in both cases they really had the same meaning, in the same sense of the word.
>
> It seems impossible for words to appear in two different roles: by themselves, and in propositions [*PTLP* 2.0122].

I do not know what these enigmatic remarks amount to. Prima facie Wittgenstein's thought seems to be guided by the notions of logical form —given by syntax, sense—given by truth-conditions, and meaning—determined by some method of projection. The sense of a sentence is a function of the *Bedeutungen* of its constituent names. The role of a name in a sentence is to contribute to determination of its truth-conditions. Outside the context of a sentence it has no such role. So it can no more be said to have a meaning outside a sentence than an ink bottle can, even though the fact that the ink bottle is on the table might be used to signify that I am at home. It is only in use that a sign is a symbol (*TLP* 3.326–3.327).

Thus far the differences between Frege and Wittgenstein do not turn on the nature and rationale of the holistic dictum itself, but upon circumambient matters. Did Wittgenstein, at this stage, add anything to Frege's discussion? One matter, much discussed in recent years, appears explicitly in the *Tractatus* but was at best implicit in Frege's writings. This is the application of the holistic principle to explain the 'creative powers' of language and language users. The issue is discussed at 4.02–4.03. To understand a proposition is to know its truth-conditions, and it is understood if one understands its constituents. It is of the essence of a proposition that it can convey a new sense by a structure utilizing old expressions. The meaning of the (elementary) constituents must be explained to us, but once that is grasped, the sense of sentences constructed from them will be understood without further ado. Wittgenstein is manifestly committed to the view that understanding any sentence of a language consists in knowing its constituents and the combinatorial rules of the calculus of language (to be sure, understanding is a mystery carried out in the remarkable medium of the mind—and the 'theory of understanding' is a task for some future science of the mind). The ability acquired when the meanings of names are grasped is not distinct from the ability to construct, out of those names, sentences with a new sense. Here we do, indeed, move to a central element of the holistic principle. It would be quite misguided, as already intimated above, to interpret the principle as assigning primacy to sentence meaning,[17] just be-

17. Cf. W.F. Quine, "Two Dogmas of Empiricism," in *From a Logical Point of View* (Cambridge, Mass.: Harvard University Press, 1953), p. 39, discussed by M. Dummett, "Nominalism," p. 492.

cause this would render unintelligible our ability to construct and understand new sentences. Conversely, semantic atomism is unintelligible just because it assumes that understanding the meanings of words is a distinct and independent ability from understanding sentences, that it is at least intelligible that one should know what the words of a language mean, but not know how to construct sentences out of them. This is analogous to knowing what the chess pieces are *called*, but not knowing their powers. But the analogy for knowing the meaning of a word is knowing how to *move* the chess pieces, and to know how to move the pieces *is* to know how to play chess, just as to know the meanings of the words of a language is to know how to *speak*.

This insight, perhaps tacit in Frege, was explicit in the *Tractatus*. But it was not to come to fruition until later (the above analogy with chess, of course, comes from Wittgenstein's later work). For it is only in the post-*Tractatus* period that Wittgenstein realizes the centrality, for a philosophical account of meaning, of notions such as understanding, speech, and communication. And it is only then that the rationale for the dictum shifts away from its Fregean foundations in the calculus model, the truth-conditional principle, and mathematical analogy, to the more fundamental grounds of understanding, speech and communication.

Wittgenstein: The Post-1929 Writings—the Repudiation of Frege

In his lectures between 1930 and 1933 Wittgenstein remarked that the Fregean holistic dictum "is true or false as you understand it."[18] The principle is discussed in the *Philosophical Remarks*, the "Big Typescript," *Philosophical Grammar*, *The Blue Book*, and mentioned approvingly in the *Investigations*. This preoccupation with the principle is significant for it suggests that Wittgenstein's understanding of it evolved,

18. "Wittgenstein's Lectures in 1930–33," in G. E. Moore, *Philosophical Papers* (London: George Allen & Unwin, 1959; New York: Collier Books, 1962), p. 261.

that its rationale and consequences needed rethinking, that the place of the principle in the philosophy of language had not, initially, been correctly located.

This should not be surprising, for the Fregean foundations for the principle are either repudiated or shifted. First, the functional, mathematical, analogy—so crucial to Frege's philosophy of language—was rejected as completely misleading. The argument/function structure which Frege claimed to be "founded deep in the nature of things"[19] is in fact a *sublimation* or *abstraction* from the subject/predicate form in grammar, as the notion of point-mass in physics is of a material object (*PR,* pp. 119ff; *PG,* pp. 202ff). Secondly, the distinction between object and concept *is* the distinction, duly refined, between subject and predicate. Yet, in the first place, the subject/predicate form is what we map reality onto, it is a norm of representation, a mould into which we squeeze the proposition. Moreover, being a norm of representation it conceals countless different logical forms; the uniformity of form of representation conceals the diversity of methods of projection. It is analogous to the case of projecting different geometrical figures from one plane to another with the convention that only circles should occur on the second plane. In this case it is the diversity of the methods of projection which will illuminate the nature of the figures on the first plane, not the circularity of the figures onto which they are mapped. The 'part of speech' which characterizes an expression is determined by *all* the rules for its use, and the ability to occur in the subject position is only one. Hence Frege's 'concept' and 'object' are not discoveries, not results of 'analysis' but a projection of grammatical moulds. Thirdly, the Fregean use of 'object' is aberrant. To say that the simultaneous occurrence of an eclipse of the moon and a court case is an *object* is misguided (*PR,* p. 137). Fourthly, Frege construes a concept as a sort of property, but is is unnatural to construe sortal nouns as names of pro-

19. Frege, "Function and Concept," in *Translations from the Philosophical Writings of Gottlob Frege,* p. 41.

perties of a substratum. An object can be conceived as bearer of a colour, a lump of clay as bearer of a shape, but how are we to conceive of a red circle if both colour and shape change? (*PR*, p. 120). 'The lump (of clay) changes its shape', and 'The patch changes its shape', are both subject/predicate sentences, but of completely different logical form. Fifthly, the Fregean (and *Tractatus*) conception of the sentence as *necessarily* complex or articulated is repudiated. In the above cited lectures Wittgenstein claimed that a sentence can be replaced by a simple sign if the simple sign is 'part of a system'. In the *Investigations* (*PI* §§19ff.) he examines the possibility of imaginary languages in which symbols satisfy the criteria for word and sentence alike, and again in §49 he argues that a symbol may be used now as a name, now as a description—a proposition. Sixthly, the functional analogy led Frege and the author of the *Tractatus* to a misguided analysis of quantifiers as logical sums or products, whereas generality is as ambiguous as the subject/predicate form (*PG*, p. 269). There are as many meanings of 'some' and 'all' as there are proofs, grounds for assertion, of existence or generalization. Finally, the calculus model of language that lies at the heart of Frege's semantics and its *Tractatus* development is adamantly rejected. The classical holistic conception generates an unbridgeable gulf between our actual practices of explaining meaning and the alleged determination of meaning by the axioms, formation, and transformation rules of language conceived as a calculus. If meaning is what is given by our explanation of meaning then it is false that *every* sentence has its meaning determined by its parts and structure (although it may be possible to reconstruct it thus). Similarly, in the absence of a rich theory of categories, classical holism allows the construction of indefinitely many sentences which, by our ordinary criteria of meaning and understanding, are nonsensical (see below). But such a theory of categories is chimerical. Classical holism sublimated and idealized the systematic character of language out of all recognition.

Each of these claims stands in need of thorough examination. This cannot be done here—all that is necessary for present purposes is to establish the point that Wittgenstein's holism is neither dependent upon, nor gives support to, the Fregean conception of the functional structure of language. However, it is not this alone that is being repudiated. For it is no part of Wittgenstein's conception of language that the notion of truth-conditions plays the pivotal role in a general account of meaning. In the first place identity of truth-conditions does not ensure identity of meaning (*BBB*, p. 115), what is requisite is identity of use. Secondly, Frege's truth-conditional principle involved a transcendent conception of truth. On his conception of sense it is intelligible that we should grasp the sense of a sentence, know its truth-conditions, and yet it be wholly impossible to specify what would count as determining the sentence to be true. For Frege sense is one thing, how we know a thought to be true quite another—and the latter is irrelevant to the former. For Wittgenstein, by contrast, what verifies a sentence is part of its grammar. We cannot grasp what it is for a sentence to be true independently of grasping a means of establishing it to be true. Thirdly, Frege's insistence on definition of complex concept-words by *Merkmale* is repudiated by Wittgenstein's stress upon family-resemblance concept-words. But the former just is the truth-conditional principle relativized to complex concept-words. Fourthly, the claim that the sense of a sentence is given by its truth-conditions yields a wholly trivial explanation of the sense of elementary sentences containing simple predicates. For Wittgenstein explanations of meaning cannot be trivial, for they provide the grammar of the expression explained, the rules for its use. This applies both to physical object statements such as 'A is red' which are criterionlessly assertable and to psychological statements such as 'X is in pain'. In the former case the explanation of meaning involves ostensive definition by reference to samples, in the latter behavioural criteria. Fifthly, Frege never extended his analysis to moods other than the assertoric and interrogative. Maybe it can be stretched to cover imperatives—but undoubtedly the meaning of imperatives would have to be explained by reference to that of the corresponding assertoric sentence. Wittgenstein frequently insists upon the intelligibility of a language consisting only of commands, and here, presumably, the meanings of such sentences could not be thus explained.

Again, to be sure, each of these issues requires lengthy elaboration to carry conviction against the conventional philosophical wisdom derived from Frege. All that is established is that Wittgenstein's holism cannot rest on the same foundations as Frege's. A final fundamental difference between the two philosophers turns on the matter of assertion. Wittgenstein's main critical contentions are two. Firstly, the assertion sign in Frege's analysis is the external mark of an internal, psychological act—an act of judgement. So an assertion must consist of two actions, entertaining a thought, and expressing one's judgement that it is true. Wittgenstein repudiates this: we do not determine whether something is asserted by checking to see whether the utterance was accompanied by an experience, as if, were we to discover the absence of the relevant experience, we would be confronted only with a supposal. Secondly, Wittgenstein emphasizes the point previously mentioned and indeed implicit in the first criticism, namely that assertion, for Frege, is something that gets added to the thought. So there is no internal relation between the sense of a sentence and its assertability, or more generally, between its meaning and its use. One can thus have a complete grasp of the sense of a sentence, but no idea what to do with it. For Wittgenstein, by contrast, assertion is "not something that gets added to the proposition, but an essential feature of the game we play with it. Comparable, say, to that characteristic of chess by which there is winning and losing in it, the winner being the one who takes the other's king" (*RFM*, p. 49). To be sure, this does not mean that the assertion sign can have no role. It can function as a punctuation mark, signifying the beginning of a sentence, and it can mark the difference between a declarative sentence and a sentence question (*PI* §22).

Wittgenstein: The Post-1929 Writings—the Foundations of His Holism

The holistic dictum is "true or false as you understand it."

We can envisage a language in which the word/sentence distinction cannot be drawn—or rather, in which symbols in use satisfy the criteria for being a sentence and for being a word. There can be non-complex, one-word sentences which are not elliptical (*PI* §§19f). And, of course, it is manifestly false that there are no significant extra-sentential uses of words in our language. How then is the dictum to be understood as true?

Given a language in which we can contrast word and sentence (as well as one-word sentences conceived as elliptical), the sentence is—over a vast range of speech activities—the minimal unit by which a move is made in the language-game. It is only with sentences that we actually *say* anything. Understanding a sentence is knowing what it *says*, and understanding begins with the whole sentence (*PG*, p. 44). There are no 'half propositions' (*Satz*)—half a sentence (*Satz*), like a word, has a meaning only in the context of a whole sentence ("BT", p. 1). Half a proposition does not stand to a proposition as half a bread-roll to a bread-roll, but as a 'half a knight's move' to a knight's move, and there is no such thing as 'half a knight's move' (*PG*, p. 39); but it by no means follows that the meaning of every sentence is explained by explaining the meaning of its constituents and its structure. The vast range of our speech activities are reported by propositional verbs which are operators on *sentences*. The sentence is, in general, the unit of communication—the 'integer of speech' as Bentham called it.[20] This elementary insight, this truism, which, to be sure, has exceptions, has wide ramifications.

First, it follows that in one sense *a sentence* has no meaning in isolation. A sentence is akin to a move in chess, and a move is only a move in the context of the game. Understanding a language is the background against which a sentence acquires meaning, as understanding chess is for a move. A sentence belongs to a language, and it is units of language we call sentences. A sentence, Wittgenstein insists, is a position in the game of language (*PG*, p. 172), hence to understand a sentence is to understand a language (*BBB*, p. 5; *PI* §199). This

20. J. Bentham, *Works*, ed. J. Bowring (Edinburgh: Tate, 1843), p. 188.

contention can be taken in two ways, absurdly or sensibly. Absurdly, it could be taken to imply that one cannot fully understand any sentence without understanding the entire language to which it belongs. This flies in the face of obvious facts. It is not necessary, in order to be justified in saying of a speaker (whether child or foreigner) that he understands, can speak English, that he understand every single sentence of English. Likewise this interpretation is tantamount to denying that language consists of hierarchical structures the understanding of the 'superior' elements of which presupposes a prior understanding of the 'inferior' or more primitive elements, but not vice-versa. It is reasonable to argue (and Wittgenstein does argue) that the concept-word forming operators on concept-words 'appears', 'seems', 'looks', presuppose a prior understanding of the 'base' concepts upon which they operate. It is absurd to argue that an understanding of, e.g. 'red' or 'square' or 'hot' presupposes an understanding of 'looks red', 'seems square', 'appears hot'. So too for more complex operators such as predicate-forming operators on sentences, e.g. 'believes that', 'wonders whether', 'conjectures that'. One would not want to deny a child an understanding of 'the cat is on the mat' on the grounds that it does not understand the sentence 'He conjectures that the cat is on the mat'.

Taken sensibly the dictum 'to understand a sentence is to understand a language', is a consequence of the holistic principle hitherto discussed, and is indeed implicit in Frege. The understanding of one sentence is not independent of the understanding of other similar sentences. A person may know that a string of Chinese symbols is a sentence, and may know, parrotwise, that that particular string means such and-such. For all that we may deny that he *understands* that sentence, even though he knows what it means. For to understand a given sentence requires that one understand many similar sentences of the same, and inferior, 'levels' within the language hierarchy. How extensive the fragment of language which must be mastered before one may say of a person that he understands a given sentence will depend upon the complexity and 'level' of that sentence. It will also, undoubtedly, be only vaguely circumscribed. The mastery of abilities in general, as well as of linguistic abilities, is a matter of degree.

This moderate holism is common to both Frege and Wittgenstein. But in Wittgenstein it rests on different foundations. Moreover it ramifies in different directions precisely because Wittgenstein's account of what understanding a sentence consists in differs fundamentally from Frege's.

If a sentence is analogous to a move in chess, a word is analogous to a chess piece with its powers (*PG*, p. 121; *PR*, p. 61). To know the meaning of a word is like knowing the powers of a chess piece, it is knowing how to do something with it, how to use it in sentences to say something. Knowing the meaning of a word, understanding a word, is akin to an ability, an ability to use the word correctly and also to explain it correctly. The criteria for whether a person knows the meaning of a word include his using the word *in sentences* to make a 'move in the language-game' as well as his responding appropriately to others' uses. They also include giving correct explanations of the word (since meaning is what is given by explanations of meaning [*PG*, pp. 59f., 68f.]) and, other things being equal, of *sentences* in which it occurs.

The Fregean holistic dictum, Wittgenstein wrote (*PR*, p. 58), amounts to the claim that it is only in a sentence that a word functions as a word, as a cog functions as a cog only in a machine. But the capacity of a cog-wheel so to function lies in its physical shape. The capacity of a word to function as a word lies in the rules for its use, its combinatorial possibilities, and its contribution to the conditions for the use of sentences in which it is embedded. Some combinations of words are clearly nonsensical, e.g. 'is has good'. Others 'sound right', but are illegitimate, because the particular combination yields no specifiable conditions which would justify asserting such a combination. No stipulation has been made about how the sentence 'I'm cutting red into pieces' or 'I feel in my hand that the water is three feet underground' (*PG*, pp. 126f.; *BBB*, p. 9) is to be used. We know what a word means in *certain contexts*, but not in these. For these combinations of words yield no circumstances which would justify their assertion, no conditions which would verify these apparent propositions. So they are senseless. Where Frege would countenance indefinitely many syntactically acceptable sentences as having a sense (e.g. 'I am cutting red into pieces' is true if and only if I am cutting red into pieces), Wittgenstein draws the bounds of sense much more restrictively. An 'hypothesis' that transcends all possible experience is not backed by meaning (*BBB*, p. 48), and unless we know what experience, what cognizable circumstances, would support the assertion of such a sentence, we have no use for it. For no application has been fixed. Indeed the very phrase "to transcend any possible experience" seems to make sense only because it is constructed on the analogy of meaningful expressions (*Z* §260). Yet Frege's severance of meaning from conditions of possible cognition implies that the bounds of sense can far outstrip the limits of possible knowledge.

Of course, as emphasized previously, there are many meaningful extra-sentential uses of words in our language. There is no difficulty budgeting for this. For such uses of words are not independent of their use *in sentences*. 'Sodium Chloride' on a labelled container names the contents whereas 'shake well' does not because of the way in which 'sodium chloride' is used in sentences. Numerals are used on pages, licences, houses, but these uses are not independent of their use in sentences. Exclamations, with their wide range of different uses (*PI* §27), have the distinctive roles in language which they do because of the conventions determining what is done by uttering them. Sometimes this is related to sentential uses ('Water!'), sometimes not ('Ow!', 'Hurrah!', 'Aha!')—but the employment of these terms is rule-governed, and to know their significance is to know the appropriate conditions for their use.

Conclusion

Knowing the meanings of words, understanding sentences, speaking a language are different facets of one vastly complex human ability to engage in the rule-governed activity of speech. Word-meaning and sentence-meaning are coordinate—

to assign absolute priority to the one or the other would vitiate the holism which was one of Frege's, and Wittgenstein's, primary insights. We may claim, as Dummett does,[21] that words are primary in the order of recognition and sentences primary in the order of explanation. But this is precisely to affirm the interdependency of word- and sentence-meaning.

Today, almost a century after Frege's *Foundations* and a quarter of a century after the *Investigations*, the holistic dictum appears so obvious as to be hardly worth mentioning. It is salutary to remember for how many generations of philosophers the obvious was not evident. Moreover, if the principle is taken as obvious, we will not stop to enquire after its rationale, and we will not stop short of subliming the principle to meet the illusory demands of the calculus picture of language. Hence we will not appreciate that in its initial emergence, in the works of Frege, it was flawed. Similarly, if we take the principle to be a truism we will not see the different ways in which it can be built into such totally distinct conceptions of language as Frege's and the later Wittgenstein's. Just how different these are, and just how extensive are the ramifications of locating the holistic principle on a different shelf in the philosophical archives (cf. *BBB*, p. 44) is a very long story, which will be told elsewhere.[22]

21. Dummett, *Frege: Philosophy of Language*, p.4.

22. This theme is developed at length in G. P. Baker and P. M. S. Hacker, *Wittgenstein: Understanding and Meaning*, Volume 1 of an analytical commentary on the *Philosophical Investigations* (forthcoming).

9 *Verehrung und Verkehrung:* Waismann and Wittgenstein

GORDON P. BAKER

In this essay I shall assess the philosophical influence of Wittgenstein on Friedrich Waismann. It is enormous, direct, and very visible in Waismann's published works. Much of it is explicitly acknowledged. On the other hand, its exact form and its extent are not correctly understood. In particular, Waismann's book *Logik, Sprache, Philosophie* (published in English under the title *Principles of Linguistic Philosophy*)[1] is not widely understood to be the culmination of a lengthy period of collaboration with Wittgenstein during which Waismann's principal aim was to produce a systematic presentation of Wittgenstein's philosophy. Because of the crucial position of this book in assessing Wittgenstein's influence on Waismann, much of the discussion will be focused on it.

It would be desirable also to assess the extent and nature of Waismann's influence on Wittgenstein. This will not be attempted here. Although it is plausible to conjecture that there was some such influence, it is difficult to establish and was never acknowledged by Wittgenstein himself. Its most important form is perhaps the least visible, the impact of Waismann's attempt to weld together into a systematic whole the material from typescripts and conversations with Wittgenstein. This can hardly have failed to concentrate Wittgenstein's attention on points where arguments needed to be filled out and inconsistencies removed. Waismann's systematization of Wittgenstein's thoughts must have been an important stimu-

1. *Logik, Sprache, Philosophie*, eds. G. P. Baker, B. F. McGuinness, and J. Schulte (Stuttgart: Reclam, 1976); *Principles of Linguistic Philosophy*, ed. R. Harré (London: Macmillan, 1965).

lus to their further development. This was what Waismann himself saw as his distinctive contribution to his collaboration with Wittgenstein:

> And how much I contributed on my own [to *LSP*]—in particular, how I have, by dint of arduous work, constructed an orderly whole out of his countless thoughts that in his own work form a chaotic muddle—Wittgenstein does not know and probably never will know, since he says himself that he is quite unable to read any philosophy, even his own writings.[2]

Since Wittgenstein's work always required a source of negative entropy in order to progress, it might be Waismann's work on *LSP* that made possible the rapid evolution in Wittgenstein's thinking over the period 1928–1935. Irremediable ignorance about the content of their conversations makes it impossible to find any detailed confirmation of this conjecture. Waismann may also have made more localized contributions to Wittgenstein's work, e.g. in the philosophy of mathematics.

There are various reasons why it is important to have a correct assessment of Wittgenstein's influence on Waismann's work. First, to straighten out some issues in the history of ideas. One of these is the influence of Wittgenstein on the Vienna Circle. There is a deep-rooted reluctance to acknowledge the extent to which logical positivism was inspired and guided by ideas derived from Wittgenstein's contemporary thinking. This was well-known to the members of the Circle (and resented by some of them). Yet it comes as a surprise, indeed a shock, to many present-day philosophers to be

2. "Und was ich alles aus eigenem hinzugefügt habe, vor allem, wie ich aus seinen zahllosen Gedanken, die ja bei ihm ein chaotisches Durcheinander bilden, in mühevoller Arbeit ein geordnetes Ganzes aufgebaut habe, weiss Wittgenstein nicht und wird es wahrscheinlich auch nie wissen, da er sich für ganz ausserstande erklärt etwas Philosophisches zu lesen, auch seine eigenen Manuskripte" (letter to Carnap, 4 March 1937; all translations in this essay are my own). The letters from Waismann to Carnap, and those from Neurath, Schlick, and Springer Verlag to Waismann are among Waismann's papers in the Bodleian Library, Oxford. The letters from Waismann and Wittgenstein to Schlick, and the letter from Schlick to W. Köhler are in the Vienna Circle Archive at the Institute for Foundational Research in Amsterdam (directed by Dr. H. Mulder).

reminded that the principle of verification is rightly to be called *'Wittgenstein's* principle of verification'.[3] It did not stem from the *Tractatus*, but from Wittgenstein's conversations with Waismann, Carnap, and Schlick in 1928–1929. Waismann was the person who first applied it within the work of the Vienna Circle and first published it to the world at large. Another similar task is to clarify the place of Waismann's book *LSP* in the literature of philosophy. It is commonly treated, and even misrepresented in the preface to the English text, as derivative from Wittgenstein's *Philosophical Investigations*. This is demonstrably false. It is derived rather from earlier typescripts and conversations. Wittgenstein had broken off real philosophical contact with Waismann before he began to work on the *Investigations* late in 1936. Although Waismann read the 1937 typescript of the *Investigations* sometime in the academic year 1938–1939, most of the text of *LSP* was already in its final form by then and hence unaffected by his reading this typescript. In any case, what Waismann read was only a fragment of the published version (roughly identical with §§1–189), and it is most unlikely that he saw the rest of the *Investigations* before its posthumous publication. Even without the use of external evidence, this could be confirmed by close analysis of the text of *LSP*, especially by observing that it lacks the arguments that distinguish the *Investigations* from Wittgenstein's earlier, relatively polished works (especially *The Blue and Brown Books* and the "Big Typescript" [TS 213]).

Recognition of Wittgenstein's influence on Waismann's work has great importance for the study of Wittgenstein. A careful use of Waismann's writings, particularly *LSP*, throws light on the development of Wittgenstein's own thinking. For Waismann was an independent, close, and well-informed witness of these changes. When used with caution, Waismann's work can also be used to clarify the interpretation of disputed and obscure remarks in Wittgenstein's writings. But the most important moral for scholars is the most general: Wittgen-

3. It is so described by Rudolf Carnap in his "Intellectual Autobiography" in P. Schilpp, ed., *The Philosophy of Rudolf Carnap* (La Salle, Ill.; Open Court; London: Cambridge University Press, 1963), p. 57.

stein's collaboration over a period of years on a project to give a systematic presentation of his thinking puts it beyond doubt that his polemics against philosophical theorizing cannot be interpreted as opposition to systematic philosophizing. If his view had been (as it is often claimed) that philosophy consists of a miscellany of conceptual therapies with no internal connections with each other, he could not have taken any part in an attempt to mold his philosophical remarks into a systematic framework. Yet he did take part in this project at the very same time that he was writing some of his notorious attacks on philosophical theorizing ("BT," §§86–93). This is conclusive proof that it cannot be mistaken in principle to try to fit Wittgenstein's remarks together into a philosophical system even though it is something that he never succeeded in doing to his own satisfaction. Other aspects of Waismann's work support the same conclusion. An example is Wittgenstein's early application (later repudiated) of the principle of verification, not only to empirical statements, but also to mathematical propositions, apparently on the assumption that any acceptable theory of meaning must be completely general or comprehensive. The effects on Wittgensteinian scholarship of recognizing the degree of Wittgenstein's influence on Waismann may be very far-reaching as well as quite specific.

Finally, recognition of Wittgenstein's influence on Waismann gives the possibility of two complementary forms of philosophical clarification. On the one hand, one can directly connect remarks in Waismann's writings with problems and solutions discussed by Wittgenstein, and this sometimes makes an important contribution to understanding the issues involved. Examples might be found in Waismann's discussion of whether nicknames of a person have the same meaning as his 'proper' proper name; in his analysis of the logic of questions; and in his introducing the notion of a sentence-radicle in connection with the distinction between rules and normative statements, not in connection with speech-acts. One might even treat the text of *LSP* as the most complete realization of Wittgenstein's attempt to produce a 'philosophical grammar'. It is derived largely from the same material as the book published under the title *Philo-*

sophical Grammar, but its systematic format and the range of issues it discusses give it a much clearer claim to this title than the actual titleholder. On the other side, developments that are associated with Waismann can be shown to have a wider philosophical context that is decisive for their correct appreciation. This is particularly clear for the concepts of open texture and language-strata. Both grew out of Wittgenstein's concept of hypothesis and the theory of meaning that he elaborated on this basis. It is doubtful whether either of them makes sense, or has any viability, independent of this foundation. This has seldom been recognized.

In the next section, I describe the nature and extent of Wittgenstein's collaboration with Waismann. In the subsequent two sections, I give more detailed information about the composition of *LSP,* and then analyze the accuracy of Waismann's representation of Wittgenstein's ideas. At the end of the paper I summarize my findings and draw some morals for scholars of Wittgenstein.

Verehrung

In the center of the group of philosophers known as the Vienna Circle stood Schlick. His influence was decisive in the formation of the group. He guided the direction of its discussions and its development. And as chairman of its meetings he not only exercised some control over discussions, but also fostered a spirit of cooperation that made the work of the Circle the consuming interest of most of its members. Waismann was one of its active younger members. He had great admiration and respect for Schlick, almost veneration, and Schlick himself seems to have given considerable responsibility to Waismann. From 1929 to 1936, Waismann described himself as acting as Schlick's assistant. Certainly many of the projects that he undertook in this period were done at Schlick's request.

Schlick was an admirer of the work of Frege and Russell and of what he saw as its flowering in Wittgenstein's *Tractatus.* He it must have been who directed the discussions of the Circle into a close exegetical analysis of the *Tractatus* in the two consecutive years 1924–1925 and 1925–1926. Associated with this study was his attempt to arrange to meet Wittgenstein in order to discuss questions raised by consideration of the book. But it was not until February 1927 that Schlick succeeded in this plan. The initial discussion went satisfactorily, even if, as Wittgenstein remarked to Engelmann, each of them thought the other quite mad.[4] Wittgenstein agreed to further meetings and consented to Schlick's request to bring some of the members of his group to them. He brought Waismann to the next one. Thereafter Waismann attended nearly all the discussions until they were given up in this form at the end of 1928. Others of Schlick's group were less regular attenders; they included Carnap and Feigl. Waismann was as close to Wittgenstein and as intimate with his work as anybody else, with the possible exception of Schlick himself. His being in this position seems a direct outcome of Schlick's influence.

From the beginning these meetings with Wittgenstein effected a communication of his ideas to the members of Schlick's Circle. His ideas were certainly discussed there, and Wittgenstein must have been aware of this practical implication of his discussions. At the beginning of 1929 Wittgenstein returned to Cambridge to resume work on philosophy, having completed his sister's house in Vienna. This change was linked with a change in the form of his communication with the members of the Circle. No longer was he content to meet with anyone other than Schlick and Waismann. By the middle of the year he had conceived the scheme of holding more formal discussions with these two. Waismann, it seems, was to make records of these discussions and to communicate them to the other members of the Circle. The first recorded discussion took place on 18 December 1929. Whatever the stimulus to make this change, it was reinforced by Wittgenstein's distaste for the manifesto of the Vienna Circle published in September 1929.[5]

4. Paul Engelmann, *Letters from Ludwig Wittgenstein with a Memoir,* trans. L. Furtmüller, ed. B.F. McGuinness (Oxford: Basil Blackwell, 1967), p. 118.

5. See his letter to Waismann in the summer of 1929, excerpts of which are quoted in *Ludwig Wittgenstein und der Wiener Kreis* (Oxford: Basil Blackwell, 1967), p. 18.

Waismann's role in communicating Wittgenstein's views became more formal and more crucial. He kept shorthand records of the meetings with Wittgenstein and at least sometimes had them typed out. He was also singled out for the role of publishing or broadcasting Wittgenstein's ideas more publicly. He wrote a paper developing Wittgenstein's views on probability and delivered it at the conference in Prague held between 15 and 17 September 1929. (It was later published in *Erkenntnis* 1 (1930–1931), 228–248, under the title "Logische Analyse des Wahrscheinlichkeitsbegriffs"). This contains the first publication of some of Wittgenstein's 'new' philosophy, in particular the first formulation of the principle of verifiability. This material must be derived from some of the conversations with Wittgenstein prior to September 1929, not from similar material recorded in Waismann's later shorthand notes.

Sometime before the close of 1929[6] a more ambitious project was conceived. Waismann was to write a book giving a systematic exposition of Wittgenstein's philosophy as the first volume in the publications of the Vienna Circle (Schriften zur wissenschaftlichen Weltauffassung). He was singled out for this task both because he was already familiar with Wittgenstein's work and because he had a great ability for "lucid representation."[7] Schlick clearly attached great importance to this work. It seems reasonable to conjecture that he was the prime mover behind the project and that he was responsible for Waismann's selection to carry it out. Indeed, Waismann's enthusiasm for the task, or even his willingness to undertake it, may have derived from Schlick's own enthusiasm for the project and his desire to meet Schlick's wishes in this matter.

The nature of the projected book is apparent from the original advertisement in *Erkenntnis* 1 (1930–1931):

Logik, Sprache, Philosophie.

Kritik der Philosophie durch die Logik. Mit Vorrede von M. Schlick.

6. In a letter to Wolfgang Köhler, dated 13 March 1934, Schlick mentions that the preface to this work was written in 1928; it was printed in 1929.

7. Carnap, "Intellectual Autobiography," p. 28.

(Schr. z. wiss. Weltauff., Bd. I) Springer Verlag, Wien (in Vorbereitung).

Diese Schrift ist im Wesentlichen eine Darstellung der Gedanken von Wittgenstein [*TLP*]. Was in ihr neu ist und worauf es ihr wesentlich ankommt, ist die logische Anordnung und Gliederung dieser Gedanken.

Inhalt:

I. Logik (Sinn, Bedeutung, Wahrheit, Wahrheitsfunktionen, Wesen der Logik)

II. Sprache (Analyse der Aussagen, Atomsätze, Logische Abbildung, Grenzen der Sprache)

III. Philosophie (Anwendung der Ergebnisse auf Probleme der Philosophie)[8]

That Waismann went some way in working out a book realizing this scheme is apparent from comparing this advertisement with his "Thesen" and contemporary lectures. It would have been a systematic presentation of the ideas of the *Tractatus* updated by the addition of material on the principle of verification and the notion of hypothesis from recent conversations and dictations.

LSP was never completed in this original form, although there were various times when its completion seemed imminent. Waismann wrote to Schlick on 15 August 1930 to report that the manuscript was nearly finished: with several weeks of undisturbed work it would be ready. (This was ostensibly forestalled by his receiving an invitation to give the lecture on Wittgenstein's philosophy of mathematics at Königsberg in September 1930.) In a letter to Waismann dated 10 September

8. "Logic, Language, Philosophy
A critique of philosophy through logic with a preface by M. Schlick.
(Schriften zur wissenschaftlichen Weltauffassung, Vol. 1) Springer Press, Vienna (in preparation).
This work is in essentials a representation of the ideas of Wittgenstein's *Tractatus*. What is new in it and what essentially distinguishes it is the logical ordering and articulation of these thoughts.
Contents: 1. Logic (Sense, Meaning, Truth, Truth-Functions, Essence of Logic)
2. Language (Analysis of Propositions, Atomic Propositions, Logical Representations, Limits of Language)
3. Philosophy (Application of the Results to the Problems of Philosophy)"

1931, Schlick commented that he took it for granted that the text would very soon be ready for publication and that *LSP* would appear by the time of his return from California, i.e. by the spring of 1932. There must have been a fairly complete text of the book by late 1931, but, if it took the form of a finished, continuous typescript, this has not survived among Waismann's papers. On the other hand, it is possible to give an accurate account of its content. One source is a lecture "Logik, Sprache, Philosophie," delivered in Vienna on 15 March 1931, of which two drafts survive, the second being a revision of the first. The second source is "Thesen" (published in *WWK* as Anhang B), where Waismann's task was to produce an epitome of Wittgenstein's current philosophy. Both of these works are reexpositions of the fundamental ideas of *TLP*, supplemented and modified by the principle of verification and the notion of hypothesis. There was certainly more than one version or edition of "Thesen" that was duplicated and distributed to various persons. One must have been issued before the end of 1930. But as late as September 1931, Schlick urged Waismann to bring out a final complete edition of "Thesen." He added a request that Waismann send him a copy of "Thesen" in its current form to be given to Professor MacKay, whose only copy was very incomplete.[9]

Since the production of the versions of "Thesen" spanned the period in which an early version of *LSP* was brought close to completion, it is probable that there was a close correspondence in their content. This is further confirmed by the temporal conjunction of Wittgenstein's objections to the issue of further versions of "Thesen" with worries about whether Waismann in writing *LSP* would misrepresent his thinking by failing to emphasize its radical difference from the ideas of *TLP*.[10]

The composition of "Thesen" and *LSP* by no means exhausted Waismann's activities in his formal role as the exposi-

9. "Ich bitte Sie ferner, mir ein Exemplar der Thesen in ihrer jetzigen Form fuer Prof. Mackay hierher zu schicken. Sein Exemplar ist naemlich sehr unvollstaendig" (letter to Waismann of 10 September 1931).

10. Compare *WWK*, p. 184 with Wittgenstein's letter to Schlick of 20 November 1931 (quoted below in notes 13 and 14).

tor of Wittgenstein's ideas. He gave at least three papers in Vienna which developed Wittgenstein's general views: "Das Wesen der Logik" (read to a meeting of the Circle on 6 March 1930), "Logik, Sprache, Philosophie" (15 March 1931), and "Logik und Sprache" (8 November 1931). He prepared and circulated a paper on Wittgenstein's philosophy of mathematics late in 1930 (printed in *WWK* as Anhang A). He delivered a lecture at the Königsberg symposium on the philosophy of mathematics entitled "Ueber das Wesen der Mathematik: Der Standpunkt Wittgensteins" (5 September 1930). Wittgenstein himself attached great importance to this lecture. He gave Waismann an outline of what he was to say (*WWK*, pp. 102ff.), and he expressed disappointment when it briefly appeared that Waismann would not be taking part in the symposium (letter to Schlick in August 1930). This lecture should have been a very important event in the development of the ideas of the Vienna Circle, since some of the members looked to Wittgenstein for a synthesis of logicism and intuitionism that would give a constructivist account of mathematics developed on an acceptable empiricist basis.[11] In fact it seems to have had a very limited influence, partly because of Gödel's simultaneous announcement of his celebrated incompleteness theorem, and partly because Waismann failed to complete the text for publication with the other papers in the symposium. As a result, the members of the Circle seem to have ignored its fundamental message, the application of the principle of verification to mathematical statements. In all these activities Waismann was expressly acting as the exponent of Wittgenstein's ideas and the defender of his point of view.

Up to the end of 1931, Waismann played a pivotal formal role in the dissemination of Wittgenstein's ideas. He certainly saw, and was probably given, some of Wittgenstein's typescripts. He was shown, e.g. the beginning of TS 211 in September 1931 (*WWK*, p. 166), and he seems to have used *Philosophische Bemerkungen* (or some related typescript). More

11. *Wissenschaftliche Weltauffassung: Der Wiener Kreis* (Vienna: A. Wolf, 1929), § 3.1.

important, Wittgenstein participated in conversations with Waismann on the overt understanding that he would communicate their content to others. This was certainly true in respect of Waismann's reports on these conversations at meetings of the Circle. There seem to have been more specific understandings too. Perhaps earlier, but certainly during Schlick's absence in America in 1931–1932, Wittgenstein met Waismann at least partly with the explicit intention of communicating material to Schlick. Most of the conversation of 21 September 1931 exists among Waismann's papers in the form of typescripts, presumably prepared for Schlick, since Wittgenstein wrote to Schlick in March 1932 to ask whether he had yet received similar notes he had dictated to Waismann on 9 December 1931.[12]

Then quite suddenly Waismann's role seems to have changed. By mid-1932 members of the Circle noted that he was no longer bringing Wittgenstein's latest ideas to their meetings. He was also left out of later conversations or conferences between Wittgenstein and Schlick, e.g. their lengthy meeting in September 1933. It is perhaps possible to conjecture the basis of this change. Wittgenstein wrote to Schlick in November 1931, apologizing for his part in the delay in producing *LSP* and excusing it by his lack of enthusiasm for the whole project: "I am convinced the Waismann would present *many* things in a form *completely* different from what I regard as correct."[13] The source of this worry is probably that Waismann, like Schlick, underestimated the radical differences between his current thinking and the ideas of *TLP*. In criticizing some remarks of Schlick's on *TLP*, he commented: "There are *very, very* many statements in the book with which I now disagree!"[14] At this very time Waismann was working on, or had completed, a revised edition of "Thesen," copies of which

12. "Haben Sie Waismanns Aufzeichnungen, die ich zu Weihnachten diktierte, erhalten?" (letter of 4 March 1932). This is quoted and discussed in *WWK*, pp. 24–25 and 196 (n. 130).

13. "Ich bin ja überzeugt, dass W. *sehr* vieles *ganz* anders darstellen würde, als ich es für richtig halte" (letter of 20 November 1931).

14. "Ich bin mit *sehr, sehr* vielen Formulierungen des Buches heute nicht einverstanden" (ibid.).

were probably distributed. Wittgenstein seems to have been given one. This provoked his renewed criticism of "Thesen" in his meeting with Waismann on 9 December 1931. He adverted to his criticism of an earlier draft of "Thesen," remarking that theses have no place in philosophy (*WWK*, p. 183). He then added that there was no justification at all for this second edition of "Thesen." He particularly wished to repudiate the dogmatism that underlay the basic ideas of *TLP* (*WWK*, p. 184). Apparently he feared that Waismann's book would present his thought in a series of theses deemed to encapsulate its fundamental ideas; and, even worse, that these would be garnered from remarks that did not belong to any one consistent framework of thought. To forestall such a double misrepresentation of his thoughts, Wittgenstein seems to have killed off the initial project for *LSP* in December 1931.

The death of the orignal project did not bring about a cessation of Waismann's work or of Wittgenstein's collaboration in it. Rather, it was the occasion for fundamental changes in the working relationship between Wittgenstein, Waismann, and Schlick, and in the whole conception of *LSP*. There was no interruption in the business of getting on with the revised project: Wittgenstein had eleven meetings with Waismann in the Easter vacation 1932! The most fundamental change must have been dropping the presumption that Wittgenstein's contemporary views could be represented as a modification of the central theses of *TLP*. Instead, *LSP* was to begin from a clean slate in giving an account of his new philosophy. That Wittgenstein was willing to continue on this project in collaboration with Waismann seems to be due to his wish to honor a long-standing promise to Schlick to do so[15] and to his unwillingness to disappoint Schlick, who was himself keen that Wittgenstein's ideas should be made available in a systematic form. Schlick's role was pivotal in bringing about a rebirth of *LSP* from the ashes of the original project. It also became more crucial in shaping the material of *LSP*. Instead of being the channel of communication between Wittgenstein and the

15. This promise is emphasized in his letter to Schlick of 20 November 1931.

Circle, Waismann came to depend in part for material on Wittgenstein's dictations to Schlick (and perhaps also on less formal conversations). He also made use of some of Wittgenstein's typescripts: certainly of the material on mathematics printed as Part II of the *Philosophical Grammar, The Blue Book,* and the beginning of *The Brown Book,* and probably of parts of TS 211 and the "Big Typescript." Changes in the conception of the book were correlated with some changes in the nature and direction of the flow of information in the Wittgenstein-Schlick-Waismann triangle.

By Easter 1934 the scheme for *LSP* had evolved yet further. Wittgenstein and Waismann were to be coauthors. Wittgenstein would supply the raw materials (ideas and remarks) and plan out the general form of the book, while Waismann would be responsible for integrating extracts from typescripts, dictations, and conversations into a continuous text. Wittgenstein's hand in the global organization of the text was of decisive importance. It would lessen the danger that the book might seriously misrepresent his ideas or the connections between them. Therefore it made an essential difference between this project and the original one, where Waismann himself was responsible for the organization of Wittgenstein's remarks. On the other hand, this interpretation of joint authorship made Waismann uneasy about whether his name should appear at all on the title page, since it seemed to him that there was no respect in which it was *his* book.[16]

The composition of *LSP* continued actively at least until late 1935, but it seems that the book never came very near to completion during this whole period. There were two related causes for this. First, there was a veritable explosion of new ideas in Wittgenstein's work in the period 1932–1934, conspicuous in the philosophy of mathematics and in a shift of emphasis in the theory of meaning from hypothesis to criteria. Waismann was certainly made aware of this evolution in Wittgenstein's thinking. Second, there was Wittgenstein's participation and interference in the writing of the book. This was

16. See his letter to Schlick of 9 August 1934.

motivated in part by his desire to get his changing arguments straight, and perhaps in part by the very perfectionism that blocked his publication of his own ideas. Both of these factors made Waismann's task difficult. With great restraint, he described his problems to Schlick: "He has the great gift of always seeing things as if for the first time. But it shows, I think, how difficult collaborative work with him is, since he is always following up the inspiration of the moment and demolishing what he has previously sketched out."[17] From Waismann's perspective, the writing of *LSP* must have made the labors of Hercules look easy.

The project for *LSP* was not only difficult to execute, but also very puzzling. During the period 1932–1933 at the very least, Wittgenstein was working on the composition of a book, the "Big Typescript," which would itself give a systematic and comprehensive exposition of his views on the very same topics covered by *LSP*. If this work had reached a form that had satisfied Wittgenstein, e.g. if he had decided to publish the 'clean' text of the "Big Typescript," it would have superseded *LSP*, making redundant any alternative or less authoritative exposition of his views. Why then was Wittgenstein himself engaged in two independent projects that covered the same ground? (If Waismann did have access to the "Big Typescript," they were not even independent.) And why was Waismann willing to devote extensive time and energy to a project that might well eventually have turned out to be pointless? The answer to these questions must be conjectural. On the one hand, Wittgenstein was often pessimistic about completing any of his own work for publication. This perhaps made him willing to cooperate in the production of a book presenting his ideas, faute de mieux. It also had the advantage, shared with his dictation of the *Blue* and *Brown Books*, that he retained some freedom to criticize or disown the final product as a

17. "Er hat ja die wunderbare Gabe, die Dinge immer wieder wie zum erstenmal zu sehen. Aber es zeigt sich doch, meine ich, wie schwer eine gemeinsame Arbeit ist, da er eben immer wieder der Eingebung des Augenblicks folgt und das niederreisst, was er vorher entworfen hat" (letter to Schlick of 9 August 1934).

distortion of his real views[18] or as an intermediate step to more adequate formulations. On the other hand, Schlick actively encouraged both Wittgenstein and Waismann to persist with the project, particularly since he himself was intensely interested in the development of Wittgenstein's ideas. His interest is very apparent from his later papers (published in *Gesammelte Aufsätze*) and from his meetings and correspondence with Wittgenstein. His concern with the progress of *LSP* is evident from Waismann's correspondence with him, since Waismann is eager to vindicate himself before Schlick by describing the great difficulties of working on the book with Wittgenstein. The motivation for Waismann's working on *LSP* must, directly or indirectly, be derived from the belief, shared by Schlick and Wittgenstein himself, that its content was not likely to be published in any alternative form.[19] The scheme for joint authorship would also provide some protection against the obsolescence of *LSP* in the unlikely event that Wittgenstein should eventually publish his own book. Hence this arrangement had some benefits for both its parties.

Wittgenstein participated in composing *LSP* according to the revised scheme throughout the period 1932–1934, but thereafter his active cooperation seems to have tailed off. Although, for example, he was in Vienna for the Christmas vacation in 1935, he apparently had no meetings at all with Waismann. Then on 19 May 1936 he wrote a letter upbraiding Waismann's publication of the article "Über den Begriff der Identität" (*Erkenntnis* 6 [1936–1937], 56–64). Waismann had prefaced this article with a footnote in which he expressed his indebtedness to Wittgen-

18. According to Carnap, this is what he did do (Carnap, "Intellectual Autobiography," p. 28).

19. At a later date this belief is openly expressed by both Wittgenstein and Waismann. "Ich habe jetzt sieben Jahre lang schwer, und *mit Erfolg*, gearbeitet und habe nicht nur in dieser Zeit noch nichts veröffentlicht sondern bin heute noch zweifelhaft ob ich meine Arbeit je in eine Form bringen werde, in der ich glauben werde sie veröffentlichen zu können" (letter from Wittgenstein to Waismann of 19 May 1935). "Da Schlick leider nicht mehr zur Ausarbeitung der neuen Erkenntnistheorie gekommen ist, wenn ferner auch Wittgenstein, wie er mir wiederholt sagte, seine Ideen nicht publizieren wird, so bin ich heute der einzige, der diese Gedanken kennt und sie zu entwickeln vermag" (letter from Waismann to Carnap, dated 4 March 1937).

stein for his "valuable stimuli" ("wertvolle Anregungen") in respect of the ideas there developed. Wittgenstein complained that this note gave a false impression. It intimated that certain conversations with him had stimulated Waismann to reflect on the topic of identity, but that Waismann's resultant ideas were so obliquely related to these conversations that he could attribute no particular ones of them to Wittgenstein. The truth, Wittgenstein claimed, was different: the elaboration of the important thought that the term 'identical' had not a single meaning, but rather a series of closely related meanings corresponding to different "criteria of identity", stemmed from him, and not just from conversations, but also from dictations and unpublished typescripts. This should have been acknowledged. In a reply dated 27 May 1936, Waismann apologized for his unfortunate choice of words, remarked on his perplexity about knowing how to draft an appropriate acknowledgment, and proposed that a note be inserted in *Erkenntnis* specifying the exact extent of his debt to Wittgenstein as outlined in Wittgenstein's letter. (This proposal was never executed.) Wittgenstein had also suggested that Schlick be consulted about how best to patch matters up. Waismann showed him Wittgenstein's letter and took his advice in replying to it. But any further mediation was forestalled by Schlick's murder in June 1936. Shortly thereafter, Waismann entered into negotiations with Springer Verlag for the publication of *LSP* under the revised title "Das philosophische Denken,"[20] and he signed a contract, probably early in October 1936, for its publication under his own name alone. The book was to be dedicated to the memory of Schlick and published, as originally intended, as volume 1 of the series "Schriften zur wissenschaftlichen Weltauffassung."[21]

In the absence of other evidence, it would have been plausible to conjecture that the known misunderstanding about the publication of the article on identity was the cause of Wittgenstein's withdrawal from the scheme for joint publication of *LSP*. But this supposition is demonstrably false. Cessation of Wittgenstein's active collaboration predates this quarrel. Moreover,

20. Letter from Springer to Waismann of 28 July 1936.
21. Letter from Springer to Waismann of 2 October 1936.

this supposition hardly accounts for the timing of Waismann's negotiating and signing a contract with Springer. An alternative explanation must be sought. From beginning to end the role of Schlick was crucial in the evolution of the project. One of Wittgenstein's primary motives for participating in what he called "die Waismann Sache" seems to have been a repeated promise to Schlick to help produce a book presenting his views.[22] Similarly, Waismann's main motive for persisting in work that was difficult and discouraging must have been his sense of obligation to Schlick to bring this project to completion. In the last year of his life, Schlick's interests had turned away from epistemology and semantics toward ethics and the meaning of life.[23] If he was indeed the driving force behind the production of *LSP* then what would be more natural than that this change in his interests would be reflected in a tailing off of work on this book? This hypothesis, rather than that of a sudden rupture, fits the facts of the termination of collaboration between Wittgenstein and Waismann. Moreover, it also accounts for Waismann's resuming work on the text of *LSP* immediately after Schlick's death[24] and entering into negotiations for its publication. At that time he collected Schlick's papers for the publication of *Gesammelte Aufsätze*. Apart from that work, what would be more appropriate as a memorial to Schlick's philosophical activities than the publication of a book that he had fathered and nurtured, a book that covered the range of topics central to most of his published writings? Bringing out *LSP* would be an act of piety. This is evident too from its dedication to the memory of Schlick. Indeed, it would be only a slight exaggeration to say that Waismann conceived of the publication of *LSP* as a posthumous publication of Schlick's own work. What Waismann originally wrote as the first section of *LSP* he used as the opening for his philosophical obituary for Schlick in *Synthese* 1 (1936). This described the renewal or new turn in philosophy that was adumbrated by Frege and Russell and then

22. Letter to Schlick of 20 November 1931.

23. This is confirmed by Dr. H. Mulder. Among Schlick's papers was found a sketch for a book on ethics dating from this period.

24. This is mentioned in his letter to Carnap of 4 March 1937.

developed more fully by Wittgenstein. (The whole text of *LSP* was an embodiment of this new conception.) Waismann felt no incongruity in claiming that Schlick's work was "the main attempt ever made" to develop this new way of philosophizing. The work of Wittgenstein and that of Schlick thus were seen as parallel branches of the same stream. Hence *LSP*, in content as much as in genesis, would be a perfect memorial to Schlick. (This conception of the book is perhaps what licensed Waismann to add to the earlier text an opening echoing Schlick's article "Die Wende der Philosophie" (*Erkenntnis* 1 [1930–1931]) and an explicit discussion of some of Schlick's other work. The discussion of the "Abbildungstheorie" is filled out with a discussion of Schlick's thesis that only form, not content, is communicable.)

Waismann's collaboration with Wittgenstein, having petered out in 1935, never revived. The subsequent writing of *LSP* was Waismann's work alone. The stream of written material from Wittgenstein also dried up. Waismann had no later access to any unpublished manuscripts or dictations nor to any typescripts apart from the 1937 version of the *Investigations*. On the other hand, Wittgenstein's influence on Waismann persisted. It was permanent. Texts that constitute expositions of Wittgenstein's ideas continued to appear, particularly *Einführung in das mathematische Denken* (Vienna, 1938) and a number of articles incorporating parts of the text of *LSP* (see Appendix 1). Even much later articles, some published and others as yet unpublished, contain material derived directly from Wittgenstein's work; e.g. most of §1 of "Verifiability" from the chapter "Ueber Hypothesen" from *LSP*, and a manuscript entitled "Belief" (ca. 1950) from TS 211.[25] Waismann also lectured on Wittgenstein's work in Vienna until July 1937 and in Cambridge in Lent Term 1938. Turning off the current by no means ended the magnetic force exerted on Waismann by Wittgenstein's idea.

From early in 1928 to sometime in 1935 Waismann worked

25. An English translation of "Ueber Hypothesen" is published as essay 5, "Hypotheses," in F. Waismann, *Philosophical Papers*, ed. B. F. McGuinness (Dordrecht and Boston: Reidel, 1977).

in close contact with Wittgenstein, primarily in systematizing and making public his ideas. Waismann's relationship to Wittgenstein seems rightly characterized as *Verehrung*. What I have tried to show is that his *Verehrung* for Wittgenstein was derivative from his continuing *Verehrung* for Schlick; i.e. that he did not change allegiance but developed a new one on the foundation of the old. Its products were a series of lectures and articles, and two complete books, all of which more or less explicitly developed Wittgenstein's ideas. The most important of these works, *LSP*, never appeared in Waismann's lifetime, largely as a result of the timing of the outbreak of World War II, and also because of Waismann's own perfectionism expressed in endless tinkering with the German text and its translation into English. This circumstance has served to obscure the exact nature and the historical importance of his writings. An important by-product of his devotion to Wittgenstein was his alienation, in company with Schlick, from the other members of the Vienna Circle.[26] This fact may well be important in the history of the Circle, but, whatever regret Waismann had about it, he must have felt that there were very real compensations.

The Composition of *LSP*

On the assumption that Wittgenstein's criticism of the reissue of "Thesen" in late 1931 and his repudiation of many of the fundamental ideas of *TLP* brought about a fresh start on *LSP*, it seems probable that most, though certainly not all, of the writings related to the execution of this project are still extant among Waismann's papers. (The relevant contents of his *Nachlass* are described in Appendix 1.) There is enough material to make possible a study of the development of *LSP*—its development both in the large and in the small. It is generally possible to establish the order of composition of various texts on a single topic and also the order of the various global

26. Neurath specifically mentioned this fact in a letter to Waismann, dated 4 August 1939: "Die Wittgensteinsche Periode hat Sie (und in gewissem Masse auch Schlick) von unserer gemeinsamen Arbeit entfernt."

reorganizations of the book. It might well be possible to assign relative dates to most of the preserved writings.

In absence of absolute dating for any part of the text produced earlier than 1936, no particular scheme for organizing the material of *LSP* and no particular general reorganizations can *definitely* be assigned to Wittgenstein. On the other hand, it is plausible to conjecture that many global developments can be attributed to him, especially the eclipse of the notion of hypothesis and the change of emphasis on the principle of verifiability. The best guess at present is that Wittgenstein himself was responsible for the general structure of the book, even in its final form. Waismann was certainly given a plan for the book in the Easter vacation of 1934; and he later complained that his main difficulty in writing the text was Wittgenstein's changes of mind as to how the material should be organized.[27] Indeed, the practical significance of Wittgenstein's being a joint author of *LSP* seems just to consist in his having taken charge of the overall structure of the book, since there was never a time when it was not true that the content of the book was derived from his work. If Waismann's activities on the book waned with Schlick's interest in the project and then revived after his death, it is likely that he carried the project to completion by exploiting what seemed to him the best one of Wittgenstein's plans rather than by concocting a new scheme for organizing the material. Nonetheless, Wittgenstein's responsibility for the structure of *LSP* is wholly conjectural. There are, by contrast, a few changes that can definitely be attributed to Waismann alone. These include the division of Part I into chapters and the transfer of the discussion of arithmetic and geometry from Chapter VII to Chapter III; the division into three chapters of the material in Chapters X to XII, and also of Chapters XIV to XVI. Waismann is also probably responsible for the quotation and discussion of Schlick's lectures "Form and Content" in Chapter XII and Chapter XV.

Waismann's papers do allow the identification of the sources

27. Letter from Waismann to Schlick of 9 August 1934.

of the material organized into the text of *LSP* and make clear the method by which the book was composed. They confirm the accuracy of characterizing the book as "die logische Anordnung und Gliederung" of Wittgenstein's ideas. At every stage of its development, the text of *LSP* can be broken down into atoms, i.e. into ideas or remarks that are taken verbatim from texts or conversations with Wittgenstein. Unlike logical atoms, these are not unchanging; their totality seems to have evolved, both by addition and by deletion, though perhaps fairly gradually. But, by comparison with their arrangement, these atoms are at least relatively changeless. Their configurations were certainly not at all stable. Wittgenstein himself was probably the chief agent in causing perturbations. He brought Waismann to the verge of despair by insisting on wholesale redrafting of parts of the text whose form he had sketched only shortly before. As Waismann explained to Schlick, the project of writing *LSP* would make sense to him if only it were a matter of improving on the execution of a definite plan. "But, as it is, all one sees is that the structure is being demolished bit by bit and that everything is gradually taking on an entirely different appearance, so that one almost gets the feeling that it doesn't matter at all how the thoughts are put together since in the end nothing is left as it was."[28] Waismann's nightmare was that the atoms of *LSP* might be logically independent each from the others.

A complete analysis of the sources and development of every part of the text of *LSP* would be an enormous undertaking, and it would be of limited interest. I shall concentrate on two chapters that illustrate the two extremes both in the method of their composition and in their known connection with Wittgenstein's work.

The first case is Chapter III. The evolution of the text is very straightforward. (For details, see Appendix 2.) A paragraph by paragraph analysis of §§1 and 2 of Chapter III spotlights its

28. "Aber so sieht man doch nur, dass Stück von Stück des Aufbaus niedergerissen wird und dass alles langsam ein völlig anderes Gesicht annimmt, sodass man fast das Gefühl erhält, dass es ganz egal ist, wie man die Gedanken zusammengefügt, da ja schliesslich doch kein Stein auf dem anderen bleibt" (ibid.).

relation to Wittgenstein's work. (This analysis is given in the footnotes to these two sections of the published text of *LSP*.) Apart from introductory remarks and transitional remarks, the text is almost wholly constructed by stringing together *quotations* (not mere paraphrases) from Wittgenstein. Indeed, apart from the few paragraphs added in the 1938–1939 revision, there is not even a single substantive paragraph of the text of these two sections that is not a quotation (or modified quotation) from an identified source in Wittgenstein's work. Although these two sections of *LSP* are atypical in the amount of *identifiable* direct quotation that they contain, they are representative of the nature of the book as an introduction to Wittgenstein's thought. They are also peculiarly important for an analysis of the method of composition of the entire book. Waismann had special interest and competence in the philosophy of mathematics. Therefore it would seem particularly likely that here, if anywhere, he would introduce into *LSP* the products of this own thinking. Yet it is manifest that here he remained absolutely faithful to his task of presenting Wittgenstein's views, developing them in a pastiche of quotations.

The second case is Chapter VI, discussing the causal theory of meaning. The development of this text is very complicated. (For details, see Appendix 3.) The result is a text no part of which can as yet be identified as quotations from any of Wittgenstein's typescripts, but every part of which is very closely linked to his work. The arguments are familiar from *PB* and 'BT''; e.g. the criticism of Russell's account of desire. Even the examples are identical with ones in Wittgenstein's writings; e.g. the clucking hen (*Philosophical Grammar* §32). and the language game of walking according to commands whose meanings are established by a table of arrows (''BT,'' p. 26 and *BBB*, p. 95). Two different hypotheses would accommodate these facts. The first is that Waismann's text is a carefully constructed paraphrase of ideas culled from Wittgenstein's manuscripts. He quite naturally took over not only the arguments, but also Wittgenstein's examples and figures of speech in working out his text. The alternative hypothesis is that the text does consist largely of quotations from Wittgenstein, i.e. quotations from conversations and discussions with Waismann, perhaps even from dictations. This would clearly explain the striking correspondences between this text and Wittgenstein's writings, for it would be natural for him to have expressed his views in ways very similar, but not identical, to their formulations in his contemporary manuscripts. (The content of the "Diktat für Schlick" bears this sort of close resemblance to his writings.) This hypothesis would also explain the impression of fidelity to earlier formulations that is given by an examination of the various drafts of material for Chapter VI. Many sentences and paragraphs remain intact through the various redraftings, suggesting that Waismann attached particular importance to their precise wording, as if they were quotations from an unidentified source. It may be impossible to settle definitively which hypothesis should be preferred, but there is some evidence that the text of Chapter VI is a very much more exact representation of Wittgenstein's ideas than it might appear to be.

A study of the method of its composition has an important bearing on the legitimacy of using *LSP* in the investigation of Wittgenstein's philosophy. There are many places where it seems to clarify and amplify remarks of Wittgenstein's whose interpretation is problematic. To the extent that *LSP* is really an arrangement of Wittgenstein's ideas, this illumination may be real, not merely apparent or conjectural. Furthermore, the stronger the case for the fidelity to Wittgenstein's thought and expression of the traceable parts of the text, the greater the interest of its apparently 'independent' parts. Some of these do not correspond to any identified material in any of Wittgenstein's typescripts, manuscripts, or dictations. They might be aspects of Wittgenstein's philosophy that are visible *only* in *LSP*. This material includes the analysis of the grammar of questions (Chapter XX, §6) and much of the discussion of Chapters XII, XIII, and XV. Even where material can be traced to Wittgenstein, its organization in *LSP* may give it significance or point that it might otherwise not have (or not be recognized to have). Chapter VI, for example, is a much more sustained and integrated analysis of the causal theory of meaning than any to be found in his typescripts. To the extent that Wittgenstein was responsible for its organization, *LSP* may show up unfamiliar implications of familiar remarks. While its exact value as a tool for studying Wittgenstein's thought cannot yet be determined with any certainty, this is probably much greater than is commonly thought, and, without doubt, Waismann's book has a greater claim to attention in this connection than any other book not written or dictated by Wittgenstein himself.

Verkehrung

During the period 1928–1935, Wittgenstein's thoughts underwent substantial, even radical, development. Changes are reflected, though not always perfectly, in Waismann's work. To the extent that they were frequent or radical, there was a real danger that Waismann's writings, especially *LSP*, would misrepresent Wittgenstein's views. At least it would have been difficult, perhaps virtually impossible, for Waismann to keep abreast of these changes and their implications. As a consequence, it might happen that *every* stage in the evolution of the text of *LSP* would constitute a misrepresentation of Wittgenstein's *contemporary* views in spite of its being entirely and accurately derived from his communications, both oral and written. One of the primary interests of Waismann's papers is the light they throw on the evolution of Wittgenstein's thoughts during this crucial period of development. The material related to *LSP* is particularly important in this respect. Changes in content are manifested in two readily apparent ways: first, in material discarded from earlier versions of the text, and second, in the survival in the final text of arguments that are clearly inconsistent with each other. A close study of Waismann's papers gives evidence independent of the dating of Wittgenstein's papers for the study of the development of his thinking—as it were by focusing on the emission and absorption lines generated by *LSP*.

The danger that *LSP* would misrepresent Wittgenstein's contemporary views was very real. Indeed, he called a halt to the original project at the end of 1931 just because he thought that it was based on a fundamental misconception. Both

Waismann and Schlick viewed his contemporary work as an extension and modification of the fundamental ideas of *TLP*, whereas Wittgenstein saw this later work as standing in conflict with many of the doctrines of *TLP*. From his point of view, the attempt to unify all of this work into a single book was the expression of a basic misconception. In 1934 Wittgenstein might well have been worried by the thought that the final text of *LSP* would stand to his current thinking in the same relation that "Thesen" had stood to his views in late 1931.

When forced from the supposition that *all* of his work was the expression of a single coherent framework of thought, one might, adhering to the principle of least intellectual effort, adopt the view that his *later* work is the gradual elaboration of a single coherent form of philosophy. This would give the familiar picture of there being not one Wittgenstein, but two. It is not clear whether Waismann himself fell into this error or whether he was merely overoptimistic about the possibility of being able to reconcile apparent conflicts within Wittgenstein's 'later philosophy'. He certainly complained to Schlick of Wittgenstein's insisting on changes to the text of *LSP*. But this remark might be interpreted in two different ways. First, as the complaint that Wittgenstein kept introducing genuine and important changes of view midway along in the composition of parts of the book. Or second, as the complaint that these changes were relatively superficial matters of the organization and exact formulation of ideas that were essentially unchanging. What is somewhat unclear is whether Waismann himself viewed the changes as a matter of the form or of the content of Wittgenstein's views. He was certainly anxious that Wittgenstein might accuse him of misrepresentation. Indeed, this worry is his principal defense against Wittgenstein's criticism of his inadequate acknowledgment of his intellectual debts in "Über den Begriff der Identität." In his letter of apology to Wittgenstein he made this point:

I would just like to tell you why I drafted the footnote in this way. When I had completed the article, I didn't really know to what extent you would be in agreement with its contents and to what extent you would not. If I characterized the whole article or even a part of it as an exposition of your ideas, I couldn't be sure that you wouldn't tell me that I hadn't understood or that I had given a lop-sided or garbled account of your ideas. Please try to understand me by putting yourself in my place: I certainly think that I understand your ideas correctly, but I would be quite certain of this only were you to read the text and inform me of your agreement with it. Thus there still remains some doubt in my mind.[29]

To Wittgenstein's worry that Waismann's work might misrepresent his ideas there corresponded Waismann's anxiety that Wittgenstein would accuse him of misrepresentation.

There are many substantial changes of thought in the evolution of the material of *LSP*. On the assumption that Wittgenstein dictated most of the major changes in content and organization, these give evidence independent of his writings for the development of his thoughts. Moreover, each of them would constitute a modification to a text that he saw as misrepresenting his *current* views. One might even say that the value of this material consists in its misrepresentations of his views. It certainly spotlights important changes, since it contains series of texts each of which is derived from previous ones by the modification of remarks which were presumably no longer consistent with the current climate of his thought. This gives evidence for the growth of ideas in place of a vague impression of their complete transformation.

Among the fundamental changes visible in the development of *LSP*, there is the gradual movement away from the view that the essence of language is its pictoriality. Originally the philosophical clarification of language would stress the notion of pictoriality (*logische Abbildung*). In the end, this conception

29. "Ich möchte Ihnen nur noch sagen, warum ich die Fussnote so abgefasst habe. Als ich mit dem Aufsatz fertig war, da wusste ich nicht recht, inwieweit Sie mit dem Inhalt einverstanden sein würden und inwieweit nicht. Wenn ich nun den Aufsatz oder einen Teil desselben als Wiedergabe Ihrer Ideen bezeichnete, so war ich nicht sicher, ob Sie mir nicht erklären würden: ich habe Sie nicht verstanden oder ich habe Ihre Gedanken schief oder entstellt wiedergegeben. Ich bitte Sie, mich richtig zu verstehen und sich auch in meine Lage zu versetzen: ich glaube zwar, Ihre Ideen richtig zu verstehen, aber ganz gewiss wäre ich meiner Sache erst, wenn Sie das Manuskript lesen und mir Ihre Zustimmung erklären würden. So bleibt immer ein gewisser Zweifel in mir zurück" (letter of 27 May 1936).

is discussed in a separate and very critical chapter under the heading "Die Abbildungstheorie der Sprache." There is the accumulation of critical remarks about the concepts of objects, facts, and simples (some quoted from Wittgenstein's essay "Komplex und Tatsache"),[30] as well as an evolving criticism of the thesis that all language is extensional.

Second, there is the gradual softening of dogmatism about the principle of verification and a subtle shift of emphasis on its contribution to the theory of meaning. In Waismann's earliest texts it is simply asserted as constituting a complete account of the sense of a sentence. At crucial junctures in his argumentation he introduced the slogan "The sense of a sentence is the method of its verification."[31] In the earliest version of Part I, the principle of verification was originally applied in a section entitled "Verschiedene Fragen und Probleme" to the dissolution of various philosophical problems, as if it could be applied quite unambiguously to any sentence as *the* method for revealing its sense. Waismann came to recognize that matters were not so simple. If the concept of verification encapsulated in this account of meaning is identified with deductively valid proof, then many, perhaps most, empirical statements will not have any sense at all. Generalization, the past tense, and the future tense all seem to generate sentences whose truth-values cannot be demonstrated from present evidence. Moreover, the principle of verification suggests that there is but a single canonical verification for any significant sentence which is constitutive of its sense, so that any other method of verification can at best be inductive and parasitic on the canonical method. But which sense experiences are canonical evidence for particular descriptions of the external world (e.g. 'There is a book on the table' or 'My brother is in the next room')? A solution to both those difficulties was sought in the concept of hypothesis (*'Hypothese'*), and this is discussed and analyzed at great length in much of the preparatory material

30. Printed as the first part of Appendix 1 of *PR* and also as Appendix 1 to Part 1 of *PG*.

31. The slogan "Der Sinn eines Satzes ist die Art seiner Verifikation" appears in "Thesen," "Das Wesen der Mathematik," "Logische Analyse des Wahrscheinlichkeitsbegriffs," and "Ex. d. Fremdseelischen."

for *LSP*, although the notion almost disappears from the final text. An hypothesis admits of multiple independent verifications, but none of them, nor any combination of them, is conclusive. At best an hypothesis is made probable by confirming evidence, never certain. The concept of verification is thereby cut loose from certainty and internally connected with probability. This constitutes a reinterpretation of the principle of verification; indeed, an outright rejection of it according to the interpretation in which 'verification' is construed as deductively conclusive evidence.

The principle underwent another parallel modification when the concept of criteria replaced the concept of hypothesis as the principal tool in the analysis of empirical language (see below). The concept of verification was separated from probability and reattached to certainty, but without thereby assimilating conclusive evidence to evidence that entails what it supports. The multiple ambiguity thus revealed in the principle of verification should induce some skepticism about the usefulness of dogmatic assertions of the slogan "The sense of a sentence is the method of its verification." A signpost that points the way to fundamental errors can hardly be treated as an authoritative indication of the royal road to truth in philosophy. This fact makes another strategy preferable, viz. to give separate treatment to the principle of verification as a specific form of the theory of meaning. Hence Waismann discussed it in a separate chapter ("Sinn und Verifikation"), in which he also considered its capacity to dissolve philosophical problems. He reached a cautious conclusion that the explanation of how to verify a sentence is a contribution to its grammar, to its sense.[32] Apart from the ambiguity of the principle itself, there are other reasons for caution. One is consideration of nonassertive uses of language, e.g. in commands and questions, since their use, even if related to questions of verification, is not simply determined by their verification (or perhaps even of the verification of their 'descriptive content'). Waismann identifies the sense of a positive and negative sen-

32. "Die Erklärung der Verifikation ist ein Beitrag zur Grammatik des Satzes, . . . zu seinem Sinn" (*LSP*, p. 472; echoing "BT," p. 265; cf. *PI* § 353).

tence question (e.g. 'Is he standing outside?' = 'Isn't he standing outside?'), in spite of a difference in sense (and verification) of the corresponding assertions (*PLP*, p. 405). Nonetheless, explaining how a sentence is to be verified *is* a contribution to its grammar, i.e. to explaining its sense. Wittgenstein's notion of a criterion belongs essentially to this framework of thought about meaning. Even though what is to be understood by the principle of verification undergoes changes, there is a fundamental continuity through the changes. This is the negative implication of the principle, viz. the implication that the 'classical' account of meaning in terms of verification-transcendent truth-conditions is to be rejected.

Third, there is development in the philosophy of mathematics, a movement away from an orthodox, though very restrictive, form of constructivism toward 'full-blooded conventionalism'. In expounding Wittgenstein's philosophy of mathematics in September 1930, Waismann stressed the complete generality of Wittgenstein's semantics. The principles that hold for empirical language hold also for mathematics.

> To determine the meaning of a mathematical concept one must study the use that is to be made of it. . . .
>
> To establish the sense of a mathematical sentence, one must make clear how it is to be verified. I.e. . . . the sense of a mathematical sentence is the method of its verification.[33]

Wittgenstein even here may not have intended a complete assimilation of mathematical to empirical discourse. It seems that he always held that mathematics was part of grammar (e.g. *PB* §108), and it follows from his understanding of that claim that mathematical sentences cannot have sense since they are not bipolar. Nonetheless, our understanding of a mathematical sentence can be identified with our knowing what would 'verify' it, i.e. constitute a proof of it. This

33. "Um die Bedeutung eines mathematischen Begriffes festzustellen, muss man auf den Gebrauch achten, der von ihm gemacht wird. . . . Um sich den Sinn eines mathematischen Satzes zu vergegenwärtigen, muss man sich klar machen, wie er verifiziert wird. D.h., . . . der Sinn eines mathematischen Satzes (ist) die Methode seiner Verifikation" ("Ueber das Wesen der Mathematik: Der Standpunkt Wittgensteins").

amounts to an exact formal parallelism that overshadows the difference between the 'sense' of a mathematical sentence and the sense of an empirical one. But Wittgenstein criticized even this weaker assimilation of mathematics to empirical discourse as embodying a fundamental confusion (cf. *PG* p. 361): mathematical proof and empirical verification are in no way parallel. It is an essential feature of the concept of sense that one can grasp the sense of a sentence without knowing whether it is true. For empirical statements this is unproblematic. My grasping the sense of such statements may be demonstrated by my ability to describe what experiences would verify them if these were to occur, as well as my ability to recognize them as being true if they are true, as false if they are false. There is no parallel for mathematics. Grasping the 'sense' of a sentence must be a matter either of my recognizing an actual proof when I am confronted with it or of my being able to describe with as much detail as required what would count as a proof of this sentence. Since a complete description of a proof is itself a proof, either of these possibilities can be realized only if there is a proof of the sentence, i.e. if I can actually 'verify' it. Consequently there is no gap between grasping its 'sense' and determining it to be 'true'. Treating a proof as if it were parallel to empirical verification is to neglect the fact that the proof determines the 'sense' of the proved sentence, not the truth of a sentence whose sense can be grasped independently (antecedently). There is nothing parallel to sense for mathematical sentences, and nothing parallel to verification. This insight is associated in Wittgenstein's work with an increasing emphasis on one aspect of the autonomy of grammar, viz. the complete independence of every rule of grammar from every other one. Genuine verification exploits logical connections between statements; the truth of one statement makes others true (or at least probable). The absence of any parallel to verification in mathematics is equivalent to the thesis that there are no logical connections between its 'propositions' which can be exploited by proofs. Waismann's later writings reflect this change of emphasis. At a late stage in the evolution of *LSP*, he reorganized the material on arithmetic and geometry to emphasize the autonomy of grammar, viz. by incorporating it into Chapter III as a preface to a general discussion of the complete independence of any two distinct grammatical rules. Chapter XX stresses how misleading is the comparison of mathematics with empirical discourse. These themes are also prominent in his *Einführung in das mathematische Denken,* whose final version was completed in the summer of 1936.

Although these developments are clearly visible in Waismann's papers, they are familiar to perceptive scholars of Wittgenstein's philosophy from his own work. There is no blinding revelation to be found in Waismann's writing, though close scrutiny might reveal details of some interest. This is not true, however, of one of the most fundamental developments in Wittgenstein's semantics, the replacement of the concept of hypothesis by the concept of criteria. This is seldom even recognized, and certainly not widely understood. Here the study of Waismann's papers can make an important contribution to scholarship on Wittgenstein. I will focus attention on evidence for this change from Waismann's writings.

The first kind of evidence is a global reorganization of *LSP,* resulting finally in the suppression of the chapter "Ueber Hypothesen" (printed as an appendix to Part II of *LSP*). All of the early material for *LSP* makes use of the concept of hypothesis. Considerable attention is devoted to its clarification. A large fraction of the shorthand notebooks consists of discussion of hypotheses under such headings as "Hypothese," "Mehrfache Verifikation," "Hypothese und Konvention." Until a very late date the chapter on hypotheses formed part of the text. It was translated into English in Vienna in 1937 ("Logical Structure of Hypotheses") so that Waismann could deliver it as a lecture when he came to Cambridge in 1938. It was apparently suppressed in the course of producing the final text of *LSP* in 1938–1939. Waismann's motivation for making this alteration is not known. But, since the applications of the concept of hypothesis had previously disappeared from most of the rest of the text of *LSP,* this chapter was no longer an integral part of the book. Indeed, the only significant use of hypothesis is made in a passage in Chapter IV, §2, and this was physically extracted from the chapter on hypotheses and hence introduced into the text after the suppression of that chapter.[34] (It formed §4 under the heading "Lassen die Aussagen des täglichen Lebens eine endgültige Verifikation zu?")

The second kind of evidence is the changing application of the term 'Hypothese' in the evolution of *LSP*. In the earliest version of what became Chapter II, §1, Waismann explained the meaning of 'Hypothese' and then added that most everyday assertions were hypotheses.[35] Later, and presumably at this time too, this remark was taken to be true of statements about other minds and about the external world, and in this context it was explicitly applied to statements about the past. All such hypotheses have two distinguishing characteristics: first, their sense is explained by explaining what constitutes evidence for them or makes them probable, i.e. in terms of their 'symptoms' ('Symptomen' or 'Anzeichen'); and second, they are never fully verified, but only made more or less probable, by evidence that supports them. The final text of *LSP* represents a considerable departure from this position. Statements about behavior and physiological states are taken as *criteria* for the ascription of psychological states to others. It can in principle be decided with *certainty* whether two persons have the same experience in a given situation (*PLP*, p. 26), and it is *not* an hypothesis that another person has a toothache when he behaves in a certain way (*PLP*, p. 343). Similarly, the statement that memory is reliable is not an hypothesis, and therefore descriptions of past events are not hypotheses relative to statements about the present and future (cf. *PLP*, pp. 20–21). These are clear changes of view. There are only two passages in *LSP* where statements about physical objects are treated as hypotheses based on descriptions of immediate experience (*PLP*, pp. 74–76 and 222–223). Both of these come from the suppressed chapter on hypo-

34. The location of this material here conforms with, and was probably motivated by, the structure of an essay entitled "Methode" in "*Ältere Reste*." Hence it may reflect Wittgenstein's early intentions about the organization of *LSP*, though the change was effected later on Waismann's own initiative.

35. "Die meisten Aussagen des täglichen Lebens haben diesen Charakter."

theses and might be criticized as anachronisms. On the other hand, *LSP* may treat ascriptions of abilities as hypotheses; on one reading of the text, such mental abilities as knowledge and understanding are hypotheses relative to behavioral evidence (*PLP*, p. 343; cf. *PG* §41). There is such a narrowing in the range of application of 'Hypothese' in the development of *LSP* that the concept very nearly disappears from the book.

Third, the narrowing in application of 'Hypothese' and the increasing importance of the term 'Kriterium' in *LSP* is not a mere change of terminology. It is directly linked with a change in the analysis and criticism of skepticism. This is clearly visible in the development of the text for Chapter II, §1. The earliest version of this argument opened with this statement:

> The assertion 'My memory is reliable' is an *hypothesis*. Not more than that, i.e. not a piece of knowledge; and not less, i.e. not a mere unsubstantiated conjecture.[36]

It then examined the contrast between the skeptic and the antiskeptic about the past:

> The advocate of an hypothesis is able to specify the criterion whose presence he is prepared to acknowledge as a provisional verification of the hypothesis. The skeptic, by contrast, cannot specify any criterion at all whose presence he is prepared to acknowledge as a final verification of the reliability of memory or of the truth of a particular memory-claim.[37]

The eirenic conclusion is reached that these claims are really equivalent, however inconsistent they may sound. Although the term criterion ('Kriterium') appears in this argument, it is equivalent in meaning with the terms 'symptom' or 'indica-

36. "Die Aussage, *mein Gedächtnis ist treu*, ist eine *Hypothese*. Nicht mehr, also keine Erkenntnis, nicht weniger, also keine blosse unbegründete Vermutung."

37. "Der Hypothetiker vermag das Kriterium anzugeben, bei dessen Vorliegen er bereit ist, die Hypothese als vorläufig bewährt anzuerkennen. Der Skeptiker dagegen vermag überhaupt kein Kriterium anzugeben, bei dessen Vorliegen er letzlich die Treue der Erinnerung oder das Faktum des Gedächtnisses anzuerkennen bereit wäre."

tion' ('Symptom' and 'Anzeichen'): a criterion is here a fact that supports an *hypothesis.* This is not the way the term is later used by Waismann. According to this use, to state the criteria for the statement that memory is reliable is to describe what constitutes *conclusive* evidence for its reliability. This makes the skeptic's position untenable. He does not give a misleading formulation of the truth, but rather he makes a claim that is false on the assumption that he uses words in their usual sense. The question expressing his doubt about the reliability of memory is "a misuse of language, nothing more" (*PLP,* p. 21). Without clear criteria for reliability, the concept of reliability of memory is just empty. But specification of such criteria would exclude the possibility of skepticism, because the presence of these criteria establishes the truth of a memory claim with *certainty.* The expression of skepticism about the past is a logical confusion dressed up as a problem. It is crucial to this whole line of argument that the statement that memory is reliable is *not* an hypothesis, that the criteria for a past-tense statement establish its truth with certainty, not merely with varying degrees of probability. This development in the argument of §1 depends entirely on the change from hypotheses to criteria in the analysis of the sense of statements about the past.

A similar development took place in the argument of §2 of Chapter II. The earliest version, entitled "Ex. d. Fremdseelischen," contains a medley of analytical tools.

> Suppose someone tells us, 'My wife is depressed'. What does he mean by this? Well, that depends on what he regards as the criterion for the truth of this statement. For the sense of a statement is the method of its verification. So we will ask him: 'How did you recognize your wife's state of mind?' He could reply: 'Well, that is apparent from various symptoms:. . .'. In this way he has listed the criteria for the truth of his assertion.[38]

38. "Nehmen wir an, ein Mann sage uns: 'Meine Frau is niedergeschlagen.' Was meint er damit? Nun, das kommt darauf an, was er als Kriterium für die Wahrheit dieses Satzes ansieht. Denn der Sinn eines Satzes ist die Art seiner Verifikation. Wir fragen also den Mann: 'Woran hast du den Seelenzustand deiner Frau gemerkt?' Er könnte uns entgegnen: 'Nun, das geht aus verschiedenen Anzeichen hervor:. . .' Er hat uns damit die Kriterien für die Wahrheit seiner Aussage aufgezählt."

Later it is argued that this account of the sense of statements about other minds is not a form of reductionism:

> In fact who is in any position to give an exhaustive list of features that characterize sadness? And granted that one or another of these characteristics is actually present, are we even then certain that we are not deceiving ourselves? I think not. There are countless circumstances, variations, and nuances that merge, so that any attempt at their pedantic enumeration would be futile. It is best then to be perfectly frank: the word 'depressed' is used in such–and–such a case, and again in such–and–such a case, and then too in many other cases that are more or less closely related to these cited cases.[39]

Finally, Waismann argued against the thesis that all of the expressions (*Äusserungen*) of an inner state are merely indicators of a hidden something that is common to all these forms of behavior. Such a view rests on a too primitive conception of how language functions. In this version of §2, Waismann's principal contention was that statements about other minds are hypotheses whose symptoms are bits of bodily behavior. But his formulation harks back to the principle of verifiability, and it contains the seed of an analysis of inner states in terms of family resemblances among patterns of behavior. Different strands of thought exist in suspension here without properly fusing together. The two later versions of §2 ("Das Problem des fremden Bewusstseins" and the final text) advance an analysis of inner states by reference to behavioral criteria. The question 'Do two persons ever have the same experience?' is meaningless unless criteria of identity are specified for what constitutes identity of experiences, and once *any* criteria are admitted, the question is in principle capable of being answered with certainty. Moreover, unless the meaning of such sentences deviates from the normal one, the answer is

39. "In der Tat, wer ist im Stande eine erschöpfende Liste der Merkmale anzugeben, die der Trauer eigen sind? Und gesetzt, das eine oder andere dieser Merkmale liege tatsächlich vor, sind wir nun auch sicher, dass wir uns nicht täuschen? Ich glaube nicht. Es gibt hier unendlich viele Umstände, Varietäten und Nuancen, die ineinander übergehen, und jeder Versuch einer pedantischen Aufzählung wäre eitel. Es ist dann das Beste zu gestehen: Das Wort 'niedergeschlagen' wird in einem solchen Fall gebraucht, ferner in einem solchen Fall und dann noch in vielen anderen Fällen, die mit den angeführten mehr oder weniger verwandt sind."

clearly that we do frequently know that two persons are having the same experience. What are variously called 'symptoms', ('Anzeichen'), 'criteria' ('Kriterien'), and 'characteristics' ('Merkmale') in the first version constitute at best inconclusive evidence for a third-person psychological statement. By contrast, the two later versions introduce the concept of criteria as part of an argument to justify the claim that some such statements can be known with certainty.

The gradual replacement of hypotheses by criteria as the primary analytical tool in Waismann's semantics highlights the parallel development visible in Wittgenstein's writings. There too there is a progressive narrowing in the scope of application of 'Hypothese', leading to its ultimate extinction. Both *PB* and "BT" (*PG*) have separate chapters on hypotheses, and the concept is much discussed and used in *WWK*. Statements about the external world are explicitly construed as hypotheses relative to descriptions of immediate experience (*WWK*, pp. 158–159, *PB* §230). Statements about other minds are implicitly treated as hypotheses, relative to descriptions of behavior (cf. *PB* §65). Later he developed the idea that expressions standing for psychological states and abilities should be explained in terms of family resemblances between patterns of behavior (e.g. *PG* §35). It is not clear whether this step was taken while he still adhered to the hypothesis-analysis of such expressions. What is clear is that he ultimately explained the sense of statements about other minds by reference to behavioral criteria (*BBB*, pp. 24–25, 57) simultaneously with his explaining mental concepts as family resemblance concepts (*BBB*, pp. 20, 88, 114–115, 119–125, 129–135, 144–146, 152). Similarly, for a time descriptions of immediate experience are taken to function as criteria for statements about the external world (*BBB*, pp. 51–52). This position is associated with a general repudiation of the concept of hypothesis as incoherent:

> Shall we then call it an unnecessary hypothesis that anyone else has personal experiences?—But is it an hypothesis at all? For how can I even make the hypothesis if it transcends all possible experience? How could such a hypothesis be backed by meaning? (Is it not like paper money, not backed by gold?) (*BBB*, p. 48; cf. *Z* §260).

Consequently, e.g., actual performances are explicitly distinguished from symptoms and treated as criteria for the ascription of abilities to others (*BBB*, pp. 101–104, 113–114). This extinction of the concept of hypothesis is correlated in Wittgenstein's writings with a revised assessment of skepticism. This change is identical with the one noted in Waismann's papers. (Compare *PB* §§54–58 and "BT" §§101–104 with *BBB*, pp. 53–54, 56–57, 60.)

There are two salient differences in this parallel development of ideas by Wittgenstein and Waismann. The first is that Waismann's progressive restriction on the application of 'Hypothese' did not lead to its being denied any application at all, and he certainly did not criticize the coherence of the notion of hypothesis. This is linked with the second difference: Waismann never abandoned the idea that the concept of hypothesis was a useful analytical tool, even if it had restricted application. This presumably accounts for his reintroducing into the text of *LSP* the view that statements about the physical world can be treated as hypotheses relative to sense-data. He thus offers as a grammatical model to illuminate the sense of descriptions of physical objects something that on the *Blue Book* conception of the matter could only darken counsel. He also later published a substantial chunk of the chapter on hypotheses from *LSP* in his article "Verifiability." Waismann's permanent attachment to this concept makes it all the more plausible to attribute to Wittgenstein's direct intervention most, if not all, of the development toward the exclusion of the concept of hypothesis from the text of *LSP*.

In writing *LSP*, Waismann followed Wittgenstein very attentively but at a respectful distance. If Wittgenstein's thought evolved rapidly during most of the period 1928–1935, then Waismann may never have kept abreast of the changes, and he may not have grasped or accepted some of them. The product of *Verehrung* may have been *Verkehrung*, either real or perceived. This in no way diminishes the interest and value of Waismann's writings. Indeed, it gives them a unique importance in the study of the development of Wittgenstein's thinking and in the clarification of its various stages. They also have great intrinsic interest as formulations of a series of philosophical positions. It is conceivable that the road to Truth should go via Misrepresentation.

Coda

There are three important morals to be drawn from the arguments of this essay. First, Waismann's papers are a major source for the study of the phases and evolution of Wittgenstein's thought in the critical period 1928–1935—indeed, the most important source apart from Wittgenstein's own writings. They have not yet been fully exploited, partly because most of the material has until recently remained unpublished, disorganized, and uncatalogued,[40] and partly because there is little recognition of the relation of Waismann's work to Wittgenstein's. Second, Waismann's papers are the primary source for studying one aspect of the history of the Vienna Circle, the relation of their work to Wittgenstein's. This is an important and fascinating chapter in the history of ideas. Its careful study might be pregnant with philosophical consequences. On the one hand, it might help to revive serious interest in verificationist or 'antirealist' theories of meaning. And, on the other, it might help to clarify some of the obscurity enveloping Wittgenstein's account of meaning in terms of criteria. Finally, *LSP* is the best available systematic, authoritative introduction to Wittgenstein's 'later philosophy' with its distinctive method of philosophizing, and it is the single most effective antidote to the obscurantist dogma that Wittgenstein set his face against any systematic presentation of his philosophical insights. His own lengthy participation in the project of writing *LSP* is a concrete refutation of this contention.

In several different respects, Waismann's is the voice of one crying in the wilderness. Oyez! Oyez![41]

40. The entire *Nachlass* was catalogued and deposited in the Bodleian Library, Oxford, late in 1976.

41. I am grateful to the following for permission to quote unpublished material: Marie Neurath, Albert M. Schlick, B. F. B. van de Velde-Schlick, and the literary executors of the estates of Ludwig Wittgenstein and Friedrich Waismann. I am also most grateful for advice and criticisms to Professor G. E. M. Anscombe, Professor Sir Alfred Ayer, Mr. B. F. McGuinness, Dr. P. M. S. Hacker, and Professor C. G. Luckhardt. Finally, I thank Mr. T. J. Reed for improvements to my translations.

Appendix 1

Among Waismann's copious papers there is much material that is related to the composition of *LSP*. The five kinds of this material will be briefly described. It must be emphasized at the outset that the division made here is related to the type of writing and to its relation with the final text of *LSP*. The material of each kind cannot be assumed to be chronologically homogeneous, nor is there any simple uniform relation between related material belonging to the different kinds of writing.

1. Shorthand notebooks: There are several series of these notebooks. The first is a set primarily containing conversations with Wittgenstein from 18 December 1929 to 1 July 1932. Transcriptions of these conversations have been published (*WWK*). The second is a set of eight with the labels "Vorarbeit 1," . . . , "Vorarbeit 8." The first two contain polished versions of some of the recorded conversations with Wittgenstein from the first set of notebooks. The other six seem to contain material directly taken from Wittgenstein, either from conversations or from manuscripts (there are close echoes of remarks in *PB*) or both. Next there are three series, closely related to each other and to the final text of *LSP:* one labeled with (random?) Roman letters (viz. "G" and "M"), one with Roman numerals (I–IV), and one with Arabic numerals (1–3).

Their content is varied, ranging from passages of just a few lines (sometimes labeled "Nachträge") to the text for whole chapters (e.g. two complete versions of Chapter VI). Finally there are two odd notebooks, one unlabeled containing remarks on philosophy, and the other an English notebook with the shorthand German text for parts of Chapters X and XI.

The writing of these notebooks follows a standard pattern. The remarks or continuous texts are written on the right-hand page only, leaving the left page free for recording emendations, additions, cross-references, etc. This arrangement would have been very appropriate if Waismann's procedure had been to compose a text to discuss with Wittgenstein, since it would be easy to incorporate suggestions for revision on the left-hand page. Certainly much of the lefthand writing looks hurried and sketchy. This is also true of some of the writing on the right, but the bulk of it is very neat and polished. Most of this writing consists of draft texts under descriptive titles (e.g. "Disposition," "Möglichkeit," "Erinnerung"); the rest is drafts of chapters or sections of *LSP*. Waismann clearly intended that a stenographer should be able to type from these shorthand texts, and in many cases there are extant typescripts made directly from these notebooks. A large proportion of the preparatory material for *LSP* was drafted in shorthand at one or more stages in its development.

2. *Ältere Reste:* There are a large number (approximately one hundred) of short typescripts, typically one to four pages in length, most of which were gathered together in two folders bearing the titles "Ältere Reste." Most of them were typed from polished texts in the surviving shorthand notebooks. It is plausible to conjecture that the others were typed from shorthand notebooks that have been lost. Each of them bears a title, e.g. "Unsere Methode" and "Allgemeinheit I," and each is typically self-contained. Many of them are derived directly from Wittgenstein's work. Some duplicate material from Waismann's records of Wittgenstein's formal conversations with him and Schlick. Some are taken from the so-called "Diktat für Schlick." Some others must be either notes taken from typescripts that Wittgenstein put at his disposal or notes of remarks that Wittgenstein made in conversations with Waismann while working on *LSP*. In several cases the typescripts are written in the first person, although it is clear that it is Wittgenstein who is the speaker. By contrast, the ones based on the "Diktat für Schlick" are rewritten in the third person (e.g. in "Verstehen eines Bildes" the sentence "Ich vergleiche mit Recht den Satz einem gemalten Bild" is replaced by the sentence "Man kann mit Recht den Satz mit einem gemalten Bilde vergleichen"). Many of these typescripts were revised for retyping at later stages in the writing of *LSP*, and in many cases it is possible to identify later typescripts based on these earlier ones.

3. *Vorstufen:* In rewriting sections of *LSP* and in rearranging the distribution of its material into chapters, Waismann put aside discarded typescripts in a folder entitled "Vorstufen." Sometimes a chapter or section was virtually wholly rewritten,

in which cases there survives an entire earlier draft of material with a counterpart in the final version. There are two superseded versions of "Namen," one of "Vorbereitende Erörterung," and two of "Zur Logik des Fragens." More commonly, parts of the earlier versions were physically incorporated in the later ones. This leaves in "Vorstufen" only the scattered pages which were substantially altered in the revision. By inserting the reused pages in the gaps of the remaindered early draft it is possible in many cases to reconstruct the complete text prior to revision and to compare it with the revised versions. Similarly, it is often possible to recover information about earlier organization of the material of the book; e.g. there are six distinguishable rearrangements of Part I. The typescripts of this category are of the greatest value in tracing the development of the text.

4. *Die Kopie:* Most of the folders containing the typescripts of the final versions of the chapters of *LSP* are inscribed with chapter headings and the word "Kopie." This is uniformly a carbon copy, almost certainly of the typescript sent to Holland for publication in 1939. Annotations show that it was the text actually used for producing the original English translation. Some parts of it are missing, and a few sections were never included in the typed text. There are several versions of the table of contents, with notes in the margin such as "Die Kopie fehlt," "Schluss fehlt," and "Anfang im Abschreiben." Although it is not known when these comments were written, they do correspond accurately with the extant carbon typescript. In some cases there is a clear explanation for the fact that parts of the final text are missing. Waismann raided the text of *LSP* for material that was published independently, leaving only a single typescript (either the original or the carbon) to be sent to Holland. This hypothesis would account for the absence of Chapter I, §§2–3, and Chapter II, §§1–2 (published as "Von der Natur eines philosophischen Problems" in *Synthese* 4 [1939]) and Chapter XIX, §§1–2 (published as "Ist Logik eine deduktive Theorie?" in *Erkenntnis* 7 [1937–1938]). It might also account for the loss of Chapter I, §1, since Waismann's obituary of Schlick in *Synthese* 1 (1936), "De beteeke-

nis van Moritz Schlick voor de Wijsbegeerte," is in part a translation into Dutch of this text.

5. Longhand manuscripts: There are a very few parts of the book for which the final text exists only in manuscript. The only substantial portions for which this is true are Chapter III, §4, and Chapter XI, §§1 and 7. (There is a manuscript version of Chapter VII, §§4–7, but it is superseded by a typescript.) All of these manuscripts were written after Waismann came to Cambridge. They presumably date from his revision of the German text in the period August 1938 to August 1939, when he worked through the book with Mrs. Paul as she translated it into English (letter to Neurath, 8 August 1938).

Appendix 2

The first stage in the composition of Chapter III is the production of its atoms. These are shorthand notes and corresponding short typescripts, whose sources in this case are mostly the formal conversations with Wittgenstein. There are four extant typescripts of this category among "Ältere Reste": "Geometrie" (three pages, based on *WWK*, pp. 38 and 61–63), "Gesichtsraum" (three pages, based on *WWK*, pp. 55–57), 'Uebersicht" (two pages, based on *WWK*, pp. 63–66 and 76), and "Möglichkeit" (five pages, related to *PG*, pp. 125–128). The second stage is the unification of these remarks into longer essays, comparable in scope to a section of a chapter of *LSP*. No doubt this was frequently accomplished by simply clipping together several of the atomic essays in a suitable sequence. There are examples of this procedure. But, where there was more extensive rearrangement or significant modification of the material, a new typescript would be made. For Chapter III there are two extant typescripts belonging to this phase: "Rot und Grün" (eight pages) and "Rechtfertigung der Grammatik" (four pages, incorporating a modified version of "Uebersicht"). Finally, there was the stage of stringing together these molecules to form the chapters of the book. This involved frequent and major rearrangements of the material, and often required modification of the molecular essays in order to make them appropriate for a new context. The material of §§1 and 2 of Chapter III was conceived and written as §§7 and 8 of a chapter "Ueber den Begriff der Regel" (an ancestor of Chapter VII), while §3 was written as §5 of the section of Part I entitled "Einige Beispiele philosophischer Probleme und ihrer Lösung" (an ancestor of Chapter II). At the time of moving §§1 and 2 from Part II to Part I, Waismann added to the text paragraphs 5–8 and 11–13 of §1 and paragraphs 4–8 of §2. (These paragraph numbers refer to the text of *LSP*, not *PLP*.) The construction of Chapter III out of this diverse material and the writing of §4 were effected in Waismann's revision of the text in 1938–1939.

Appendix 3

There are at least nineteen sections in the shorthand notebooks containing parts of the text of Chapter VI, as well as two complete (but differing) drafts of the entire chapter. There are seven short early typescripts in "Ältere Reste" and also one longer essay ("Was ist ein Befehl?") incorporating material from several of these shorter ones. In "Vorstufen," material related to §§7 and 8 is found incorporated into an early draft of Chapter VII. All parts of the final text are reworked at several different periods in the shorthand notebooks.

10 Wittgenstein on "Moore's Paradox"

KENT LINVILLE

Wittgenstein "once remarked that the only work of Moore's that greatly impressed him was his discovery of the peculiar kind of nonsense involved in such a sentence as, e.g., 'It is raining but I don't believe it.' "[1] Despite this perplexing assessment of Moore's work and the impressive volume of commentary on *Philosophical Investigations*, neither has led to an exploration of Wittgenstein's treatment of such sentences (which he calls "Moore's Paradox") in Part II, section x.[2] The following discussion aims to remedy this neglect.

Moore claims that sentences of the form "I believe that *p*, but not *p*" (hereafter, M) would "be perfectly absurd . . . to say [assert]," although what they assert "is perfectly possible logically."[3] What puzzles Moore about such sentences, what

1. Norman Malcolm, *Ludwig Wittgenstein: A Memoir* (London, New York: Oxford University Press, 1958), pp. 66–67. These sentences were brought to Wittgenstein's attention in a paper (the identity of which is not known) that Moore read to the Moral Sciences Club at Cambridge in October 1944. For documentation and details, see Wittgenstein's letter to Moore in *Letters to Russell, Keynes, and Moore*, ed. G. H. von Wright (Oxford: Basil Blackwell; Ithaca, N.Y.: Cornell University Press, 1974), p. 177.

2. Ludwig Wittgenstein, *Philosophical Investigations*, trans. G. E. M. Anscombe (Oxford: Basil Blackwell; New York: Macmillan, 1958). Parenthetical reference will be to this work. References to Part I will be cited by section (§) number, reference to Part II by page number.

3. The actual specimen to which Moore is referring reads, "I went to the pictures last Tuesday, but I don't believe that I did" (*The Philosophy of G. E. Moore*, ed. Paul Arthur Schilpp (Evanston and Chicago: Northwestern University Press, 1942), p. 543). However, both this and the form "I believe *p* but not *p*" are treated by Moore as being problematic in the same way. (Compare his discussion in "A Reply to My Critics" and "Russell's Theory of Descriptions.") Following Wittgenstein, the discussion here treats the "I believe *p* but not *p*" form, leaving it to the reader to adapt what is said to the alternative form.

he finds in need of explanation, is the "absurdity" of asserting M. Moore's motives for giving such an explanation are clarified by placing his perplexity in a more significant historical context. This altered view of Moore's plight can be secured by imagining the following objection to one facet of Descartes's *cogito:*

> As you have it, claims such as 'I am sitting here by the fire' or 'This is a hand' are dubitable; by contrast, the claim that 'I think (believe/doubt) that this is a hand' is indubitable. You understand this difference to reflect a difference in what is asserted in the two cases. The former assertion goes beyond a mere report of sense-experience, for it purports to report something existing independently; whereas the latter assertion merely describes one's own state of mind, and so (according to your *cogito*) cannot be doubted. But if that is correct, why can't we assert the following: 'I believe that this is a hand, but this is not a hand'? Surely that would be a perfectly absurd thing to assert, although I cannot see why it should be, given the truth of your claims about what the conjuncts of such a sentence actually say!

Appreciating that Descartes shares Moore's need to explain M's "absurdity" helps identify the sensibility that governs Moore's response to M. For the assumed intelligibility of M which motivates his explanation of its unassertability rests upon an unannounced, though familiar, Cartesian assumption: namely, that the conjunct of M incorporating "I believe" is self-referential. Only if one thinks that the assertion "I believe that it is raining," e.g., reports, describes, or in some manner "tells how it is with the speaker," will one find it puzzling—in need of explanation—that its conjunction with the assertion "It is not raining" is odd. For only then does it appear that M *cannot* be logically flawed, since its conjuncts are not about the same subject matter.

Moore advances no argument in support of the assumed self-referential character of assertions incorporating "I believe."[4] To articulate the epistemological doctrines which

4. An assumption Moore makes explicitly in developing the claim that the assertion of *p* "implies" that I believe *p:* "You imply this proposition *about your present attitude* although it is not implied by (i.e., does not follow from) what you assert" (Moore, *Philosophy,* p. 542; my italics). For direct criticism of Moore's proffered solution of M's oddity, see Merrill Ring and Kent Linville, "Moore's Paradox: Assertion and Implication," *Behaviorism* 1 (1973), pp. 87–102.

make the adoption of Moore's primitive thesis natural, I shall center attention upon construals of belief found in Descartes's *Meditations*. But the scope of these remarks is intended to range beyond Descartes, encompassing (*mutatis mutandis*) other standard analyses that treat belief as a phenomenon (e.g., "a pattern of behavior," "a disposition to certain behavior," "a brain state," or "a specific array of psychic constituents correlated with (e.g., Tractarian) objects named in '*p*' "). For the idea that "I believe that *p*" expresses a condition of the speaker is an implication shared by these analyses; they differ only in what they take to constitute that condition.

In relation to Wittgenstein's discussion, I intend the following remarks to sustain three of his themes: first, that to regard "I believe" as a referring expression is to "misinterpret" its logic (cum grammar); second, that this "misinterpretation" plays a fundamental role in generating the solipsism of the first *Meditation* (and so plays a central role in traditional epistemology);[5] third, that underlying these epistemological doctrines is that "primitive conception of meaning" which Wittgenstein singles out in opening the *Investigations*, as the source of trouble for philosophy. An auxilliary enterprise, suggested by the role which I find for the concept of seeing-as in the discussion of Moore's Paradox, is to indicate that Wittgenstein conceives of philosophical paradox generally as resulting from a form of "aspect blindness."

The reading of "I believe" suggested by the *cogito* is subject to a form of criticism which Moore himself has made in another connection: namely, that on such an interpretation one is unable to account for interpersonal disagreement.[6] If, for example, "I believe that Alpha Centauri is the closest star" were about the speaker, then an interlocutor saying that he did not believe it to be the closest star would not contradict

5. A theme suggested elsewhere in the *Investigations:* "The significance of such possibilities of transformation, for example of turning all statements into sentences beginning 'I think' or 'I believe' (and thus, as it were, into descriptions of my inner life) will become clearer in another place. (Solipsism)" (*Investigations*, §24).

6. See Moore's criticism of "ethical subjectivism" in his *Ethics* (London: Williams and Norgate, n.d.), pp. 100–103.

what I say (the truth I claim), since we would not be talking about *the same thing*. In which case, when two people discovered they had different beliefs this would merely mark a contrast between them ("I feel anxious"—"I don't"), not thrust them upon a point of disagreement. When such discoveries occur in ordinary discourse, however, there is disagreement. And the resolution of such conflicts is achieved by determining the truth or falsity of *p*—in the above example, for instance, by determining the truth or falsity of "Alpha Centauri is the closest star." Thus, prefixing "I believe" to the simple assertion does not transform it into a truth claim exclusively about the assertor.

Agreeing that "I believe that *p*" cannot be read as solely the report of a datum in one's mental life, one will feel that, still, at bottom such a statement is self-referential. For the truth of such an assertion, one may reason, is not completely contradicted by the discovery that not *p*. It remains that *I did believe* that *p*. This reasoning proceeds upon the assumption that " 'I believed' must tell of just the same thing in the past as 'I believe' in the present" (p. 190). And when coupled with our earlier observation—that an adequate analysis of "I believe that *p*" must allow for interpersonal disagreement—one will urge that such assertions are about *both* the speaker and *p*. But of course it will not do to claim that these assertions are simply *conjunctions* of the claims that I believe and that *p*, if (as previously claimed) they are not falsified by not *p*.

Returning to *Meditations,* we find a second reading of "I believe" which seems to provide precisely the model needed. Consider the following from the third *Meditation:*

> If we consider them [ideas] only in themselves and do not relate them to something, they cannot, properly speaking, be false. . . . The principal and most common error which can be encountered here consists in judging [believing] that the ideas which are in myself are similar to or conformable to, things outside of myself; for certainly, if I considered the ideas only as certain modes (or aspects) of my thought, without intending them to refer to some other exterior object, they could hardly offer me a chance of making a mistake.[7]

7. René Descartes, *Meditations,* trans. Laurence J. LaFleur (Indianapolis and New York: Bobbs-Merrill, 1960), p. 36.

Descartes seems to be saying that judgments (beliefs) which are subject to error are effected by "taking" the contents of one's own consciousness ("ideas") to be *reflections* of external things. This picture is developed by Wittgenstein in the following: "At bottom, when I say 'I believe . . . ' I am describing my own state of mind—but this description is indirectly an assertion of the fact believed. —As in certain circumstances I describe a photograph in order to describe the thing it is a photograph of" (p. 190). The parallel between this and the preceding quotation from Descartes resides in the thought that in saying "I believe it is so," one is *both* describing one's own state of mind and "relating" its content to "things which are outside myself." In terms of Wittgenstein's remark, when saying "I believe it is so," one begins by describing one's own state of mind ("I believe . . . "). And continuing in one's description of *the same thing,* describing its "content" (specifying what one believes), one intends this *also* to describe something other than the state itself, "the facts." This makes it appear as though when in the state called "belief," one's mind is (or is "taken" to be) a reflective medium. As Wittgenstein mentions in connection with photographs, one may describe a mirror image, for example, in order to describe what it is a mirror image of; and as a mirror image (or photograph) may be a good or bad representation of what is imaged (or photographed), so a belief may be true or false.

The analogy breaks down, however, when one presses the putative parallel between true and false belief, on the one side, and good and bad representation, on the other. One can line up a mirror image or photograph to one's right, the thing imaged or photographed to one's left; and it is this *independent access* to both sides which gives talk about good and bad representation the sense that it has. But the comparison between what one believes is the case and what is the case is nothing like that. There is no dual access in the case of belief. To express this from within the analogy: what one believes is the case *is* one's access to what is the case.

There is a temptation to restore this Cartesian picture of belief as a state of mind which "points beyond itself," by shifting the analogy from mirror-impressions to sense-impressions. For just as one does not place one's beliefs alongside what is the case to see if they somehow fit or correspond, so neither does one place what looks or appears to be the case to the left or right of what is the case to determine if one's perception is veridical. Moreover, as it is possible to believe such-and-such when such-and-such is not case, so something can look or appear to a person to be such-and-such when it is not such-and-such. If I assert "I believe it is red" or "It looks red" when the thing is not red, I may subsequently say, "I believed then that it was red, but it wasn't" or "It looked red to me, but it wasn't." However, in opposition to this assimilation of beliefs to sense-impressions, Wittgenstein remarks, "One can mistrust one's own senses, but not one's own belief" (ibid.). And the point of this remark is to remind us that the parallel between "I believed" and "It looked" breaks down in the present tense. To conceive of belief as a kind of sense-impression is to forget that "I believed then that . . . but it wasn't" (unlike "It looked . . . but it wasn't") does not have a significant present-tense counterpart. In Moore's words, "M would be a perfectly absurd thing to say."[8]

We have argued against three readings of "I believe" that take assertions in which it plays a role to be (at bottom) about the speaker and, consequently, M to be non-self-contradictory. However, in the course of our discussion an important difference between M and paradigmatic cases of contradiction has surfaced: a change of tense or (we may here add) a change of person transforms M into an unproblematic sentence. And this fact alone is sometimes thought sufficient to establish the claim

8. Lest one is tempted to think things cannot look *that* radically different from what we believe or know them to be, it is to the point to repeat the following anecdote from Miss Anscombe's "The Intentionality of Sensation": "Often things look to us, strike us, not as they look but as they are! (Conviction that only so is 'looks' used rightly was the cause of confusion to an over-confident ordinary language philosopher . . . : F. Cioffi brought in a glass vessel of water with a stick in it. 'Do you mean to say,' he asked, 'that this stick does not look bent?' 'No' said the other bravely: 'It looks like a straight stick in water.' So Cioffi took it out and it *was* bent)" (in *Analytical Philosophy*, ed. R. J. Butler [Oxford: Basil Blackwell, 1965], p. 173).

that M, too, is logically impeccable. Such reasoning is present in the following argument by Professor Bernard Williams:

> 'I believe that it is raining but it is not raining' constitutes a paradox, which was famously pointed out by G. E. Moore. This is a paradox but it is not a formal self-contradiction. If it were, then in general 'x believes that *p* but *p* is false', would also be a self-contradiction. But this is obviously not so. Thus I can, without any paradox at all, say 'Jones believes that *p* but *p* is false'. . . . [9]

But arguing that M could be true (is not self-contradictory) because its non-first-person counterparts are unproblematic assertions is not a universally sound form of reasoning. For by analogy, one could as well argue that "I promise to meet you, but I won't meet you" asserts something logically possible, since its non-first-person counterparts can also voice straightforward assertions. However, that would clearly misinterpret the locution "I promise to . . . ," which is not employed to assert (report or describe) *that* I promise. . . . And although "to believe" is assuredly not a "performative verb," a central claim in Wittgenstein's discussion is that our understanding of "I believe" is not modeled upon the logic of other person and tense constructions of "to believe." In contrast to those latter developments of the verb, incorporating "I believe" in an assertion neither alters nor adds to its subject matter: "The expression 'I believe that this is the case' is used like the assertion 'This is the case' " (ibid.). Wittgenstein attempts to place "I believe" in a different light, to show that it is a different kind of instrument. Briefly, it attenuates assertions: "I believe that *p*" is a limited or hesitant or otherwise guarded form of the assertion that *p*.[10] Thus he warns, "Don't look at it as a matter of course, but as a most remarkable thing, that the

9. Bernard Williams, *Problems of the Self* (Cambridge: Cambridge University Press, 1973), p. 137.

10. It is against this backdrop that Wittgenstein's concluding admonition is to be read: "Don't regard a hesitant assertion as an assertion of hesitancy" (*Investigations,* p.193). A treatment of "believe" similar to Wittgenstein's is found in J. O. Urmson, "Parenthetical Verbs," *Mind* 61 (1952), 480–496. There are important differences between Urmson's and Wittgenstein's view, however. For a detailing of those differences, see Ring and Linville, "Moore's Paradox," p. 88.

verbs 'believe', 'wish', 'will' display all the inflexions possessed by 'cut', 'chew', 'run' " (ibid.).

But we are not inclined to heed that warning, for when philosophizing we succumb to "a primitive idea of the way language functions" (§2). Roughly, words are names, and language is used to report the existence of what is named. Belief is a phenomenon of human experience. So learning the various forms of the verb "to believe," we are taught to detect and announce its presence in different persons and at different times. This "realist" conception of belief provides Wittgenstein's motive for opening his discussion with the following series of questions:

> How did we ever come to use such an expression as 'I believe . . . '? Did we at some time become aware of a phenomenon (of belief)? Did we observe ourselves and other people and so discover belief? [Ibid.]

The temptation to give affirmative answers to Wittgenstein's queries is articulated in the following:

> Believing is a state of mind. It has duration; and that independently of the duration of its expression in a sentence, for example. So it is a kind of disposition of the believing person. This is shown me in the case of someone else by his behavior; and by his words. And under this head, by the expression 'I believe . . . ' as well as by the simple assertion. . . . [Pp. 191–192]

But then to make sense of the fact that one can truthfully say "I believe . . . ," one must be able to recognize this disposition in one's own case. For as here pictured, belief *is* belief, wherever or whenever it occurs. However, will it be necessary to *observe* myself, to take notice of myself as others do? To give sense to the sentence, "Judging from my actions and words, *this* is what I believe," one would have to develop a picture of behavior indicating that two people were speaking through my mouth. But then M would no longer be ruled out as "perfectly absurd." The "depersonalized" plight of mind portrayed in such a picture would also allow for the significant assertion of M (cf. p. 192). And that one "splits an ego" in working out a development of the verb in the first-person paralleling "He believes" reflects the confusion involved in thinking "I believe" and "He believes" play the same logical role. ("That . . . development of the verb would have been possible, if only I could say 'I seem to believe' " [ibid.].) Moreover, when we imagine a symmetrical form for "I believe," as in the above, there is no longer even the appearance of a contrast between M's assertability and its intelligibility, which is a necessary condition of the Paradox.

The idea that belief is a phenomenon (or, in the formal mode, that "belief" names one and the selfsame thing) dies hard. One is inclined to object that the above remarks bear upon an *epistemological* difference in the application of "I believe" and its non-first-person variants, not their meaning. All that the above considerations show is that *I* have inside knowledge: " 'One feels conviction within oneself, one doesn't infer it from one's own words or their tone' " (p. 191). Pushing the noted asymmetry to one side as irrelevant to the real point at issue, it will be maintained that if one imagines "I believe that *p*, but not *p*" and "He believes that *p* but not *p*" refer to the same person, the state of affairs being supposed or "entertained" in connection with each is the same. And this surely shows that they mean the same thing, express the same proposition![11]

Such appeals in support of the claim that a word or sentence is understood run deep in traditional philosophy, including Wittgenstein of the *Tractatus:* " 'A state of affairs is thinkable'—what this means is we can picture it to ourselves."[12]

11. One wedded to the notions of sense and reference to determine what is said will so reason. One is then inclined to think the role of the pronoun in fixing our understanding is merely that of "locating the belief in space" (identifying of whom we are predicating the belief). This picture is also at work in the still widely adopted notation "A believes that *p*," which is taken to express the same proposition—have the same truth-value—no matter what is substituted for "A."

12. Ludwig Wittgenstein, *Tractatus Logico-Philosophicus,* trans. D. F. Pears and B. F. McGuinness (London: Routledge & Kegan Paul; New York: Humanities Press, 1961), 3.001. Of course since Descartes's remarking of the concept of a chiliagon, philosophers have been warned of the confusion in thinking imaginability a necessary condition of intelligibility. But the idea that imaginability is a sufficient condition has gone largely unchecked; for example, the following from Hume: "Nothing we imagine is absolutely impossible," and conversely, it is not possible "for the imagination to conceive any thing contrary to a demonstration" (*A Treatise of Human Nature,* ed. L. A. Selby-Bigge [Oxford: Clarendon Press, 1888], pp. 32 and 95, respectively).

The *Investigations* of course goes to lengths to show that contrary to the assumption underlying that appeal, any such picture is fully as much a "sign" as written or uttered words. Any picture can be variously interpreted or applied, and thus requires rather than produces understanding (§139). But this is forgotten or ignored when considering what M asserts, as it were, apart from its assertion. For in lieu of employment within the pale of human communication, one here turns to the mind or to the imagination, and "A picture is conjured up which seems to fix the sense [of M] unambiguously [§426], . . . a picture which by itself seems to make the sense of the expression *unmistakable:* 'Now you know what is in question'—we should like to say. And that is precisely what it does not tell him" (§352).

Taking our lead from Wittgenstein's concluding comment, we shall consider the picture(s) formed to represent what M asserts. For the conjunct incorporating "believe" we think of a person speaking and acting in certain ways, or being in a particular "cognitive state" which so disposes him. To represent the other conjunct, one thinks of a state of affairs falsifying what is believed. Observing the pronoun in M, this "thought experiment" directs one to form an "idea" of *oneself believing* such-and-such, and such-and-such not being the case, side by side. But if we understand the truth claimed by "I believe it is so" to be represented in the mouth of one sincerely speaking and acting in certain ways, or being so disposed, how is the truth of M's other conjunct to bear upon what it asserts? When the words are understood ("interpreted") in this way, they are no longer able to express one's own belief. For example, assuming one acknowledges that one's belief that the cat is on the mat is false upon accepting the truth of "The cat is not on the mat," then the words "I believe that the cat is on the mat" will not declare that belief. For observing the strictures of the pronoun represented, when the meaning of these words is molded from the picture's representation of M, then as *in* the representation what they assert *in* one's own mouth or mind will be understood to be consistent with "The cat is not on the mat."

As Wittgenstein remarks in another connection, here we may say that although such pictures show how our imagination represents false belief, they do not show what lies at bottom of such presentations.[13] But, "instead of 'imaginability' one can also say here: representability by a particular method of representation" (§397). Expressing the matter this way enables one to see that in the following remark Wittgenstein is attempting to expose the "method of representation" that yields these apparitions of sense: "Moore's paradox can be put like this: the expression 'I believe that this is the case' is used like the assertion 'This is the case'; and yet the *hypothesis* that I believe this is the case is not used like the hypothesis that this is the case" (p. 190).

Stating this in terms of language-games, in normal circumstances (wherein asserting M would be "absurd") one does not conjecture or hypothesize that one believes such-and-such. If one is hypothesizing when one says "I believe it is raining," then this is a hypothesis about the weather, not oneself. But when inclined to claim that the sentence "I believe it is raining, but it is not raining" asserts something logically possible, one *must* take the former conjunct to be about the speaker. If regarded as a truth claim about the weather, clearly such a sentence is a contradiction. Since what Moore *means* to be talking about in connection with such sentences is not logically impossible, what he understands or means by M must be the hypothesis that I believe . . . , and it isn't so. But the expression "I believe" is not used to formulate the hypothesis *that* I believe. However, this expression can be *seen as* a hypothesis; and it is the "dawning" of that aspect, I submit, which inclines one to claim that M is logically possible.

We can interpret M as a hypothesis, and see it as we interpret it. As the cube illustration (p. 193) is interpreted as an inverted open box or three boards forming a solid angle, according to the context which surrounds it, so "I believe it is raining" is interpreted as something I assert or as something

13. Ludwig Wittgenstein, *On Certainty*, eds. G. E. M. Anscombe and G. H. von Wright (Oxford: Basil Blackwell; New York: Harper & Row, 1969), §90.

that is asserted about me (i.e., a hypothesis), according to the context which surrounds it. And as the following discussion tries to make clear, since "I believe that *p*" interpreted as something *I* assert makes M nonsense ("perfectly absurd"), our claiming that what *it* asserts is logically possible shows we have placed (imagined) M in a context which supplies the interpretation of "I believe" as something asserted about me. Phenomenologically, when one gazes at M and exclaims, "It could be true!" this expresses the " 'dawning' of an aspect" (p. 194).

Seeing M as a hypothesis is more like seeing  as an object that has fallen over than seeing the altering aspects of Jastrow's duck-rabbit (p. 194): "It is possible to take the duck-rabbit simply for the picture of a rabbit, . . . but not to take the bare triangular figure for the picture of an object that has fallen over. To see this aspect of the triangle demands imagination" (p. 207). Nor are we going to take a bare sentence as a hypothesis; this, too, will require imagination. Seeing M as a hypothesis is a *kind* of seeing-as which requires a story; one sees M as a hypothesis by embedding it in a fiction. In that it is like the following:

> I can imagine some arbitrary cipher—this, for instance: 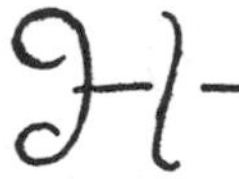
>
> to be a strictly correct letter of some foreign alphabet. Or again, to be a faultily written one, and faulty in this way or that: for example, it might be slap-dash or typical childish awkwardness, or like the flourishes in a legal document. It could deviate from the correctly written letter in a variety of ways. —And I can see it in various aspects according to the fiction I surround it with. [P. 210]

There is an important difference, however, between seeing Wittgenstein's arbitrary cipher in the various aspects he instances and seeing M as a hypothesis. The cipher, but not M, might *be* what it is seen as. The fiction enabling one to see such a sentence as a hypothesis does not characterize, what we may call, a "significant context": a context in which M is or could be what it is seen as. Thus, to so construe "I believe" is to *misinterpret* its logic—its role in speech and communication. To see this, we need to focus upon the kind of story which enables us to see M as a hypothesis.

Descartes of the first *Meditation* gives us a clearly articulated illustration of the kinds of fiction which give M the appearance of life. That the intelligibility of M is there central in Descartes's thought is evident in the following: "[Therefore] I shall consider myself as having no hands, no eyes, no flesh, no blood, nor any senses, yet falsely believing myself to possess all these things."[14] This quotation brings out clearly that the earlier skeptical reflections do not lead Descartes to change his mind (his beliefs) about anything. The beliefs which he takes to the second *Meditation* are the same as he had upon entering the "study." What is new is the avowal that he will "consider himself to believe falsely." However, to "consider" oneself believing falsely is not to declare that one's beliefs are false (e.g., it is not to *assert* that "I believe I am seated next to the fire, but I am not seated by the fire"). Rather, the recommended response to the skeptical reflections of the *Meditation* is that one entertain the *supposition* that one's beliefs are false.[15] When made in quest of "metaphysical certainty," this recommendation to *suppose oneself believing falsely* is not counsel to action ("since I am not considering the questions of action, but only of knowledge").[16] But as we have argued throughout, any picture or manner of expression which seems to enable one to suppose M as a philosophical ("metaphysical") hypothesis is articulated by modeling "I believe" on its non-first-person and non-present-tense forms. And turning to the dialectic of the first *Meditation*, we see that precisely that assimilation informs its plan and execution.

Consider the following wherein Descartes declares his intentions: "I will . . . make a serious and unimpeded effort to destroy generally all my former opinions."[17] Is not the notion of a "former opinion" *here* an invention? If what Descartes is talking about is to be relevant to his investigation, calling it a "former opinion" *cannot* mean that it is a past belief (e.g., "I

14. Descartes, *Meditations*, p. 22.
15. "If there were a verb meaning 'to believe falsely', it would not have any significant first-person present indicative" (*Investigations*, p. 190).
16. Descartes, *Meditations*.
17. Ibid., p. 17.

was formerly of the opinion that Mr. A was a good philosopher, but now believe quite the opposite"). Yet Descartes clearly is attempting to get the reader to see his own beliefs—not as currently claimed, but—as rationally unaccredited opinions, *true of* a "former self" (viz., one's plight of mind *prior* to leaving the community of common men—"vulgar opinion"—and entering what Hume was later to call "profound and intense reflection").

That partial assimilation of "I believe" to former opinions is completed in the dream argument. Suppose with Descartes that it is conceivable one might now be dreaming (surely Descartes thought that it was). Still, the most this shows is that at some (any?) future time one might be forced to say, "I believed then that *p*, but not *p*." (Why?—"I was only dreaming.") Descartes himself seems to see this as the force of the argument; to wit, the following from the second *Meditation:* "I have thought I perceived various things during sleep, which I recognized upon waking not to have been really perceived."[18]

Last, there is Descartes's evil genius: "Just as I sometimes judge that others are mistaken about those things which they think they know best, how can I be sure but that God has brought it about that I am always mistaken."[19] But this "How can I be sure but that he knows I believe . . . , but it's not so" is simply an appeal to the intelligibility of M's third-person counterpart. Generally, judging that others are mistaken takes the forms, "You (He) believe(s) *p*, but not *p*."

Now such stories undeniably do incline one to think that M is an intelligible sentence. But when we "take" M in that way, we are "seeing" it in the "grammatical dimensions" of its past-tense and third-person forms: "It is almost as if 'seeing the sign in this context' were an echo of a thought. 'The echo of a thought in sight'—one would like to say" (p. 212). Although this echo does indeed incline us to claim that we can actually think such a sentence, mean something by it, we have

18. Ibid., p. 26.
19. Ibid., p. 20.

unwittingly deprived ourselves of the contexts (and thus the understanding) which enter(s) into the use of "I believe" to *declare* one's own belief. For it is clear that even if the "possibilities" Descartes sketched were actualized, *no* sentence having the form of M would occur. Judging that what I thought I perceived was not veridically perceived takes the form, "I believed then that *p*, but not *p*"; and again, judging that others are mistaken about what they think they know takes the forms, "You (He) believe(s) *p*, but not *p*." Intelligibility thus ascribed to M results from a "misinterpretation," an illicit assimilation of M to its past-tense and non-first-person forms.[20]

We can draw the strands of this discussion together in the suggestion that Wittgenstein's exploration of seeing-as in Part II, section xi, recapitulates the principal theme of philosophical paradox developed in *Investigations,* Part I. Wittgenstein holds that in philosophical perplexity our thought is occupied by "misinterpretations of our forms of language" (§111) that arise when language is "on holiday" (§138). Sentences which generate Moore's Paradox provide an ideal (because unambiguous) example of that truncated view of words. For Moore acknowledges the absence of a technique for applying M to claim what, in philosophical reflection, he says it asserts. And *pace* Moore, one is inclined to think that although M cannot be intelligibly asserted, one can suppose such a thing. That *can* be said correctly, i.e., in a philosophically innocuous manner. But when cited to show that M could be true, I have argued that this gesture places "I believe" in the wrong "grammatical dimensions." The nature of this "misinterpretation" is given summary expression by Wittgenstein in the following:

Even in the hypothesis the pattern is not what you think.

When you say 'Suppose I believe . . . ' you are presupposing the whole grammar of the word 'to believe', the ordinary use of which

20. In "Some Remarks on the Ontology of 'Profound and Intense Reflection' " (unpublished), I attempt to show that this kind of account of Descartes's skepticism promises to conceptualize the skeptic's problematic doubt—a "doubt" that fades, much as an after-image, when we turn from the considerations that lead us to it.

you are master. —You are not supposing some state of affairs which, so to speak, a picture presents unambiguously to you. [P. 192]

The distortion Wittgenstein is referring to in the pattern of the hypothesis is taking the form of words "Suppose I believe" to be a constituent of that pattern. Although this form of words has its uses, language-games which engage our concept of hypothesizing (e.g., "Investigating to find out if . . . ," "Its seeming to be the case that . . . ," "Discovering it is the case that. . .") normally play no role in connection with this form. In the absence of such language-games, the idea that one can actually suppose M gets glossed: I can imagine or picture such a state of affairs. Undeniably, beholding M in philosophical reflection we are presented pictures which incline one to claim that although M is dead in speech and communication, it lives in thought. But to rest easy in the conviction that understanding is therein secured is to assume imaginability is a sufficient condition of intelligibility. Contra that assumption, Wittgenstein argues that "the picture is only like an illustration to a story. . . . [O]nly when one knows the story does one know the significance of the picture" (§663). And drawing from Descartes, I have tried to illustrate how the stories which articulate the pictures formed to represent what M asserts turn upon oneself imagining *him* believing such-and-such, or construing one's own (current) beliefs as *true of* one's "former self."

In the context provided by such fictions, M is *seen as* a hypothesis. With this thought, we have tried to reconceptualize Moore's initial "experience" of M: his alleged recognition of "what it asserts," accompanied by the acknowledgment that it is on permanent "holiday." The philosophical temptation to ascribe that meaning expresses the "dawning" of an aspect. In the words of Wittgenstein's kindred notion, we are "experiencing the meaning of a word" (p. 210)—viz., "believe"—in the wrong "grammatical dimensions." The "life" we there see in "signs" apart from actual or possible occasions of their use, Wittgenstein speaks of as the "secondary meaning" of words (p. 216): "The familiar physiognomy of a word, the feeling that it has taken up its meaning into itself, that it is an actual likeness of its meaning" (p. 218). It is this "organic" dimension of language that causes trouble for philosophy, that blinds us to the need of considering the application of philosophically problematic expressions to secure our understanding. However, tracing the conditions of this phenomenological facet of language leads back to Part I of the *Investigations*, and the *primacy* of use. That I take to be the thrust of Wittgenstein's remark, "When you say 'Suppose I believe . . . ' you are presupposing the whole grammar of the word 'to believe' . . . [and not] some state of affairs which, so to speak, a picture presents unambiguously to you." For the "experience" which forces such a picture upon one presupposes possession of the language: "The substratum of this experience is mastery of a technique" (p. 208); "It is only if someone *can do*, has learnt, is master of, such-and-such, that it makes sense to say he has had *this* experience" (p. 209).[21] Specifically, it is mastery of the full development of the verb "to believe," an understanding of its sense in other persons and tense, which makes possible the "grammatical illusion" (§110) that M is possessed of sense—or, alternatively expressed, which "disguises" a piece of "patent nonsense" (§464), the foundation of philosophical *Luftgebäude*. If sound, the truth Moore sees though "misinterprets" in the claim that M itself is logically possible, is that *our language* contains the possibility of those other sentences.[22]

21. I argue in "Wittgenstein at Criticism" (unpublished) that Wittgenstein's mature philosophy is best conceived of as a form of phenomenalism, as featuring a class of appearances akin to facial physiognomies.

22. I should like to acknowledge helpful criticism of earlier versions of this paper by Professors Francis Dauer, Grant Luckhardt, Norman Malcolm, Merrill Ring, and Hubert Schwyzer. To Merrill Ring I owe added mention of numerous discussions and a jointly conducted seminar in which he helped substantially in developing what understanding I have of Moore's Paradox.

11 "*Mechanism* and *Calculus*": Wittgenstein on Augustine's Theory of Ostension

ROBERT L. ARRINGTON

The early sections of the *Philosophical Investigations* have generally been understood to incorporate Wittgenstein's own negative evaluation of the role of ostensive definition in language acquisition.[1] It is acknowledged by all that in these sections he is arguing against a theory of language, expressed by Augustine and accepted by numerous philosophers, which assigns ostensive definition a pivotal role in the learning process. The possibility has not been adequately considered, however, that what Wittgenstein says against ostensive definition is to be interpreted as opposing the false or misleading Augustinian account of this form of meaning explanation and is not directed against ostension itself as it operates in our actual practices.[2] The failure to explore this possibility reflects a widespread, more general failure to see that throughout Wittgenstein's later work he is not so much offering us a theory of language—including a theory of ostensive definition—as engaging in therapy, that is to say, dissolving problems created by misuses and misunderstandings of language. This often involves a criticism of views held in the history of philosophy, and Augustine's theory of ostension is for Wittgen-

1. Such an interpretation has recently been called a "philosophical commonplace"—see Bernard Harrison, *Meaning and Structure: An Essay in the Philosophy of Language* (New York: Harper & Row, 1972), p. 50.

2. An exception to what I consider inadequate readings of Wittgenstein's reflections on the topic is P. M. S. Hacker's excellent essay, "Wittgenstein on Ostensive Definition," *Inquiry* 18 (Autumn 1975), 267–287. Another good but brief discussion of the issues is to be found in E. K. Specht, *The Foundations of Wittgenstein's Later Philosophy* (Manchester: Manchester University Press, 1969), pp. 63–71.

stein one of the most significant of these historical 'sicknesses'. To be sure, therapeutical criticism indirectly provides us an illumination of our own linguistic practices, but the confusion of historical therapy with linguistic theorizing has often led to an inadequate grasp of this illumination. In the case of ostensive definition, I wish to argue, such confusion has generated a standard account of 'Wittgenstein on Ostension' which is inaccurate and in some ways quite opposed to what Wittgenstein shows us.

The standard interpretation of Wittgenstein's investigation into ostensive definition takes him to establish that a definition of this sort is incapable of imparting or communicating by itself the meaning of any term whatsoever, even that of a basic color term. Kenny, for example, after indicating that Wittgenstein distinguishes between the bearer and the meaning of a name, characterizes his assessment of ostension in the following way:

> Though bearer and meaning are distinct, the meaning of the name is sometimes explained by pointing to its bearer: that is precisely what an ostensive definition is (*PI*, I, 40). But if such explanation is to be successful the learner must not only be acquainted with the bearer, but also grasp the role in language of the word to be defined. Thus, if I know that someone means to explain a color-word to me, the ostensive definition 'That is called "sepia" ' will help me understand the word (*PI*, I, 30; *PG*, p. 88). But the ostensive definition will not suffice by itself, because it can always be variously interpreted. For instance, suppose that I explain the word 'tove' by pointing to a pencil and saying 'This is called "tove" '. The explanation would be quite inadequate, because I may be taken to mean 'This is a pencil' or 'This is round' or 'This is wood' or 'This is one' or 'This is hard' and so on (*PG*, p. 60; *BBB*, p. 2). So in the acquisition of the understanding of a word acquaintance with the word's bearer is not so important as mastery of the word's general use.[3]

Kenny implies that for Wittgenstein an ostensive definition can only point out the bearer of a name, and insofar as this pointing is ambiguous in the sense of being compatible with

3. Anthony Kenny, *Wittgenstein* (Cambridge, Mass.: Harvard University Press, 1973), p. 157. For other presentations of what I call the standard interpretation or account see G. Pitcher, *The Philosophy of Wittgenstein* (Englewood Cliffs, N.J.: Prentice-Hall, 1964), p. 241; Harrison, *Meaning and Structure*, pp. 49–52; and Robert J. Fogelin, *Wittgenstein* (London: Routledge and Kegan Paul, 1976), pp. 102–107.

different uses of the name, the definition does not convey the name's use or meaning. In order for the use to be imparted, further explanation is required in the form of nonostensive rules. Thus Wittgenstein is taken to view ostensive definition as an inherently incomplete, insufficient, and inadequate explanation of meaning.

I shall argue that this standard interpretation is wrong in principle and in detail. It fails to come to grips with what Wittgenstein in general is doing and with what, specifically, he means when he talks about the ambiguity of an ostensive definition. In his eyes ambiguity poses a problem for a certain theoretical account of ostensive definition, the Augustinian account, but not for the definition itself. When we have a proper grammatical understanding of how ostension works in actual practice, which is what Wittgenstein provides us, we will see that the Augustinian theory of language is wrong not because it relies on an inadequate instrument for explaining meaning, but because it misunderstands the nature of that instrument.

Much of the confusion surrounding Wittgenstein's treatment of ostensive definition results from a failure to make clear the different questions which arise, or can arise, with regard to this way of explaining meaning. There are two issues which especially need to be kept distinct. First, there is the question whether this form of definition can *in fact* produce by itself an understanding of the meaning of a term it purports to explain. Here the definition is to be judged in its function and capacity as an instrument in the teaching process. Is it, or is it not, an adequate *mechanism* for the purpose of instilling understanding? Wittgenstein makes an explicit distinction between ostensive teaching and ostensive definition (*PI* §6, §27).[4] The question of the adequacy of ostension as a mechanism is the question of the adequacy of ostensive teaching. When the issue is correctly defined, we will see that Wittgen-

4. He does not elaborate this distinction in the *Investigations* aside from saying that ostensive definition is involved in a language-game of its own, a game in which the definition is the correlative of asking something's name. My task later in the paper will be to clarify what this language-game is, at which point I will borrow heavily from what Wittgenstein says in the *Grammar* about the role of ostensive definition in a calculus. It would also be

stein does not place any significant limitations on ostensive teaching. Second, there is the matter of ostensive definition proper, the role of ostension in a *calculus* or language-game. Negatively, Wittgenstein discusses the way in which other philosophers—those who advocate a version of the Augustinian theory of meaning —have misunderstood the grammar of ostensive definition. In doing this he is not criticizing the ostensive form of definition itself but rather a grammatical misunderstanding of it—specifically one which mistakes the role it plays in a mechanism for the role it plays in a calculus. Positively, Wittgenstein gives us a grammatical analysis which explicates the role of ostensive definition as a rule that determines the sense of a term. Although, as it turns out, the ostensive rule is only one of several rules determining sense, this does not imply any inadequacy on its part, for all the rules are internally related.

With regard, then, both to ostensive teaching and ostensive definition proper, my thesis will be that Wittgenstein finds no reason to reject, criticize, or limit in a significant fashion these forms of meaning explanation. To justify this line of interpretation it will be necessary to proceed slowly and by steps. In Section II I shall spell out in more detail the different issues surrounding ostensive definition and also counter the reasons given for the standard interpretation. In Section III, I shall argue that Wittgenstein has no objections to the adequacy of ostensive teaching. Section IV will contain a discussion of the Augustinian misunderstanding of the grammar of ostension, as well as a description of Wittgenstein's positive characterization of the grammatical role ostensive definitions play in a language-game. Section V will be devoted to Wittgenstein's elucidation of the internal grammatical structure of an ostensive definition.

II

Wittgenstein's discussion of ostensive definition in the *Philosophical Investigations* is part of a more comprehensive

---

possible to think of ostensive *teaching* as (part of) a language-game, only a different one. I do not, following Wittgenstein, speak of it this way.

investigation of the Augustinian theory of meaning.[5] According to this theory the basic unit of language is the word in its capacity as a name. This name designates an object in the world, which object is its meaning (*PI* §1). Children learn a language by taking note of the fact that certain names are used in the presence of certain objects or kinds of object. Ostensive teaching and definition are merely more formalized procedures for drawing a language learner's attention to the object signified by a word, and hence to the word's meaning. The teaching and the definition establish an association between the word and the object or an image of the object (*PI* §6).[6] Once the learner has attached a name to an object—once the association has been established—he can use that name to refer to the object and talk about it (*PI* §27).

In response to the doctrine of ostension involved in the Augustinian account, Wittgenstein makes a number of critical comments, two of which have been especially influential. First, he questions whether ostensive teaching can be said to produce an understanding of a word merely by establishing an associative mechanism whereby an image of the object named by the word comes before the mind when the word is heard (*PI* §6). Having this image, he implies, is not tantamount to understanding the word. He goes on to say:

> Don't you understand the call "Slab!" if you act upon it in such-and-such a way?—Doubtless the ostensive teaching helped to bring this about; but only together with a particular training. With different training the same ostensive teaching of these words would have effected a quite different understanding. [*PI* §6]

This certainly appears to claim that ostensive teaching is only partially effective in bringing about understanding when understanding is taken to involve proper use. Second, Wittgenstein notes that an ostensive definition is ambiguous, i.e., that it is subject to multiple interpretations:

5. Wittgenstein's reference to this theory in the work of Augustine is to *Confessions*, Bk. I, chap. 8.
6. For Augustine's discussion of the role of images in understanding see *Confessions*, Bk. X, chaps. 8–15.

> The definition of the number two, "That is called 'two' "—pointing to two nuts—is perfectly exact.—But how can two be defined like that? The person one gives the definition to doesn't know what one wants to call "two"; he will suppose that "two" is the name given to *this* group of nuts!—He *may* suppose this; but perhaps he does not. He might make the opposite mistake; when I want to assign a name to this group of nuts, he might understand it as a numeral. And he might equally well take the name of a person, of which I give an ostensive definition, as that of a color, of a race, or even of a point of the compass. That is to say: an ostensive definition can be variously interpreted in *every* case. [*PI* §28]

Wittgenstein proceeds to draw the following conclusion from the fact of this ambiguity: "So one might say: the ostensive definition explains the use—the meaning—of the word when the overall role of the word in language is clear" (*PI* §30). Here again he appears to be saying that ostensive definition is in itself inadequate to instill understanding, that it requires supplementation: in addition to receiving the ostensive definition of a word one must in some other way come to know the role or use of that word in language.

Before we conclude that these passages render the standard interpretation obviously correct, let us remind ourselves of the context in which they appear. Wittgenstein is, after all, examining the Augustinian theory of meaning. It may be the case, I have suggested, that he is criticizing a certain picture of ostensive teaching and definition that figures in the Augustinian theory, and not saying anything against ostensive teaching and definition themselves. The inadequacy to which he refers would in this case be the inadequacy of the theory and not of the role of these forms of meaning explanation in language as it is. Furthermore, it will be of value to inquire what kind of remarks Wittgenstein is making in these critical passages. Are they grammatical or empirical remarks? How we should interpret what he says may depend on the matter of *which kind* of statement he is willing to make.

With these cautionary points in mind, let us reflect again on the passages just cited. Wittgenstein suggests that understanding a word is not the same as having an image of the object it names (*PI* §6). But this can be taken in two different ways. It could mean that the Augustinian theory is in error in equating the operation of the associative mechanism (the having of an image of the object named) and understanding the word. This criticism would amount to a grammatical remark which claimed that having an image of an object is not what is *meant* by understanding the meaning of the word that names this object. This would not be a criticism of ostensive teaching itself, but a criticism of a grammatical theory about it. On the other hand, Wittgenstein's suggestion that the operation of the mechanism is not tantamount to understanding the word could be a claim to the effect that the ostensive teaching and the association it establishes are not causally sufficient to produce understanding. If this were the nature of Wittgenstein's criticism, then he would indeed be criticizing ostensive teaching, but he would be doing this only by putting forth an empirical claim.

Next consider the comment that with different training the same ostensive teaching of 'Slab' would produce a different understanding of it (*PI* §6). Again there are the same two ways of taking this. It could be a straightforward empirical claim, in which case Wittgenstein would be saying that ostensive teaching is not causally sufficient but requires supplementation by "training." But his point could be different. He could be contending that we would be willing *to say* of two students that they have a different understanding of a word even if the same ostensive teaching has been given them, especially if they have also been given different training along with the ostensive teaching. This would be another grammatical argument against the Augustinian theory. In identifying 'understanding a word' with 'having an image of the object named by the word' this theory would be committed to granting the same understanding if the same ostensive teaching had been given (i.e., if the same associative mechanism worked). Insofar as in ordinary language we are willing to speak of a different understanding while granting the same image, our way of talking would be different from the Augustinian way. This would be a comment on the notion of ostensive teaching that occurs within the Augustinian account, not a comment on ostensive teaching itself.

Finally, consider the famous passage (*PI* §28) in which Wittgenstein tells us that an ostensive definition can be variously interpreted and that it explains the use only if the overall role of the word in language is clear. He could be saying, on the one hand, that ambiguity always plagues such a definition and can never be overcome by further ostensive definitions alone, e.g., that repeated assertions of 'That is called "red" ' will never allow us to detect which of several uses of the word is intended, its use to name a color, to name a shape, to name a piece of paper, etc. This would be an empirical claim, and one about ostensive definition itself and not merely about an Augustinian conception of such. But the passage could equally well be seen as a grammatical remark directed against an Augustinian misconception, in this case the misconception of the definition as being "perfectly exact." If the definition were perfectly exact, the demonstrative 'that' would have to have a univocal sense which precisely fixed the overall sense of the ostensive definition itself. In good Augustinian fashion, it might mean something like 'the object of my attention' or 'the referent of my pointing'. But, Wittgenstein could be saying, the ambiguity of the ostensive definition shows us that it, and its constituent terms, do not have such a fixed sense. Rather, its sense varies with the sense (the use) of the word being defined. The claim that the overall role of a word must be clear if the ostensive definition is to explain its use may, then, be a tautology, a way of saying that understanding the ostensive definition itself involves understanding the use which the word being defined is being given and that this understanding is not accomplished by grasping some univocal sense of 'that' or by attending to the object at which someone points. To argue in this fashion would not be to criticize ostensive definition as inadequate or incomplete at all, but simply to elucidate what such a definition *is*.

I suggest, then, that there are different ways of reading the comments which so often have led to the claim that Wittgenstein demonstrates the limitations of ostensive definition. Note that Wittgenstein can be taken to show this in each case only if his remarks are *empirical* ones. But Wittgenstein denies that he is engaged in an empirical inquiry (*PI* §109; *PG*, p. 66) and explicitly claims to be conducting grammatical investigations (*PI* §90). This should incline us to view the passages in question as criticisms of an Augustinian misconception and hence as having no direct negative implications for the role of ostensive definition itself in language acquisition.

It might be argued that the simple grammatical-empirical distinction employed above does not catch all of the possible ways of treating the issue of ostensive definition. I would agree. To get clearer about these matters it will be necessary to examine in more detail the various ways in which the Augustinian theory can be interpreted and the various ways in which it might be criticized. This will enable us to have a better idea of the kind of investigation Wittgenstein himself is engaged in.

First of all, one can take the Augustinian account *itself* as either a grammatical or an empirical rendering of language. It can take the form, that is to say, of either a meaning analysis or a causal theory. If it is a grammatical account, then it professes to tell us what 'meaning' means, and what it means to explain the meaning of a word. Specifically, it would claim that by 'the meaning of a word' we mean the object in the world which the word designates, and that when we speak of explaining the meaning we have in mind singling out and exhibiting the object designated. Furthermore, it would analyze 'understanding the meaning' as 'the effect of the associative mechanism between word and object' or perhaps as 'having an image of the object'. The Augustinian theory would unpack the meaning of a particular ostensive definition by interpreting the demonstrative component as meaning 'the object of the speaker's attention or act of pointing', for this object would be the meaning of the term defined. To rebut this theory grammatically, one would have to show that 'meaning', 'explanation of meaning', 'understanding', and 'ostensive definition' are not taken by us as the theory makes out. The inadequacy of its picture of ostensive definition would then refer to the fact that an ostensive definition is not the only thing that we *call* an explanation of meaning, that it does not explain meaning by pointing us to an object we *call* the meaning, and that its words do not have a fixed, univocal sense.

As an empirical account the Augustinian theory appears quite different. It becomes an attempt to explain meaning and the acquisition of language in a causal way, by getting outside language and explaining how linguistic phenomena arise from nonlinguistic procedures and events in the world. It attempts in this way to answer such questions as: How does it come about that a person learns the meaning of a word? and How does it come about that a person can correctly use a word to mean an object in the world? The former question is answered by an appeal to ostensive teaching, and the association between word and object that is established by means of the ostensive teaching becomes the link between word and object whereby a person can correctly use the word to mean the object. To object to this empirical theory *on empirical grounds* one might try to show that no amount of ostensive teaching would be causally adequate to generate the ability to use words, or that no causal link is correlatable with correct use.

One might additionally object to the empirical theory on *grammatical grounds*. It might be argued, for instance, that it contained or implied a grammatically incorrect account of 'meaning' or 'teaching' or 'learning' or 'understanding'. Such a criticism would show that, however well substantiated empirically, the theory could not explain what *we mean* by language and its acquisition. One could say either that it was conceptually confused or conceptually irrelevant. I think it likely that many defenders of the standard account concerning Wittgenstein's treatment of ostensive definition see him as arguing in this fashion. They perceive a conceptual 'gap' between human conceptual understanding and the mechanism of association or stimulus-response.

There is still another possibility. The empirical theory qua empirical theory may pass inspection grammatically, and yet may produce a certain causal explanation of language learning which comes to be mistaken by philosophers for a grammatical account. For instance, it may be the case that language learning, at least with regard to some words such as color terms, proceeds by means of association. Taking note of this fact, a philosopher might conclude that the occurrence of the association is the *criterion* of 'understanding what a color term means'. But even if the factual theory is true it does not follow that the grammatical claim is also correct. Hence the Augustinian theory might be interpreted as a grammatical theory which mistakenly identifies causal conditions of learning and understanding with grammatical conditions of these processes and abilities.

In which of these ways does Wittgenstein view and criticize the Augustinian theory? In light of his own methodological claims (*PI* §90, §109) it is obvious that he sees himself as involved in a grammatical inquiry and not an empirical one. This need not rule out, however, a grammatical criticism of an empirical theory—"We are not interested in any empirical facts about language, *considered as empirical facts*" (*PG*, p. 66, my emphasis). The next task before us is to see whether Wittgenstein would reject on grammatical grounds the Augustinian empirical learning theory which understands language acquisition to proceed in large part by means of association and which takes ostensive definition to be an adequate teaching instrument. Once this is done we can then turn our attention to the grammatical criticisms which Wittgenstein makes of the Augustinian grammatical theory, especially the criticism that it has misassimilated empirical and grammatical elements.

III

Although Wittgenstein does not directly address himself to the viability of the Augustinian empirical learning theory, he does, as we noted above, make a distinction between ostensive teaching and ostensive definition (*PI* §6, §27), and he speaks of the former in ways which certainly appear to assimilate it to a mechanism. "Here the teaching of language is not explanation, but training," he tells us (*PI* §5). In *On Certainty* he points out that our learning of language (and facts) has the form "that is a violet" and "that is a table" (*OC* §450), and he goes on to say that language does not emerge "from some kind of ratiocination" (*OC* §475). Rather: "The child . . . learns to react in such-and-such a way, and in so reacting it doesn't so far know anything" (*OC* §538). It would seem quite natural to explain this training, and the reactions it produces, in terms of a causal mechanism of the form described by the Augustinian theory. To be sure, Wittgenstein does not say as much. Nevertheless, we can glean from his thought various grounds for rejecting the claim that ostensive definition, interpreted as a mechanism, is *incapable* of being the sole instrument involved in teaching language. These grounds are not themselves empirical. They demonstrate, rather, that there is nothing grammatically absurd in the empirical thesis that language acquisition does or may proceed solely by means of ostensive teaching. Wittgenstein does not endorse this empirical thesis; nor does he reject it. He merely approves it as a grammatical possibility. To show this, I propose to construct several criticisms which have been brought by philosophers against this learning theory and to indicate why Wittgenstein would reject these criticisms.

There are those who argue, and perhaps think of themselves as following Wittgenstein in doing so, that ostensive teaching fails to be an adequate explanation of meaning because it fails to account (1) for our understanding of what it means *to point,* (2) for our understanding of what it means for something to be a *name,* (3) for our grasp of the *intralinguistic rules* of language, (4) for our grasp of *grammatical categories,* and (5) for our mastery of *use.*[7] I shall consider each of these objections in turn.

Take, first of all, the case of pointing. It has been argued that pointing cannot explain meaning and language because it itself already involves or presupposes the linguistic notions of reference and designation.[8] But this is not Wittgenstein's position. He tells us that it is a natural fact about human beings that they respond to the pointing gesture in the way they do (*PG,* p. 94)—this being one of those natural facts which, in his view, do not explain but make possible the forms of language

7. Most of these points are made by Bernard Harrison, and I will often cite *Meaning and Structure* as an excellent source to consult for a systematic presentation of the arguments.

8. Ibid., p. 57.

we have. Pointing is not something which itself needs explanation and hence does not presuppose linguistic reference. Explanation by pointing, then, cannot be ruled out as grammatically circular.

Second, consider the case of naming. It has been said that the inductive abstraction of a common element from a group of ostensive objects would not permit us to grasp that the word associated with this common element is its name.[9] At best, the argument goes, such a procedure would lead us to have an inductive expectation that the common element would accompany the name. But this claim seems to assume that understanding what a name is amounts to having some particular mental experience, specifically a mental experience other than that of inductive expectation. For Wittgenstein, on the contrary, the criterion for understanding what a name is consists of the correct use of a word as a name. There may be many ways to bring this about, including the inductive abstraction of a common element that is associated with the sound of the word. For Wittgenstein the teaching process per se is no part of the grammar of a word: "The way in which language was learnt is not *contained* in its use. (Any more than the cause is contained in the effect)" (*PG*, p. 80). The teaching process is a part of "mere history" (*PG*, p. 86). He often points to various ways in which a student may learn something about language: by having it explained to him, by applying a list of rules, by observing others using the language, by guessing at what is going on. There is nothing inconsistent, then, in teaching a person what a name *is* and *means* by putting him through a series of ostensive definitions. He may pick these things up, and therefore use the word as a name, or he may not. While it is undoubtedly true that Wittgenstein would place some limits on the types of language acquisition which can correctly be called 'learning', there is no reason for thinking that, in his eyes, acquisition by ostension and abstraction does not qualify.[10] Such acquisition is not grammatically absurd.

9. Ibid., pp. 54–55.

10. Cf. Peter Geach, *Mental Acts* (London: Routledge & Kegan Paul, 1957; New York: Humanities Press, 1971), pp. 18ff.

Third, let us look at the claim that a procedure of ostensive teaching cannot succeed in teaching someone the intralinguistic rules of language. It has been argued in this context that an understanding of a term such as 'blue' requires a grasp of "restrictive rules" which relate it to other color terms, e.g., ' "Blue" is not " . . . " '.[11] This restrictive rule cannot be picked up ostensively, it is said, because the procedure of ostensive teaching would at best instruct one in a rule of correlation of the sort 'The word "blue" applies to anything like the objects to which it has been applied in the ostensive definitions'. This latter kind of rule is inadequate, however, to explain the meaning of a color term, for if it were the sole rule operative, it would authorize us to apply the word to objects which, although they resemble the ostensive or paradigm objects as much as these paradigm objects resemble each other, are not correctly designated by the term. Mauve, for instance, may resemble the various shades of blue as much as they resemble one another, but it is not correctly called 'blue'. Thus it is concluded that in order to understand 'blue' we must grasp the nonostensive, restrictive rule ' "Blue" is not "mauve" '. Nature, we are likely to be told, does not come to us separated into natural nameables.[12] *We* must decide where the limits of a color are, and hence what the signification of a color term is, and this we can do only by setting forth rules which arbitrarily define those limits. The procedure of ostensive teaching alone could provide us with our language only if the world did consist of discrete natural nameables—in that case we could pin our words onto the nameables, and their discreteness and distinctiveness would themselves guarantee that the limits of a name's sense are determinately given. But in our world this is not possible, and thus ostensive teaching alone cannot explain a name's sense or its restrictive relations to other names. So goes a very popular, and persuasive, argument.

How would Wittgenstein react to this demonstration of the limits of ostensive teaching? In the first place, it is totally

11. Harrison, *Meaning and Structure*, pp. 58ff.
12. Ibid., pp. 63ff.

inconsistent with his later philosophy to derive linguistic or grammatical facts from metaphysical doctrines, and the thesis that discrete natural nameables do not exist *is* a metaphysical doctrine. Without its support the argument from rules is decidedly weakened. In the second place, while Wittgenstein would certainly grant the existence of restrictive rules of the sort described above, he would question the relevance and the necessity of appealing to them in explaining the acquisition of verbal understanding. In the *Philosophical Grammar* we find him saying:

> But when we learn the meaning of a word, we are very often given *only* the single rule, the ostensive definition. So how does it come about that on the strength of this definition we understand the word? Do we guess the rest of the rules?
>
> Think also of teaching a child to understand words by showing it objects and uttering words. The child is given ostensive definitions and then it understands the words.—But what is the criterion of understanding here? Surely, that the child applies the words correctly. Does it guess rules? . . .
>
> I might also say of a little child "he can use the word, he knows how it is applied." But I only see what that means if I ask "what is the criterion for this knowledge?" In this case it isn't the ability to state rules. [*PG*, pp. 61–62]

It is not as components of the learning process that rules (necessarily) figure in language. A person doesn't have to be given rules in order to understand the meaning of a word, and he doesn't have to recite them in order to demonstrate this understanding. Furthermore, correct usage of a word is not usage that is somehow causally guided by rules, either explicit or implicit ones. Using a word correctly may indeed be using it in agreement with its restrictive (and other) rules, but Wittgenstein certainly suggests in the above passage that such correct usage can be generated by doing nothing more than giving the student an ostensive definition.

It would be interesting in this context to speculate *in an empirical frame of mind* whether there could be a causal mechanism based on ostensive teaching alone that would suffice to inculcate intralinguistic rules. Our conjecture might take the following form. In addition to providing the student a series of ostensive definitions of the same term, let us provide him an ostensive array, a systematically arranged set of such definitions for a variety of terms—say, color terms. This procedure would lead the student to call a certain ostensive or paradigm object 'mauve' even if it could be said to resemble the paradigm objects called 'blue' as closely as they resemble one another. Furthermore, this procedure would lead him to say that the mauve object is *not* blue—telling him 'This is not blue' might itself be called a kind of ostensive definition or thought of as a form of negative feedback. In this fashion the student would come to distinguish between blue and mauve; even if they could be said to resemble one another, the difference in the teacher's linguistic response to them would become a significant difference between them which would allow the student to 'see' or 'guess' the appropriate restrictive rule. At the very least, it would be sufficient to bring the student to use 'blue' and 'mauve' in agreement with the restrictive rule ' "Blue" is not "mauve" '.

One objection to this empirical conjecture might be that such an ostensive array could at best produce an awareness that blue and mauve are empirically distinct. It could not produce an awareness that blue and mauve are *necessarily* distinct. But, the objection goes, it is precisely this latter form of awareness which, grammatically speaking, one must have in order to understand the intralinguistic rule ' "Blue" is not "mauve" '. No awareness of contingent differences could lead to the grasp of necessary, rule-generated truths. Hence ostensive teaching cannot yield intralinguistic rules.

Wittgenstein would reject this argument. In the *Remarks on the Foundations of Mathematics* he argues time and time again that there is nothing in the vehicle of a proof or the vehicle of an experiment that serves to distinguish them.[13] We can use five marbles to prove that two plus three equals five just by arranging these marbles in a certain configuration. One may

13. See *Remarks on the Foundations of Mathematics,* trans. G. E. M. Anscombe (Oxford: Basil Blackwell, 1956; Cambridge, Mass.: M.I.T. Press, 1964), pp. 13–30, 36, 75–77, 81, 163.

ask, does not such a configuration show merely that in this particular case two added to three yields in point of fact five objects? How can this be a proof demonstrating a necessary truth about any group of two and three objects as opposed to an experiment supporting a contingent truth? Wittgenstein's answer is that the modality of the operation is a function, not of the operation's vehicle, but of our way of taking it. We can take the arrangement of marbles as a proof that two plus three equals five, and we can teach others to take it this way. How? By taking the arrangement as paradigmatic, by putting it in the archives, by appealing to it in order to judge the correctness of particular sums, by refusing to deviate from its result. The necessity is not in the objects and their configuration but stems from our way of responding to them. All of these things can equally be said about an ostensive 'proof' that blue is not mauve. Hence an ostensive array can be used to impart the necessary truth that blue is not mauve. The grammatical fact that rules involve necessary truths does not make it grammatically absurd to claim that rules are conveyed by ostensive teaching.

Fourth, let us consider that criticism which has figured prominently in the standard interpretation of Wittgenstein's treatment of ostensive definition. In the passage from Kenny quoted at the beginning of the paper, it appears that one problem with an ostensive definition is its inability to explain the grammatical category of the term being defined. An ostensive definition is ambiguous, and hence 'That is called "red" ' might be used to assign the word 'red' to the color, the paper, the shape, etc. In and of itself, the argument seems to go, the definition is incapable of conveying the grammatical category. For a person to understand the meaning of 'red' on hearing the definition, the grammatical category must be provided in addition to the definition. It is this grammatical category, Wittgenstein is taken as asserting, which must already be understood if the ostensive teaching is to explain the use of the word. Hence the teaching itself cannot explain, but presupposes an understanding of, this element of grammar.

Such a reading of Wittgenstein is inconsistent with the very text of his comments on ostensive definition. A close examination of *Philosophical Investigations* §29 will show that he does not think that ostensive definition—as a teaching instrument—is limited or impaired in its ability to instruct one in the grammatical category of a term:

> Perhaps you say: two can only be ostensively defined in *this* way: "This *number* is called 'two'." For the word "number" here shows what place in language, in grammar, we assign to the word. But this means that the word "number" must be explained before the ostensive definition can be understood.—The word "number" in the definition does indeed show this place; does show the post at which we station the word. And we can prevent misunderstanding by saying: "This *color* is called so-and-so," "This *length* is called so-and-so," and so on. That is to say: misunderstandings are sometimes averted in this way. But is there only *one* way of taking the word "color" or "length"?—Well, they just need defining.—Defining, then, by means of other words! And what about the last definition in this chain? (Do not say: "There isn't a 'last' definition." That is just as if you chose to say: "There isn't a last house in this road; one can always build an additional one.")
>
> Whether the word "number" is necessary in the ostensive definition depends on whether without it the other person takes the definition otherwise than I wish. And that will depend on the circumstances under which it is given, and on the person I give it to.

Several points emerge from this quotation. To begin with, introducing the grammatical category into the ostensive definition *may not* be necessary. The student may be able to identify the referent of 'red' without being told that it is a color. In that case he connects the word 'red' and *the color red*, which means that he takes the demonstrative 'this' to indicate the color red. This shows that, if understanding 'red' requires understanding its grammatical type, ostensive teaching—or ostensive definition in its role as a teaching instrument—is capable of achieving this. The grammatical type, as an element of the use of the word, is not incapable of being conveyed by ostension. Next, 'This *color* is called "red" ' is itself an ostensive definition. To argue that the problems attendant on 'That is called "red" ' require us to supplement it with an indication of the grammatical category is simply to recommend one form of ostensive teaching over another. Finally, Wittgenstein notes that the grammatical category must itself be understood and explained, and he hints that its explanation cannot be given solely in terms of words but must include ostensive definition. This is far removed from urging the explanatory insufficiency of ostensive teaching.

Fifth and last, let us reflect on the charge that ostensive definition is incapable of teaching the meaning of a word because, given that meaning is use, it is obvious that an ostensive definition in pointing us to the bearer of a word does not show us its use. In substantiation of this charge we might be referred to *Philosophical Investigations* §27, where, after noting the Augustinian view to the effect that once we define our terms ostensively we can use them to talk about things, Wittgenstein remarks: "As if what we did next were given with the mere act of naming." Is he not here saying that an ostensive definition only shows us a word being used as a name, and thus fails completely to reveal the various uses to which we put words after having named objects with them? To understand the ostensive definition, i.e., to understand what a word names, is not to understand that word's meaning, its use. The remark about ambiguity might in this context be interpreted as showing that the ostensive teaching is compatible with a great diversity of uses (the different grammatical categories marking different uses) and hence does not succeed in explaining the particular use of the term being defined.

In response to this charge we need to remember that, according to Wittgenstein, a single ostensive definition may succeed in engendering the correct use of the term defined (*PG*, p. 61), just as it may succeed in engendering an understanding of the grammatical category without explicitly mentioning that category. If ostensive definition is being evaluated as a teaching instrument, then its adequacy is a function of its ability to achieve the desired goal, in this case correct use. And it can and often does, as a matter of fact, achieve this goal. Hence the fact that, grammatically speaking, the ostensive definition itself does not involve a use of the definiendum beyond its naming use does not prove that it cannot generate the ability to use this term in some way other than simply as a name. To be sure, if a language learner responded to our ostensive definition by doing nothing more than uttering the name when in the presence of the ostensive object, we would probably conclude that he did not yet know how to use it and hence had not fully learned the meaning of the word (*PG*, p. 83). But whether he responds to the definition in this peculiar, uncomprehending manner, or whether after one or more such definitions he begins to employ the term in the variety of ways constituting its use—that is a contingent matter. It has not been shown that the second alternative is grammatically impossible, and it is not, for Wittgenstein, within the province of the philosopher to show that it is empirically impossible.

We may conclude this phase of our inquiry by noting that the ambiguity of an ostensive definition is itself no grammatical bar to its adequacy as a teaching instrument. As Wittgenstein puts it: "That it is ambiguous is no argument against such a method of definition. Any definition can be misunderstood" (*PI*, p. 14). No instrument of teaching is guaranteed to be successful. Grammatically, its adequacy does not depend on its success on any particular occasion. That an ostensive definition can be misunderstood is no sign that it cannot also be understood, and hence achieve its goal. If we are viewing it as a teaching instrument, then understanding it means getting its point, which in turn means being able to use correctly the word it defines. This end is often achieved.

IV

We have established that there is nothing grammatically wrong with conceiving ostensive definition to be an instrument of teaching, and often in fact a successful and sufficient instrument. That is, if we interpret the Augustinian theory merely as an empirical theory, there is no real philosophical objection we can bring against it. Conceived in this way, the theory contains a concept of ostensive definition as a method of instruction which grammatically cannot be faulted. But the Augustinian account is more than an empirical theory; it is also a grammatical one, and it is as a grammatical theory that Wittgenstein takes objection to it. He points out, for instance, that the general theory is in error in equating the meaning of a term with the object named by that term. If this were a correct equation, we would have to say that the meaning of 'N' died if Mr. N died, but we do not say this (*PI* §40). He also points out, I have suggested, that 'understanding the meaning of a word' does not mean the same as 'having an image of the object named by the word' (*PI* §6).

More important for our purposes, Wittgenstein judges that the Augustinian grammatical theory is incorrect in its understanding of ostensive definition as it is used within a language-game or calculus. As a grammatical theory it views ostensive definition not merely as an adequate teaching instrument, as does the empirical version, but also as a necessary condition of meaningful speech. It proposes not just that this form of definition is instrumental in teaching a language, but also that it *must* be employed in order for this language to designate the world and convey information about it. The Augustinian grammatical theory sees ostension as the means whereby our words are connected to the world such that in understanding these words we pass from language to reality. In its view this connection is a causal one. Empirically, ostensive definition is a mechanism which relates word and world by establishing an associative connection between them so that an object or its image contingently calls forth the name of this object. This causal connection is taken over by the grammatical theory and proposed as the necessary condition for linguistic reference to the object. For example, the word 'red' means a red object only insofar as its use is the causal consequent, via ostensive definition, of a red object. And a person can be said to use the word 'red' correctly only insofar as he is prompted to use it by a perception or memory image which is similar to the perception associated with 'red' on the occasion of its ostensive definition. In this way his use would be the product of the causal connection between red objects and 'red' which was established by the definition in the first place, and he would thereby be using it to refer to a red object. In general, then, the Augustinian grammatical theory maintains that one uses words correctly and informatively only if one uses them as a causal consequence of ostensive definitions. In fact, it may be taken to maintain that 'correct and informative use' *means* 'use which is the causal consequence of ostension'. What we now need to do is to examine Wittgenstein's reasons for rejecting this grammatical theory.

At one point Wittgenstein explicitly raises the question whether ostensive definition is a necessary condition of language or meaningful speech. He writes:

> Does our language consist of primary signs (ostensive gestures) and secondary signs (words)? One is inclined to ask, whether it isn't the case that our language *has* to have primary signs while it could get by without the secondary ones.
>
> The false note in this question is that it expects an explanation of existing language instead of a mere description. [*PG*, pp. 88–89]

Wittgenstein is not denying that ostensive definition is necessary for our language to describe the world; he is saying rather that we may misunderstand the sense in which it is necessary. *Looking for an explanation* we expect from ostensive definition some mechanism which causally ensures that we are talking about the world. We confuse the 'must' of grammar with the 'must' of causation. If instead we asked for a (mere) description of our language we would see that this form of definition is in a sense necessary, but not in the way postulated by the Augustinian theory. It is not as a causal mechanism that ostensive definition plays a grammatical role in a language-game; not as a causal mechanism that it connects word and world.

> "The connection between words and things is set up by the teaching of language." What kind of connection is this? A mechanical, electrical, psychological connection is something which may or may not function. *Mechanism* and *Calculus*.
>
> . . . .
>
> It gives the wrong idea if you say that the connection between name and object is a psychological one. [*PG*, p. 97]

More positively:

> The connection between "language and reality" is made by definitions of words, and these belong to grammar, so that language remains self-contained and autonomous.
>
> . . . .
>
> The correlation between objects and names is simply the one set up

by a chart, by ostensive gestures and simultaneous uttering of the name etc. It is a part of the symbolism. Giving an object a name is essentially the same kind of thing as hanging a label on it. [*PG*, p. 97]

So ostensive definition *does* establish a connection between words and world, but this connection is not a mechanical, psychological, or causal one (*PI* §689). Why is the connection not causal and what kind of connection is it?

In the first place, the causal effect of the operation of ostensive definition qua mechanism is not always, in our grammar, a justifying condition of word use.

Can one say that the word "red" needs a supplement in memory in order to be a usable sign?

If I use the words "there is a red book in front of me" to describe an experience, is the justification of the choice of these words, apart from the experience described, the fact that I remember that I've always used the word "red" for this color? Does that *have to* be the justification? [*PG*, pp. 94–95]

These are certainly rhetorical questions. I have an experience, and without further ado I call it the experience of a red object. Often I am perfectly justified in doing so. If I need any justifying reason at all, it is simply that I have learned English (*PI*, §381). The question of a memory image traceable back to the occasion of 'red' being ostensively defined does not arise. Hence ostensive definition does not always, in our grammar, justify word use by being a causal antecedent of this use; as a causal antecedent ostensive definition is not, therefore, a necessary condition of correct use.

Nor is it a sufficient condition of correct use. The associative mechanism set up by the definition must produce the *right* image and/or the *right* word. That is to say, the mechanism can go awry (*PG*, p. 97); it can cause one to have the wrong memory image or to utter the wrong word. As Wittgenstein tells us, a mechanical or psychological connection may or may not function. If I rely upon the memory that this is the same perceptual quality named in the ostensive definition, it is always possible that I incorrectly remember the perceptual quality or incorrectly remember the name attached to it, and consequently I may use the wrong word. But in what sense wrong? After all, it is the word I am caused to utter by the mechanism generated by the ostensive definition. If the operation of this mechanism were the grammatical determinant of correct use, then it would make no sense to say that it generated an incorrect use. In that case, I would truly be at the mercy of the mechanism:

> If the use of the word "red" depends on the picture that my memory automatically reproduces at the sound of this word, then I am as much at mercy of this reproduction as if I had decided to settle the meaning by looking up a chart in such a way that I would surrender unconditionally to whatever I found there. [*PG*, p. 95]

Just as the chart may fade, the memory image may fade and the associative connection degenerate. But if either the chart or the image were the final, grammatical determinant of the meaning of a word like 'red', then that word would change its meaning as the fading commenced. 'Red' would mean whatever state in the world or memory image in the mind happened at the moment to be causally connected with my utterance of 'red'. In that case I *could not say* that the present memory image I was having was no longer red. I do say this—I *can* say it—from which it follows that the memory image does not (does not always) determine the meaning of 'red'. It and the associative mechanism behind it are not, then, a sufficient grammatical ground for the correct use of 'red'.

If it be replied that the correct use of a term is given by the original causal connection between it and an object in the world, not some degenerate causal connection, this merely raises other problems. How do I know that the original causal connection is or is not now operating? How do I know that the color I remember to have been called 'red' was indeed the color that was called 'red'? If I can't answer these questions, then my grammatical ground is useless, for I would not know when the justifying condition prevailed. If I can answer these questions, then I know, independently of the operation of the mechanism, what color was or is called 'red' and I do not have to rely on the associative connection at all. The knowledge of the color that was or is called 'red' would itself be a sufficient ground for using the word.

The causal explanation involving ostensive definition is an attempt to explain how one can talk about the world. Wittgenstein's argument against this attempt is not that it fails as a causal explanation but that it fails as a grammatical one, a grammatical explanation which happens to take a causal form. A grammatical explanation must provide the conditions under which one can be said to have correctly referred to or described some object. It must provide, that is, a criterion of correct use. Wittgenstein's objection to the Augustinian grammatical theory is that it does not succeed in this task. As we have seen, we do not always or normally justify the use of a word by appealing to the operation of a mechanism of ostension. And even if such a mechanism does exist, it is not sufficient to justify the use of the word; it must be certified by some other criterion to be the correct mechanism.

Moreover, a grammatical explanation must explicate what is meant by saying that a word designates a given object. Once again, Wittgenstein challenges the Augustinian theory's ability to meet this requirement. His objection is well illustrated in a passage in which he speaks of someone making the empirical discovery that a person will bring sugar if a certain sign is given—a button, say, is pressed—and the cry 'Su' is also given. He asks whether this shows that 'Su' is the correct sign for sugar, and he responds by saying "I do not use 'that is the sign for sugar' in the same way as the sentence 'if I press this button, I get a piece of sugar' " (*PG*, p. 188). A causal process, which may indeed operate, has been mistakenly identified as implicated in the meaning of the assertion that a word designates an object. Thus the Augustinian grammatical theory fails on another count.

If the connection between words and things is not a causal connection, not even a causal connection enshrined in grammar, then what is it? Wittgenstein's answer, we have seen, is that the connection is made by definitions belonging to grammar, by correlations between objects and names set up by a chart or by ostensive definitions (*PG*, p. 97). This connection or correlation, he tells us, "is part of the symbolism" (*PG*, p. 97). So grammar connects words and world by means of ostensive definitions, but these definitions operate as part of the language-game or calculus, not causally, not as part of the mechanism of nature. What we need to do is understand how such a definition operates noncausally, grammatically, within the calculus:

> How does an ostensive definition work? Is it put to work again every time the word is used, or is it like a vaccination which changes us once and for all?
>
> A definition as a part of the calculus cannot act at a distance. It acts only by being applied. [*PG*, pp. 80–81]

So the definition does not act like a vaccination—that would be for it to act at a distance and hence to be no part of grammar. But when the definition works 'up close' it is not working as a causal mechanism. It works by being applied as a part of the symbolism. This implies that in the calculus or language-game ostensive definition has a role, a use, which is part of its own grammar and which determines its meaning. What is this role? Wittgenstein gives us a clue in the following: "Suppose I am now asked 'why do you choose *this* color when given this order; how do you justify the choice?' . . . I can answer 'because *this* color is opposite the word "red" in my chart' " (*PG*, p. 96). Here the chart constitutes the criterion for correct use, and the same can be said for an ostensive definition. There are occasions when we *give* an ostensive definition to determine the sense of a word; occasions when we *appeal* to it to adjudicate the correct use of that word; and times when we request an ostensive definition as a *test* of someone's understanding. These are its functions as part of the calculus, that is, the functions defined by the calculus as its use and meaning. Appeals to ostensive definition or to the samples introduced by them are, by definition as it were, appeals which determine meaning, justify use, and connect language and reality.

But it is always easy to slip back into a misinterpretation of the way in which a definition works as a part of the symbolism and to see it once more as a causal condition of correct use.

> Isn't it like this? First of all, people use an explanation, a chart, by looking it up; later they as it were look it up in the head (by calling it before the inner eye, or the like) and finally they work without the chart, as if it had never existed. In this last case they are playing a different game. For it isn't as if the chart is still in the background, to fall back on; it is excluded from our game, and if I "fall back on it" I am like a blinded man falling back on the sense of touch. An explanation provides a chart and when I no longer use the chart it becomes mere history.
>
> I must distinguish between the case in which I follow the table, and the case in which I behave in accordance with the table without making use of it.—The rule we learnt which makes us now behave in such and such a way is of no interest to us considered as the cause or history behind our present behavior. [*PG*, pp. 85–86]

The ostensive definition functions as part of the calculus only as long as we continue to appeal to it to settle questions of meaning and correct use. In terms of the distinction made in the *Blue Book,* it is not enough that use merely *accord* with the definition; we must put the definition to work as an instrument—we must employ it to settle questions of meaning and correct use (*BBB,* p. 13). *Then* it is being applied. When it acts in this fashion, questions simply do not arise about whether we have remembered a previous definition correctly, whether the chart has faded, and whether the associative connection has degenerated. These are matters of the past, but an ostensive definition is applied in the present, with the authority we give it in the present, to determine sense and adjudicate use.

The question which remains is how the definition *can* have these functions. The objections raised by the standard interpretation against the role of ostensive definition in teaching can be raised as well against its role in a calculus. Is an ostensive definition not ambiguous? Is it not a mere ceremony of giving a name to an object? Does it not fail to specify syntax? How then can it define use and meaning? What we require is an extended grammatical investigation of ostensive definition which illuminates its meaning and its role in a calculus and which will put to rest these objections. Wittgenstein provides us with this.

V

Wittgenstein makes it exceedingly clear in the *Philosophical Grammar* that he is not interested in a mechanistic or psychological explanation of the acquisition of language or of any other aspect of it: "An explanation of the operation of language as a psychophysical mechanism is of no interest to us. . . . We need an explanation which is *part of the calculus*" (*PG*, p. 70). That is to say, the only explanation he wishes to offer is a grammatical one, an explanation which does not show us *how* someone comes to use words and mean them in a certain way, but one which explains *what* they mean. "Misled by our grammar, we are tempted to ask '*How* does one think a proposition, *how* does one expect such and such to happen?' " (*PG*, p. 103). What the philosopher should do is concern himself with the *content* of what is said (*PG*, p. 63), and the only explanation of meaning that should concern him is the one which unpacks this content, which tells us what it *is*. Thus Wittgenstein's interest in ostensive definition lies in the fact that such a definition is often part of this grammatical explanation of meaning: "By 'explanation of the meaning of a sign' we mean rules for use but above all *definitions.* The distinction between verbal definitions and ostensive definitions gives a rough division of these types of explanation" (*PG*, p. 60). An ostensive definition is part of the grammatical background of many words, and as such it serves to define their senses (*PG*, p. 153). Therefore it tells us *what* we mean, not how we mean. The proper task for the philosopher is to display more perspicuously the role of ostensive definition in a grammatical determination of meaning.

One question which can be asked in this spirit is whether ostensive definition is a sufficient grammatical determination of meaning. To ask this is to inquire whether such a definition provides a complete account of the sense of a word. In answer, Wittgenstein writes:

> I can ostensively define a word for a color or a shape or a number, etc. etc. (children are given ostensive explanations of numerals and they do perfectly well); negation, too, disjunction and so on. The *same* ostension might define a numeral, or the name of a shape or the name of a color. But in the grammar of each different part of speech

the ostensive definition has a different role; and in each case it is only *one* rule. [*PG*, p. 61]

So the ostensive definition is one rule among others, and hence only one part of the grammatical determination of what a word means. It is not, then, a sufficient grammatical account in the sense of being a complete account. This is one of those grammatical theses Wittgenstein talks about which, if expressed, everyone will accept (*PI* §128, §599): *of course,* even with regard to a simple term like 'red' we have in addition to its ostensive definition restrictive and syntactical rules which relate it to other terms. But, as we will see, it is exceedingly difficult to remain content with this (obvious) grammatical fact.

In denying that ostensive definition is a complete grammatical account, Wittgenstein is saying something that is consistent with his overall evaluation of the Augustinian theory of meaning. This theory, he maintains, describes language as simpler than it is (*PI* §3; *PG*, p. 57). Not all words function in the way in which 'pillar' and 'block' function. Similarly, it is to oversimplify matters to say that the meaning of any word is given solely by its ostensive definition; other rules also specify the meanings of our words.

In spite of the obvious truth of the grammatical remark that ostensive definition is only one of the things we call 'explaining the meaning of a term', it is difficult to be satisfied with this fact of grammar. Some are tempted to question or deny it, and Wittgenstein expresses one such temptation in the following way: "It may seem to us as if the other grammatical rules for a word had to follow from its ostensive definition; since after all an ostensive definition, e.g. 'that is called "red",' determines the meaning of the word 'red' " (*PG*, p. 60). It is in response to this challenge that, in the *Philosophical Grammar,* Wittgenstein brings up the matter of ambiguity: "But this definition is only those words plus pointing to a red object, e.g. a red piece of paper. And is this definition really unambiguous? Couldn't I have used the very same one to give the word 'red' the meaning of the word 'paper', or 'square', or 'shiny', or 'light', or 'thin' etc. etc.?" (*PG*, p. 60). Because an ostensive definition is ambiguous, he seems to be saying, it cannot generate the other grammatical rules.

What is Wittgenstein's argument here? One might begin by asking how the questions he poses are to be answered. Is 'That is called "red" ' really unambiguous? If it is, this could only mean that, given the rules of the language employed in it, only one interpretation of its meaning is possible. If, on the contrary, it is ambiguous, this would mean that, given the rules of the language employed in it, multiple interpretations are equally legitimate. If it is ambiguous, 'That is called "red" ' could be used to assign the word 'red' to different things, perhaps to the color, to the substance, to the shape, and so on, insofar as 'that' might, in light of the rules governing it, be used to single out the color, the substance, the shape, and so on. In this case, from the mere words of the ostensive definition alone we could not determine to which of several things the term being defined was being assigned. This would be a logical 'could not', not a psychological one. Now one might ask, under what interpretation of the words in the definition, and especially the word 'that', could the definition be unambiguous? This could be the case only if 'that' meant something like: 'the object to which I am pointing' or 'the object whose front surface intersects with a straight line drawn outward from my pointing finger (or which would so intersect if I did point)'. It may be absurd to say that this is the meaning of 'that', but it would have to be the meaning if, as Kenny and others have claimed, the ostensive definition referred us to the *bearer* of the name. Surely the bearer is that object to which we assign the word 'red', and that object would be one intersecting a line drawn outward from my pointing finger. But, again, if 'that' did mean 'the object whose front surface intersects . . . ', then the ostensive definition would not be ambiguous, and Wittgenstein clearly implies that it is. From which it follows, contra Kenny and the standard interpretation, that an ostensive definition does not refer us to the bearer of the name being defined. Furthermore, if 'that' were provided with a univocal sense in the fashion indicated, it would be very doubtful that 'That is called "red" ' could function as a definition, as the determinant of the sense of the word. It would be a contingent matter of fact that the entity intersecting a line drawn outward from my finger is called 'red'. Wittgenstein, however, denies that an ostensive definition is a contingent statement (*PG*, p. 68; *BBB*, p. 2). He writes: "An explanation of meaning is not an empirical proposition and not a causal explanation, but a rule, a convention" (*PG*, p. 68). As a rule determinative of sense, an ostensive definition is not bipolar. It cannot be falsified.[14] Thus we can conclude that in pointing out that 'That is called "red" ' is ambiguous, Wittgenstein is drawing attention to the fact that it is not equivalent to the contingent proposition 'The object whose front surface intersects with a line drawn outward from my finger is called "red" '.

How, then, is the ostensive definition to be interpreted? Wittgenstein gives us a fairly clear answer:

> The ostensive definition may be regarded as a rule for translating from a gesture language into a word language. If I say "the color of this object is called 'violet'," I must already have denoted the color, already presented it for christening, with the words "the color of that object" if the naming is to be able to take place. For I might also say "the name of this color is for you to decide" and the man who gives the name would in that case already have to know what he is to name (where in the language he is stationing the name). [*PG*, p. 88]

As a rule of translation, the ostensive definition equates the meaning of the demonstrative gesture and the meaning of the word. The gesture—'that' or 'this color' together with the pointing—must already then mean red. The speaker *uses* the words and the act of pointing to mean *the red color*. But because the word 'that' could equally be used to refer to the paper, its shape, its thinness, etc., and because 'this color' could be used to refer to the shade or the brightness, the ostensive definition that employs these words is ambiguous. Of course the person using these words and giving the definition means one thing rather than another by them; the definition has for him a determinate sense. It follows that when

14. Hacker, "Wittgenstein," p. 283.

'That is called "red" ' is uttered as a definitional rule which determines the sense of 'red', the red color is already being singled out or denoted by 'that': the person giving the definition and the person receiving it must understand it in this fashion. So the student, the learner, must already be able to use language to talk about—to denote—red if he is to understand the ostensive definition of 'red'. He must be able to use the word 'that' or the words 'this color' to denote the color red. Hence we can see the real point of Wittgenstein's concluding remark concerning the ambiguity of an ostensive definition: "I might say: one must already understand a great deal of a language in order to understand that definition. Someone who understands that definition must already know where the words ('red', 'ellipse') are being put, where they belong in language" (*PG*, p. 61). This statement and its correlate, *Philosophical Investigations* §30, are not empirical or grammatical postulates concerning the inability of ostensive definition to inculcate meaning; they are grammatical propositions about 'understanding' which follow from what an ostensive definition *means.*

Now we are in a position to see why the other rules of grammar cannot be derived from the ostensive definition. The reason for this is not that the ostensive referent fails to be a discrete natural nameable. The reason is that the meaning of the ostensive definition presupposes the meaningful use of language to denote the color red, which use involves the grammar of 'red' and all terms synonymous with it. We cannot grasp the ostensive definition and *then* read off from the ostensive referent the other grammatical rules governing 'red' for the simple reason that we can't grasp the ostensive referent or the meaning of the ostensive definition without already understanding, and *employing,* these rules. To be sure, the ostensive definition determines the meaning of the word 'red', as the objection we are considering maintained (*PG*, p. 60). But it does this only because we already employ other words—'that' or 'this color'—to talk about, to denote, the color red, and we determine the meaning of the *word* 'red' by equating its use with the previously mastered use of these other words.

Let us see in more detail how the ostensive definition of 'red' grammatically implicates the syntactical rules governing 'red'. The meaning of the definition cannot be understood—not in a psychological sense but in the sense that it cannot be defined or determined—without appeal to these syntactical rules. As we have seen, 'that' or 'this color' must be used to single out or denote the color red; to be used in this fashion requires that it be used in agreement with rules of syntax. If 'that' were not used in agreement with the rules of syntax governing 'red', then its use would not be a meaningful use of language *to talk about red.* Talking about red is using language in agreement with the rules which determine the sense of 'red'. If, as Wittgenstein tells us, "an explanation of a sign can replace the sign itself" (*PG,* p. 99), it then follows that 'that' or 'this color' used in explanation of 'red' can replace 'red', and they can do this only if they follow the syntactical rules governing 'red'. The word 'red' can be used to single out or denote the color red; it can also be used to describe something as red. Denoting and describing are at least in part syntactical functions, interrelated ones at that. In the ostensive definition 'that' or 'this color' is being used to perform the function of denoting. These words can also be used to describe something as red, e.g., 'The table is *that color*'. If denoting or naming is, as Wittgenstein says, a sort of preparation for describing (*PI* §49), then the syntactical form employed in denoting is grammatically connected to the syntactical form employed in describing. Hence 'that' or 'this color' in the ostensive definition directly involves the syntactical form used in denoting the color red, and indirectly involves the syntactical form used in describing something as red. To understand 'That is called "red" ' is by definition, then, to grasp these syntactical rules (in the sense of having the ability to use 'red' in accordance with them). The ostensive and syntactical rules form a system, a calculus; there is an internal relation between them.

Another example, and a related point concerning grammatical categories. Consider the grammatical category: piece in a game. When Wittgenstein tells us "the words 'This is the king' (or 'This is called the "king" ') are a definition only if the learner already 'knows what a piece in a game is' " (*PI* §31), he is specifying what it means for 'This is the king' to be a definition and to be understood as one. A learner understands the definition only if 'he knows what a piece in a game is'. Note the single quotation marks Wittgenstein uses in describing the condition of understanding: they show that this is a condition within a language-game and not, as it were, a condition within nature, not a condition which functions as a causal condition of understanding. In surrounding the condition with quotation marks Wittgenstein can be seen as highlighting the fact that the relationship between 'understanding the definition "This is the king" ' and 'knowing what a piece in a game is' is a grammatical one which serves to explain the meaning of the former expression. He goes on to say that 'This is the king' is a definition only if the learner "has already played other games or has watched other people playing 'and understood' " (*PI* §31). The claim being made is that we would *say* that a person understands the definition only if we would *say* that he understood what a piece in a game is. And we very properly say these things because 'this' in the definition means 'this piece' and a person has not understood the definition if he has not understood the meaning of its constituent terms.

Thus we can say that in our language basic color terms and certain other terms are adequately defined ostensively. It is true that their meaning is also specified by other rules, rules specifying syntax, restrictive relations to other terms, and grammatical categories, and it is true that these rules cannot be derived from the antecedently determined ostensive referent. But these rules are implicated, directly and indirectly, in the ostensive definition itself, so that they are not something we need to grasp *in addition to* the ostensive definition. The divorce of semantic and syntactic considerations, encouraged by the false interpretation which takes the ostensive definition as acquainting us with only the bearer of the name and not its use, is far from Wittgenstein's intention, as we can see when he writes:

One is inclined to make a distinction between rules of grammar that set up "a connection between language and reality" and those that do not. A rule of the first kind is "this color is called 'red',"—a rule of the second kind is "~~p=p". With regard to this distinction there is a common error; language is not something that is first given a structure and then fitted on to reality. [*PG*, p. 89]

Neither, we might add, is language something that is first fitted onto reality and then given a structure. An ostensive definition is an adequate determination of meaning because it is internally related to *all* the other rules which govern the term defined.

Finally, it should be noted that when an ostensive definition operates as a part of a calculus or language-game within which it plays its designated role, there is an internal relation between understanding the ostensive definition and understanding the term defined. If the sense of a word is determined by an ostensive definition, then it is a grammatical and necessary truth that one understands the term only to the extent that one understands its ostensive definition. When ostension is thought of as an instrument within a teaching mechanism it is only a contingent truth at best that understanding the term is the result of understanding its ostensive definition: no teaching instrument is necessary. In the context of teaching, it is only a contingent truth that an ostensive definition explains the meaning of the term defined; in the language-game of ostensive definition it is a necessary truth that the definition explains this meaning.

We are now in a position, given an understanding of the grammatical structure of an ostensive definition, to see what Wittgenstein means when he writes: "The connection between 'language and reality' is made by definitions of words, and these belong to grammar, so that language remains self-contained and autonomous" (*PG*, p. 97). The meaning of 'red' is not determined by going outside of language, examining objects, and *coming to see* what the color red is by some extralinguistic form of awareness. The meaning is determined by a definition, and in this definition language is already being used to single out the color red. The meaning of 'red' is given by equating its use with the use of another bit of language: 'that' or 'this color' or similar expressions. Hence even in an ostensive definition the meaning equation is purely linguistic. We remain within language; it speaks for itself (*PG*, p. 40) and thus is autonomous and self-contained. As Wittgenstein tells us: "An answer to the question 'How is that meant?' exhibits the relationship between two linguistic expressions. So the question too is a question about that relationship" (*PG*, p. 45). This, we have seen, is as true of ostensive definition as it is of verbal definition. It would not be true if the standard interpretation or the Augustinian theory were accepted. If, as the standard interpretation suggests, the demonstrative 'that' referred us to the bearer of the name 'red', the ostensive definition would relate the bearer and a linguistic expression. If, as the Augustinian theory suggests, the demonstrative 'that' meant 'the object whose front surface intersects with a line drawn outward from my pointing finger', the ostensive definition could not without absurdity equate the meaning of 'red' with the meaning of the demonstrative expression—all color terms on that hypothesis would mean the same thing, and none of them would mean what they do mean. Both the standard interpretation and the Augustinian theory misunderstand the grammar of ostensive definition.[15]

15. I would like to thank Peter Hacker for his helpful comments on an earlier draft of this paper.

Index of Wittgenstein's Works Cited

Index of Names